The Definitive Job Book

The Definitive Job Book

Rules from the recruitment insiders

Anne Watson

CAPSTONE

Copyright © Anne Watson 2008
First published 2008 by
Capstone Publishing Ltd. (a Wiley Company)
The Atrium, Southern Gate, Chichester, PO19 8SQ, UK.
www.wileyeurope.com
Email (for orders and customer service enquiries): cs-books@wiley.co.uk
The right of Anne Watson to be identified as the author of this book has been asserted in accordance with the
Copyright, Designs and Patents Act 1988

Designations used by companies to distinguish their products are often claimed as trademarks. All brand names
and product names used in this book are trade names, service marks, trademarks or registered trademarks of
their respective owners. The Publisher is not associated with any product or vendor mentioned in this book.
This publication is designed to provide accurate and authoritative information in regard to the subject matter
covered. It is sold on the understanding that the Publisher is not engaged in rendering professional services. If
professional advice or other expert assistance is required, the services of a competent professional should be
sought.

Although all information contained in this book was verified at the time of going to press, the publisher and
author cannot take responsibility for any changes in the products or services subsequently made by any of the
retailers included herein.

Other Wiley Editorial Offices: Hoboken, San Fransisco, Weinheim, Australia, Singapore and Canada.
Wiley also publishes its books in a variety of electronic formats. Some content that appears in print may not be
available in electronic books.

Library of Congress Cataloging-in-Publication Data
Watson, Anne
 The Definitive Job Book: Rules from the recruitment insiders / Anne Watson.
   p. cm.
Includes index.
ISBN 978–1–84112–781–1 (pbk. : alk. paper)

1. Job hunting. 2. Résumés (Employment) 3. Employment interviewing. I. Title.
HF5382.7.W38 2007
650.14--dc22
                          2007039319
ISBN   978–1–84–112781–1

Typeset by Sparks in 10.5 pt Baskerville (www.sparks.co.uk)
Printed and bound in Great Britain by TJ International Ltd, Padstow, Cornwall

This book is printed on acid-free paper responsibly manufactured from sustainable forestry in which at least two
trees are planted for each one used for paper production. Substantial discounts on bulk quantities of Capstone
Books are available to corporations, professional associations and other organizations. For details telephone John
Wiley & Sons on (+44) 1243–770441, fax (+44) 1243 770571 or email corporatedevelopment@wiley.co.uk

To my father Eric Watson, an inspiration to all who knew him.
Love's last tribute.

ACKNOWLEDGEMENTS

I am indebted to so many people for helping me create this book, something that always seemed to me to be the logical outcome of so many years in recruitment. I would particularly like to thank all of the recruitment insiders who were so generous with their time, sharing their thoughts and experiences with me and broadening immeasurably the scope of the book. Thanks also to Louise Triance, who introduced me to areas of online recruitment where I had never been. While in Hong Kong I experienced the kindness of strangers, Jeremy Hobbins, Pieter Schats, Philip Eisenbeiss, Peter Dove, Chris Strachan and Oliver Hemmings. They each took time out of their hectic schedules to talk to me about their recruitment experiences, giving me invaluable insights into their corporate worlds and their individual viewpoints.

I am also very grateful to the whole Capstone team and in particular to Emma Swaisland for her belief in the topic and for retaining her critical perspective, keeping me on track. Thanks to Scott Smith, a role-model amongst network-ers, and to Iain Campbell and Kate Stanley for their creative energies.

My love and thanks to the Hawkins family, Martin, Tom and Eleanor, who are always supportive, encouraging and patient, dutifully laughing at my jokes and never complaining when yet another weekend is lost to the keyboard.

Finally, thanks to all of the people I have interviewed over the years that have shown me that everyone has unique talents – all we have to do is iden-tify them and use them.

CONTENTS

Throughout the book you will find words of wisdom and cautionary tales from recruitment insiders who will give you some insight on life from their side of the desk and what it means for you.

Chapter 1: The decision to move   1
Result: call to action!

Chapter 2: Crafting the perfect CV   25
Result: the perfect marketing tool

Chapter 3: Get the letter right   81
Result: an invitation to interview

Chapter 4: Where and how to apply   105
Result: you target the job you want

Chapter 5: High performance interviewing   153
Result: you are seen at your best

Chapter 6: Negotiating the best deal and managing the job offer process 207

Result: the right job with the right employer

Chapter 7: Techniques to help you make the best of who you are   225

Result: more powerful communication

Appendix A
Anne's 10 top tips to stay one step ahead of the crowd and make the recruiter love you ...   251

Appendix B
Resources you may find helpful   255
Result: a well-informed and effective job hunt

Index   261

FOREWORD BY MILES TEMPLEMAN, DIRECTOR GENERAL OF THE INSTITUTE OF DIRECTORS

The 21st century has brought with it a different and more challenging working environment. Daily developments in technology mean that the working day is now 24 hours and a person working in Shanghai is as accessible to us in the UK as someone working in Sevenoaks. Competition emanates from the four corners of the world and in this global, fast-paced environment, the UK has to continue to develop a leading and powerful role that will ensure it retains its position as an entrepreneurial and innovative business centre where ethics are strong and values run high. Businesses need to grow and they need to provide the financial resources that will allow the UK to continue investing in its infrastructure, its services and its people

We need to make sure that we are creating a business environment where there is support, the freedom to fail, the skills and the tools to do the job; but most importantly, the clarity of objective. If you give people a clear objective and say, 'Look, you find a good way of doing it', lo and behold, they will do it. The sure way to make this happen is to ensure that people are constantly learning and advancing knowledge and skills. People need to feel that they can express themselves and use their ideas without fear of failure. This way they will continue to innovate and both the individuals and business will thrive.

If you are seeking business growth, look for people around you who can help you develop your ideas. Use all the available resources in terms of getting the knowledge, building the skills, focusing in on particular areas. Great steps forward come from intense focus, and they don't come from anything else. If you want to get on in life and business, you have to say: 'Here's where I am going to go for it', and 'Here's how I am going to achieve it', and then concentrate on that.

Part of the remit of the Institute of Directors has always been to help businesses achieve their potential and this can only happen through the personal growth of people who run those businesses. What the industry wants from its universities is intelligent graduates with relevant skills who understand the economic drivers facing business and industry today, thus making sure that they are prepared for the workplace of today. We need a step change in performance at all levels if we are to meet the demands of the global business environment. The starting point of that excellence of corporate performance is high-performing individuals with ambition and determination, underpinned by a thirst for constant learning.

DRAMATIS PERSONAE

THE RECRUITMENT INSIDERS

The people listed below are all those who kindly shared with me their views on the world of recruitment, interviewing and job hunting. They are all people whose careers are focused on this area, in one field or another. You will find their advice, comments and contributions throughout the book on everything from CVs to confidence, rejection to resignation, networking to negotiating – and more. I hope you will find their insights as valuable as I have. Allow me to introduce them.

Andrew Harley, Management Consultant, Aquarius

After graduating in 1975, Andrew's working career started in human resource management in pharmaceuticals and then in distribution. After a period with Merck Sharp and Dohme he moved to Rowntree plc in York where he specialized in the provision of assessment centres for graduate recruitment as well as development centres for senior managers. He then joined an HR consultancy and became their practice leader for assessment and development in the north-east of England and in Scotland. His work has included the design, development and delivery of assessment and development centres. He has carried out individual assessments and coaching assignments at board level for a diverse client base.

Sheila Burgess, Director, SBI International

Sheila Burgess is based in Paris where she has developed her business as a bilingual secretarial/PA Recruitment Consultant over the past 20 years. Her name is synonymous with 'going the extra mile'. She is also known as the most frightening interviewer in Paris. Originally based in Brussels and London, Sheila now works closely with prestigious international companies to recruit 'les perles rares' required by the Anglo-French workforce, i.e. fluent English/French speakers with strong bicultural backgrounds, the very practical qualities and skills associated with this kind of work and who are looking for long-term positions. A linguist herself, Sheila also works with a well-known UK-based international head-hunter and is involved in cross-cultural training sessions for management. In her spare time, she keeps bees.

Jane Chapman, Development Consultant, Financial Services

Jane Chapman has enjoyed many challenging and exciting years working in a large financial services business as a Development Consultant. She is both a chartered accountant and a psychotherapist and combines business expertise with facilitation and coaching skills.

Her coaching clients value her insight, interest and encouragement, and the vast knowledge and experience she brings to them. Her one-to-one coaching encompasses self-awareness, skills development and career and role changes as well as resolving difficult issues in the workplace (e.g. conflict, stress, under-performance).

Tim Elkington, Managing Director, Enhance Media Limited

Tim Elkington is the Managing Director of the online recruitment communications agency Enhance Media Limited, which he founded in 2001. Prior to that, Tim was Head of Research at Workthing.com and was part of the core team that launched the site from the Guardian Media Group. Prior to Workthing, Tim worked in the planning department of the *Guardian* where he was responsible for research and sales support material across the Guardian network of sites, including Guardian Jobs.

Tim initiated The National Online Recruitment Audience Survey – the UK's largest online recruitment research project. Tim is a regular speaker at online recruitment conferences and a respected commentator regarding online recruitment through both trade and national publications.

Tim's blog, Online Recruitment – the bigger picture (http://timelkington. typepad.com/tims_blog/), features commentary on industry news and aims to look at online recruitment developments in the wider context of the UK media industry.

Rachel Hannan, Director, Gatenby Sanderson

Rachel is a Director of Gatenby Sanderson, a leading search and selection consultancy specializing in local government senior appointments, a role she moved into after 12 years' experience in senior search and selection, in both the public and private sectors.

She set up and developed the company's research function and has taken a lead on Children's Services work for the organization and has been involved in major restructuring and improvement work in local government.

She is a generalist with a broad portfolio of clients and has been responsible for well over 60 senior appointments in local government alone, including chief executives of County and Metropolitan Borough Councils and numerous directors and heads of service across the whole range of functions. Outside of local government and her private sector experience, Rachel has worked in regeneration, which has included work with economic development partnerships and also with health and the voluntary sector.

Andrew Harris, Director, Matthews Harris Consulting Limited

Andrew Harris graduated with a first class honours degree in sociology from the University of Leeds and completed a postgraduate diploma in personnel management at Leeds Polytechnic in 1979. He started his career in human resource management at The Burton Group, joined Magnet Kitchens in 1987, achieved his first Personnel Director position at the age of 32 and resigned as Group HR Director of a FTSE 250 company in 1996 to set up his own executive search and human resource consultancy, Matthews Harris Consulting Limited. Over the last ten years this company has helped appoint over 350 senior executives in nine countries; has employed over 25 people and generated a fee income in excess of £3m. Having sold the business at the end of 2006, Andrew has accepted an opportunity to join one of the leading executive search firms in Australasia and will be emigrating to New Zealand.

Clare Howard, Director of e-coaches.co.uk

Clare Howard is the Director of e-coaches.co.uk, specialists in the fields of personality type, leadership, career development, training and development and e-learning. She is currently a leading light in careers and learning for a web-based careers, learning and lifestyle site open to upwards of two million participants in the 14–24-year-old range. This includes the free provision of an i-portfolio™ and toolkit tests, and information to help its users identify career and learning choices.

Her philosophy is that you can invent your own future, wherever you start from. So, her professional life has taken her from researching medieval Florentine entrepreneurs, international traders and spin-doctors, through to hands-on project management of computer development teams, and an ability to hold her own in conversations about web 2.0 and all things e-.

Her interest in things technological has its origin in self-interest – because with the aid of a phone and high-speed Internet she can spend as much time as possible living her alternative lifestyle in her house and garden in the south of France. A virtual bottle of wine and bowl of olives just don't hit the spot. Vive la différence.

Gareth James, Director, People Plus

People Plus was set up by Gareth in 1993 after an 18-year career as a Personnel/HR generalist, his final role being an International HR Director for a sector of the Rhone Poulenc group, covering Africa, Asia, Australasia and Latin America as well as the UK.

Gareth's passion is the development of people and People Plus provides a portfolio of services for clients across the private and public sectors both in the UK and overseas. Gareth's main area of activity is organizational development and change management, career management, executive coaching and team development.

Gareth's personal development has included 12 programmes in psychometrics and assessment, 360° Feedback, Transactional Analysis and NLP.

When Gareth is not working he will be found either inside a theatre, opera house or concert hall or travelling to exotic places (87 countries visited and he's not finished yet!).

Kevin Johnson, Financial Adviser

Kevin Johnson has been a Managing Director and Director of several consumer goods companies. He has operated at main board level for over 25 years in a wide range of companies which have marketed and manufactured white goods, electrical accessories, speciality branded chemicals, building products, kitchens and apparel. He has also worked for several privately owned companies where he led major restructuring programmes, which in turn led to profitable exits for their owners.

Throughout his career he has always been fascinated by the way that business professionals and entrepreneurs concentrate on their business performance and balance sheets but fail to manage their own wealth and security.

Kevin wished to address this situation and has now become an FSA-approved financial adviser where he combines his business experience with investment skills to help business professionals and entrepreneurs secure and build their personal wealth.

Nadine Jones, Head of Human Resources, Baugur

Nadine's retail career spans 16 years, having worked with businesses such as Safeway, ASDA (George), Austin Reed and Thomas Cook.

Nadine has a wealth of experience in major systems implementation, change management and outsourcing, Nadine has worked with senior teams to improve capability and profitability across the retail businesses she has worked with. Nadine's aim is to improve the bottom right-hand corner of the P&L with her comprehensive experience and practical approach to managing people. A true generalist, Nadine has managed all aspects of HR and has been described as 'as comfortable at board strategy day as at a new starters' induction'.

Nadine describes herself as a 'frustrated ops director' and a 'retailaholic', with a key role to deliver measurable added value from the HR function.

Sarah Lacey, Managing Partner, Sarah Lacey and Associates

Sarah Lacey has managed an executive research business since 1994. Her career in executive research began with Boyden International in the late 80s, moving on to the London office of Heidrick and Struggles where she was a research associate. Soon after starting a family, she established SLA, one of the first outsourced research companies in the marketplace. Her team of researchers quickly grew to five, working across a range of industry sectors from financial services to retail, and on senior level positions including a number of high profile CEO and COO appointments for leading PLCs. The business has grown through recommendation and remains one of the better-known suppliers of quality executive research both nationally and internationally.

Zaria Pinchbeck, Managing Director, ZPR Ltd

Zaria Pinchbeck is Managing Director of ZPR Ltd, a Soho-based PR company that specializes in the retail sector with clients such as Selfridges, Superdrug, The Peacocks Group, Lakeland Ltd, Mamas & Papas and the AS Watson Group. Zaria started her career in the recruitment industry (working with and trained by the best) before joining ASDA where she worked for eight years with business leaders such as Archie Norman, Allan Leighton and George Davis, moving from recruitment into internal and external communications. She was Head of PR for ASDA when she decided to leave to set up ZPR in June 2001.

Jan Shaw, Associate Director, Barracuda Search

After an earlier career as a consultant with the National Institute of Industrial Psychology, Jan moved into the Corporate HR world with Rank Xerox International, British Airways and ultimately Wal-Mart ASDA. There, he was part of the original senior team working directly with Archie Norman, Allan Leighton and George Davies and he was a vital part of the team that turned this formerly ailing retailer into the £1 billion+ turnover apparel worldwide Wal-Mart brand. The development of a progressive operating and customer-focused company culture was aided by Jan's successful recruitment of the recovery management team. The current CEOs of Sainsbury, Somerfield, HBOS, Alliance Boots and ASDA were some of his original successful appointments into ASDA Wal-Mart.

Martine Robins, European HR Director, Cookson Electronics

Martine Robins is the European HR director for Cookson Electronics, responsible for 13 countries. Cookson Electronics is a global organization and the leading supplier of advanced surface treatment, plating chemicals and assembly materials to the automotive, construction and electronics markets.

Martine is a member of the Chartered Institute of Personnel and Development and has considerable international HR experience obtained predominantly from working in engineering and technology organizations.

Heather Summers, Director, WorkMagic

Heather Summers is an experienced Senior Executive who now runs her own successful human resources and management consultancy business. As well as strategic consultancy, she specializes in executive coaching, personal growth coaching and training. Heather believes we all have much more potential than we give ourselves credit for. All the training she does helps people find and fulfil that potential.

Heather holds an MBA, has an MA in English Literature and French, is qualified in Psychometrics and is a Master Practitioner of NLP. Together with Anne Watson she wrote *The Book of Luck* and *The Book of Happiness*.

Rob Walker, Senior Consultant, Gaulter Russell

Rob Walker currently works as a Senior Consultant for Gaulter Russell, a top level executive search and selection business in Auckland, New Zealand. He was dragged into executive search straight after university where he studied Economics and has always brought his unique style to the job – unconventional, relentlessly optimistic and an ability to produce results in the blink of an eye. Fast-paced and restless for the next task, he is renowned for speaking his mind and getting it right. He is currently enjoying the great outdoors that is New Zealand, spending too much time at the beach and proving that assessment of people and delivering results crosses all cultures effortlessly.

INTRODUCTION

This is your personal head-hunting call

I have discovered that head-hunting is much more than just a different form of recruitment. When I target someone for a specific role and ring them up, I am disrupting their lives. People who are head-hunted are busily doing their job, minding their own business, totally involved in what they are doing – they are not job hunting. They are often very surprised to receive a call and sometimes they have to be persuaded to listen. Some people are more reluctant than others and they need to be convinced to listen and to engage in the process. Gradually they begin to question what they are doing in their job and they compare it with what appears to be on offer. This whole process of comparison causes them to think about their careers, their future, their salary and where they are going in life. Statistics show that the majority of people who have been head-hunted leave their job within 12 months – whether for the company they were initially approached for or for another. The call is unsettling and challenging – 'Are you where you ought to be?'

The next big question becomes 'Could I be doing better than this?' A candidate who got through to the final shortlist for a head-hunted position told me that the whole process had been disturbing, unsettling and caused him sleepless nights. Although he did not get the job, he did not regret the time he spent in the interview process as he felt that he had been forced to think through everything about his life. He now felt more confident about his abilities, recognized that he had a worth in the outside world and that he could broaden his horizons if he wanted to.

Buying this book is, for you, the equivalent of that head-hunting call. I am asking you to think about your career and to work out if you should be contemplating a move. Change isn't usually very comfortable so this book will help you through the process. Do not be wary of the Neuro-Linguistic Programming (NLP) techniques that I use throughout the book, these are simply a tool to help you in your job change process. NLP is just about finding a better way to communicate; what can be wrong with that? These techniques are not obtrusive or obvious – just subtle ways of making sure you put forward the best picture of who you are.

There are different ways of approaching this book. You can either start at the beginning and read it all the way through or you can pick and choose the bits that interest you. Whichever route you take, use it as a way of challenging yourself about what you think and what you do. The one clear message for all job hunters is this: it is down to you to find the answer to your career direction. You can invite the opinions and the advice of as many people as you like but it is up to you to achieve the ultimate accolade of success – a contract of employment for a role that you find fulfilling. Other people will advise, help, sympathize and introduce you to others, but ultimately the responsibility for all of this lies with you. Job offers don't come on a plate and the way to find one is to take control.

Losing your job for whatever reason, whether it was because you decided to leave, because your role was made redundant or because you were fired, leads you to an immediate crossroads. Alternatively, you may be a new graduate and at the very beginning of this job-hunting process. Nearly all of us need to work to earn money to live. The more money we have, the more likely it is that our lifestyle will improve. Losing that income hits at the roots of our security and sense of identity. No matter how good you are, how qualified and experienced, you will have those moments in the middle of the night when you wonder whether you will work again and when your money is going to run out, and you will allow your imagination to run riot, anticipating doom and disaster. A clear job-search plan and the knowledge that you are doing all of the right things will bring the certainty that your strategy is right and you will get the results that you need. Stick to the job hunting programme and you will get results. A new job will bring about difference in your life and will improve it. Ruts can be boring so allow yourself to be stimulated and stretched by the ideas and advice offered and seek out the right place for you.

How this book will help you

There are apparently three things you can do in your life that will bring you the maximum amount of stress and pressure: one is to get divorced, another is to move house and the third is to find a new job. I am therefore inviting you to bring pressure into your life and move to a more rewarding role. Now is the time to consider whether or not you are in the right role and if you need to change. If you are a recent graduate, the world of job hunting will be a relatively new one for you and it has many pitfalls you may not even be aware of. You may already be in a role and be actively job seeking and wondering why the right job is not falling into your lap. You may not know what you could be doing to improve your skills in job hunting. You may not even realize that you ought to do something about your life and your career. Now is the time to start! Hiring top people who will add value is what every organization should be doing; adding to their talent bank and improving the calibre of their workforce. How do you make sure that you are considered to be talent and that someone wants you?

Set the goal

A satisfying job, working with like-minded people, that allows you to grow and develop your skills and talents has got to be a goal for most people. Add to that the need to be rewarded financially and you will then have the foundations for a successful professional life that will fuel a rewarding and rich home life. Research shows that many people are in jobs that they do not enjoy or feel indifferently about. The number of waking hours we spend at work is greater than the number at home so if you are one of those people who feel a degree of dissatisfaction about their current job perhaps it is time to reconsider your career choices. Maybe you would be happier in a different company but fulfilling the same role. Maybe you need to learn new skills and pursue a different career path. Maybe you want to unleash the entrepreneur that lurks deep inside you. Perhaps you have found yourself out of work later in life and you are encountering obstacles that you did not even know existed.

Wherever you are in life, sitting at your desk and wondering what to do is unlikely to bring about life changing actions. Thinking in a vacuum is very difficult so using this book in the right way for you will provoke thought, lead you to form an action plan and allow you to take control of your life.

It will give you the chance to develop a strategy for your own career. Jeremy Hobbins, Group Managing Director of Li & Fung Retailing, a $10 billion turnover business, believes that a career and a job search strategy should be no different from developing a business strategy. You begin with an end in mind and you work your way towards it, knowing what you are looking for. Only once you have established this goal can you begin to develop the plan to achieve what you want. If you are ambivalent about what you want or if you have done insufficient market research and soul searching, you could end up somewhere you don't want to be. If you know what you want, then you can use this book for the practical tools and skills to help you get there. However, if you don't, then before you embark on a colossal campaign of interview chasing, take the opportunity to explore and reflect.

Once you have a compelling vision of your career goal, then you can start to work towards it. You will be sure of what you want and you will be focused and clear minded, not deflected or deterred. You may alter your view slightly as you go along and adapt as you need to in line with market conditions but if you embark on a job search with too broad a remit, you run the risk of accepting the wrong role for the wrong reasons. A written job offer with a contract of employment is difficult to refuse, particularly if you are not sure what you want and therefore can have no particular reasons to refuse. It is flattering to be selected and to have beaten off the competition. Pressure will be brought on to you to take the job so it is vital that you know you will recognize the right job offer when it arrives. An uncompromising determination to get the absolute best for yourself in career terms will serve you well. You will know when to say yes and when to say no.

Look at the process

The purpose of this book is to address the whole of the job hunting process, considering everything about who you are, what the right job for you is and then how to nail it. My experiences over the years have led me to meet people who are skilled and talented in the job search process and others who are helpless, not knowing where to begin and how to go about the most fundamental parts of the job search. We seem to be awash with information on the Internet and on bookshelves about how to create the perfect CV and how to answer smart interview questions and all of this, while useful in parts, can also be contradictory. How do you know what to believe and what to ignore?

I believe that the most important part of any search is to ensure that you do it with integrity, making sure you remain true to yourself and who you are. There is no point in having a perfect CV if it doesn't reflect the real you. There are traps along the way for the unwary so a vital part of the job search process is to be aware of the needs of potential employers as much as you are of yourself. Detail, planning, research and rehearsal will win the day.

This book will allow you to consider what you can do that will make your job search unique and true to you. Some of this may seem obvious common sense while those of you going for your first interviews may be glad to look at the whole process from beginning to end. The most someone can get out of this book is the right kind of career role that will bring the utmost fulfilment and personal satisfaction. Together, we will forge a job-seeking strategy that will ensure that you get what you are looking for in life, rather than ending up where fate takes you. We will create a unique CV, not one that has fallen off a production line and that could apply to anyone. We will equip you with the knowledge to perform at your best at interview and the knowhow to negotiate the best package for yourself. Some of you will be sophisticated and experienced job hunters who know a lot about the process and how to be successful. There will be thought-provoking elements in this book for you that will allow you to fine-tune your approach. If you are new to the job market, then this will provide you with unparalleled insights into a hitherto unknown world.

I believe that when you are out there looking for a job, the biggest fear is that of the unknown. Am I getting it right? Is my CV good enough? How do I come across to others? How can I be assertive and get what I want, without being aggressive? What am I doing wrong?

I have also discovered that everyone gives conflicting advice. What is perfectly fine for one person is a major or minor transgression of someone else's rules. For 20 years I ran a research business where we provided the research services for other head-hunters. I found out then that everyone has their own way of assessing candidates and their own way of making decisions.

What I have done, therefore, is to talk to people who are working in the business of recruitment, either within the human resources function of a company; within a recruitment company; or consulting to recruitment companies or chief executives, who know that people are the most important asset they have. I asked them for their own ways of working and making decisions in order to share them with you.

These luminaries in the business, HR and recruitment world have generously given their own tips and advice to people who are out there looking for the right role. The advice you will get will therefore not be just from my perspective but will encompass a whole range of views and opinions. Take the advice that suits you and fits well with the person you are. The best way to present yourself is as the authentic you, not who you think you ought to be. Remember that what you are doing will not suit everyone so be sure that it is the best that you can do and that you have evaluated the alternatives. Make sure you are not making elementary mistakes that mean your application will be discarded. As Rachel Hannan of Gatenby Sanders says, 'Do not give anyone any excuse to discount you from the process'.

It is not a job for life

Today's job market is a very different place to that of 20 or even ten years ago. There is no longer a job for life; now global economics influence your workplace in the UK. The manufacturing base of the UK has all but disappeared and we are all thinking differently about life and work. We have seen whole companies and sectors disappear and we have to recognize that most people will have at least one significant career change during their working life, and perhaps substantially more. We are in the age of the portfolio career and we need to adapt accordingly. School leavers used to be encouraged to follow certain career paths such as the civil service, coal mining, teaching, apprenticeships, banking or multinationals in manufacturing. These were jobs for life with safe pensions at the end of it. Now that we are all likely to have a number of jobs in our lifetime we need to have the flexibility and mindset to adapt to this level of change. Self-confidence and a realization that your career lies in your own hands and no-one else's are the foundation stones of any career.

You may start out in your working life in one kind of role and then change to something different. You may start off as an employee and move into running your own business. You may opt out altogether and settle for the downscaled life in rural parts of France. Whatever it is that you do, it means you have to be ready for change. You need to know what the requisite tools for the changing job market are. You need to know what people are looking for and how to show people that you have got what it takes. This book tackles all the individual elements that make up the skills of the successful job hunter. Not everyone will need to read every word. After all, many of the skills required in getting a job are pure common sense. However, it is good to be reminded of what you are doing and how you could be going about it.

Above all, reminding yourself how best to equip yourself for a job search, how to present yourself and how to maximize your impact will all help give you the best chance of success.

Raise your game and put forward the best possible impression of who you are and a better job will ensue. When you have done the right kind of research and sent in the best possible CV, you will be confident that it is giving a great picture of who you are. Be ready to incorporate new thinking and new ideas into your search and the result will transform your life.

The choice to work where you want

Twenty-six years in the world of recruitment and thousands of interviews later has introduced me to some people who flourish in their roles, whilst others meander along and some seem destined to years of frustration and disappointment. In order to excel in your role, you have to be in the right one in the first place. Many of our waking hours are spent at work so wouldn't life be much more agreeable if that time were spent in a happy and rewarding environment? This job has got to be within your control, not someone else's. You can choose where you want to spend most of your waking hours so make sure you choose wisely

Start with who you are

Self-knowledge is the best starting point in any job search. You are unique and only you have that particular combination of training, experience and personality. How do you find the job that will allow you to excel? It is definitely out there and the information in this book will help you to find it and secure it.

Maybe you already have a job and the question is how you will have the courage to decide to leave what you are doing and find move to another role with all that this entails. People who take risks and make bold decisions are more likely to achieve success, particularly if this risk-taking ability is built on a foundation of achievements, research and a high level of self-confidence.

Graduates are leaving universities with the world at their feet yet saddled with debt. You are now looking at endless possibilities, with graduate recruitment fairs, enticing online advertisements and hurdles to overcome in order to secure the right job for you. Before you even think about what you are applying for, you need to think carefully about what skills and qualities you bring with you. The best starting point is to think about what you can offer an employer rather than working out what you want from them. How can you know this if you haven't thought about yourself, what you are good at and what you enjoy? Trust me, you are bound to be asked this at interview so it is better to start formulating thoughts way in advance.

Tools and resources

One purpose of this book is to provide you with tools and resources at a number of levels. Some of these will be the fundamental tools that are needed for a job search – the CV and the letter you send accompanying it. Many of you will already have a perfectly good CV saved neatly on your PC that you update regularly and you may feel that it doesn't need any upgrading. However, everyone can improve and do better so have a look at yours and see if it is the 5-star effort it needs to be in today's competitive marketplace. A generic CV is just not what it takes to get yourself noticed so prepare for hard work.

No matter how brilliant your marketing tools might be, they need an application. Identifying the best route to your selected market is a vital stage and you need to review the network that you have and how you can build on it. The most likely route to a new job is via someone you know or someone you are introduced to. An avalanche of CVs whizzing round the Internet just won't get you what you want so get ready for plenty of e-mails, telephone calls, cups of coffee and the opportunity to talk.

Be patient as you read the book – what is blindingly obvious to one person will be a new insight for another. When I tell you the correct way to spell Curriculum Vitae, don't laugh scornfully at this statement of the obvious. An analysis of CVs I reviewed over the last three months showed that 43% of the people who proudly entitled their CV 'Curriculum Vitae' actually spelt it incorrectly. Not such a good start!

Talent spotters

If you open up the annual report of any public company someone, be it the chief executive or the chairman, will make the point that 'people are the most important part of our business'. No matter how brilliant your products are or how stunning your service is, without the people to drive the business and deliver the process, your business will fail.

In 1991 when Archie Norman was spearheading the renewal of Asda, bringing it back from the verge of bankruptcy, part of the cultural change that drove the success of the business turnaround was putting people as one of the core values of the organization. This included treating people with respect, reflected by referring to them as colleagues, not employees; recognizing that all colleagues should be able to have input and suggest improvements, part of which was the immensely successful 'Tell Archie' scheme, focused on providing legendary customer service.

Businesses need talent. They need entrepreneurial people; they need creative people; they need steady people who will continue to deliver the same standard of performance; they need people who will dot the 'i's and cross the 't's. In short, they need a broad mix of people across the spectrum. The good news is that this means that there is a job for you in almost any organization. Whatever your skills and whatever your ambitions, there is a niche for you. The challenge for employers is to make sure that their business has this eclectic mix in the organization and that they have consistent performance. Just as you are sitting wondering where the right job is for you, the employers are scratching their heads wondering how to find you.

Everyone is capable of doing more than one kind of job. The world is full of exciting possibilities that we have not got enough time to explore. Make sure that when you retire and you look back at your working life, you do not regret lost opportunities and think wistfully of what might have been. Now is the time is to look at your life and to think about making dreams a reality.

CHAPTER 1

THE DECISION TO MOVE

RESULT: CALL TO ACTION!

Fed up with your job: you know you need to move

Did you know that, according to research carried out by www.gumtree.com (the UK's biggest website for local community job classifieds), 53% of British workers are in their current roles purely by chance? Only 8% of them said they were doing something they've wanted to do since they were young. A further survey of 1500 users showed that half of them would not swallow a salary sacrifice to take their dream job, preferring to stick with the work they were doing, even if they were in it by accident and didn't really like it anyway.

If you are reading this book, it must be because you have a feeling, however mild, that there may be something else you could be doing. Now is the time to take control of your life and do the job that you want to do rather than stay where you have ended up. What is your dream job? And why aren't you doing it? Avoid the comfort zone of being a victim. Take responsibility for your own life and for your own career. It is up to you how you choose to earn a living and how you choose to use your talents. Don't fall into the trap of blaming other people for how your career is going.

For most aspects of our lives, we make positive choices about what we want. We choose our homes, our holidays and our cars. We choose the people that we want to live with and we decide actively about most of our interests and leisure pursuits. Isn't it astonishing, therefore, that so many of us drift into a job and later on we wonder how it happened?

My one and only formal job interview was at the age of 22 when, having got through the civil service exams and interview panel, the final stage was an interview in the immigration office in Hull. Apparently I had ticked a number of boxes on my original application form for Executive Officer, a grade that covered a myriad of possibilities within the civil service. I had indicated that one of the roles I was willing to be considered for was that of Immigration Officer. I didn't even recall doing this, so the box must have been merrily ticked in a fit of ill thought through enthusiasm. The next five years of my life were spent in the world of immigration because I had mindlessly ticked a box and then shown enough initiative to buy a copy of the Immigration Act 1971 that I had artlessly peeping out of my handbag at the Hull interview. This initiative impressed the inspector of immigration so much that I got the job that I wasn't sure I even wanted. Although I loved working with the intelligent and quirky people I met there, the Civil Service working environment was absolutely wrong for me as I was born to break rules. I often wonder what would have happened if I had put some thought into my job search and actively thought through what I wanted to do and what I would be good at.

Redundancy and coping with the shock

You might be reading this because your role has been made redundant and you are wondering what to do to create a new future and a new career. While you are dealing with this, you are also coping with the emotional impact of this life-changing event. People will be telling you how you must view it as an opportunity. They will be reassuring you that you will easily find another job and that it is bound to be something better. They will tell you that it will be an exciting adventure that will lead to a better paid and more rewarding job. They will be reminding you that you often used to complain about the job and wished you could leave. This may well be true but it is always easy to shout encouragement from the sidelines. It is alright for other people, dishing out advice from the secure position of a salary cheque landing in their bank accounts at the end of the month. They still have the security of their daily routines whereas you are adjusting to a life that you never imagined. Routine is a word you no longer recognize and I bet that at three o'clock in the morning you lie awake wondering if you will ever work again. Even if you are absolutely confident about your marketability and your skills, occasionally doubts creep in. Losing your job hits at the very roots of your security and, unless your redundancy cheque is seven figures, you know that eventually it will run out and you will have to find a way to pay the mortgage. The weight on your shoulders is a heavy one and it is a lonely place to be.

Accept that it is perfectly natural to have down days when you just can't be bothered to make one more telephone call or to write one more email. While it is important to maintain the momentum of a high energy and focused job search, you also need to make sure that you have a break and maintain your personal well being and equilibrium. Take time for exercise, whether this is going to the gym, attending a pilates class, Tai Chi, five-a-side football, running, walking or going for a swim. One of the best ways of combating stress is to burn it off through physical exercise. Rest, relaxation and a change of scenery also help you to regain your motivation as well as the confidence and the pace you need. Go for a coffee or a drink with a friend because it is as important to find the time for reflection as it is to be immersed in the nitty gritty of job hunting. The encouragement and companionship of others will lift your spirits and help you return to your tasks with a lighter spirit.

As well as the job search, you have to cope with the redundancy situation itself. You might be quite delighted to be leaving your job and you may regard this cheque as a bonus. However, you may be vulnerable to feelings of rejection, insecurity and lack of confidence. No matter how resilient you may normally be, your self-confidence has been given a nasty dent and it is from this lonely position that you have to start a job search and be performing at your absolute best. This is the time when you require every vestige of self-confidence that you can muster. You need to be full of self-belief and eager to look forward. In order for this to happen, you need first of all to resolve the issues of the old job and the redundancy so that you can put it behind you and move on. If you don't, this could hold you back and it may spill out in one way or another during interviews. Before you know it you will be talking too much about the redundancy, using all the wrong words, and sounding critical and bitter. Get rid of all of this before you start the job hunt. If possible, go away on holiday and give yourself the leisure time to absorb what has happened to you and to work it through in your head. The temptation will be to launch into action immediately, to start the telephone calls and the networking, but sometimes the best course of action is to do nothing and to create a period of calm where you can begin to restructure your thoughts about your future.

Pieter Schats, Managing Director of Toys LiFung (Asia) Limited, says:

I believe that everyone should lose their job once in their career. It focuses your mind on your own performance and it redefines the meaning of security.

However, it is also important to look at corporate performance and to recognize that it just may not be your fault. Other people in the organization will look at how the redundancy has been handled, hopefully with dignity and respect, and the whole process will speak volumes about the employer.

Finally, once you have experienced a redundancy situation yourself, you will make sure that no-one ever has to feel like you felt and you will be a better manager and better boss as a consequence.

Walking out on your job

Perhaps you have just walked out on your job or you have resigned without a job to go to. You may have marched into your boss's office and had the satisfaction of slapping your letter of resignation on the desk. However it happened, you are now living with the consequences of a brave decision. Whether it was something you had thought about carefully beforehand or if you responded to the impulse of the moment, the result is the same. You need to get a job – and you probably need to get it fast.

Everyone will tell you that it is always easier to get a job from a position of employment and perhaps it could be true. However, maybe this is an example of the rigid thinking of the 20th century, not the flexible and more tolerant views of the 21st. Of course, this depends on the reasons why you decide to leave. You might have decided to leave because you were faced with an unacceptable situation at work that caused you a moral dilemma. Maybe you were at odds with the company's values and you could not fit in. Maybe you realized that you had no future with the company and you were so unhappy that you just had to go. Whatever your reason, so long as you can justify it with clear examples of what drove you to this decision, prospective employers will understand. They may even be impressed by this demonstration of your strength of character and your self-confidence.

If you plan to find a job that matches your skills in a better way than the role you have just left, you will need to dedicate full-time resources to it. Job-hunting while you are working is a hard act to manage. You can spend your days off doing research and creating your CV and letters of application, but you need time during the normal hours of the working week to make telephone calls as well as attend informal meetings and interviews. Now that you are liberated from the day job, you can leap straight into action and secure that next role.

Bearing in mind that you need to leave a company in the right way, just as you need to join one properly, you may need to reflect on whether you need to build any bridges with your former employer. If you left in the heat of the moment and perhaps said things that now, in the cold light of day, you may now regret, find an opportunity to sort things out. You may not change your decision to leave but you can change the impression that you have left behind. You never know when your paths may cross again at some point in the future so make sure you have not left behind any unfinished business.

And if you were fired?

Generally good employers work within HR best practice and if they are experiencing problems with your performance at work, you will be made aware of it through feedback, both informal and formal. Disciplinary procedures and processes are in place and these are usually adhered to. Occasionally individuals ignore the process, tempers flare and the result could be your sudden and ignominious departure. However it happens and whatever action you may decide to take through the employment tribunal system, you are still left in an unhappy and probably emotional situation. You need to manage how you feel as well as rousing yourself to create a brilliant job-seeking strategy. It will be even worse if you are coping with lawyers, disciplinaries, statements and a personal cash crisis from the lack of salary. If this is the case:

- Talk the situation through with someone you respect.
- If you need it, get legal advice. Get in touch with your local Citizen's Advice Bureau, ACAS, your union representative or a friend who has knowledge of employment legislation. Find the extra resources you need to help you deal with the unknown.
- Check your insurance policies to see if they cover repayments on your mortgage.
- See if you can find someone who would be happy to act as a negotiator or a go-between to help find a solution.
- Beware of friends who encourage you to litigate. In the end you are the one who will be facing the long-drawn-out process to find a legal resolution. It is a long, lonely, risky and expensive road. Evaluate what

impact the attendant publicity could have on your career and your future employability. Make a pragmatic decision, not an emotional one.

- Start looking forward and take the first step to create a new career.

The graduate

After years of education, the final year with all of the stress and strain of deadlines and exams, followed by the triumph of the graduation ceremony itself, the moment of truth has arrived. The gap year has been completed in all of its Australasian glory and it is now time to get a job. A quick scan of the finances shows that student loans and overdrafts are at varying levels of awe-inspiring terror and the short-term jobs that have bailed you out up until now are just not up to this kind of financial task. It is time to get serious and start your career.

You may have a clear vocation and know that you are going to be a doctor, a lawyer, a nurse, an artist, a dancer, an actor, a teacher, a care worker, a vet or a social worker.

On the other hand, you may be like most graduates who have been in full time education for at least 16 years and who don't have a clue what to do next. You may have tried the university careers advisory service and have gone around recruitment fairs. You have probably spent hours on the Internet, looking at company websites and applying online for their graduate trainee scheme. It may seem at times that you are just trying for anything so now is the time to bring focus and clarity to the job search area.

Jan Shaw, Associate Director, Barracuda Research, says:

When choosing a career, remember that there are two very different career tracks. One is within a large corporate and the other is in a small, privately owned and entrepreneurially led organization. The two tracks are different and offer different kinds of career benefits. A major point of consideration is that whilst you can move later on from the large corporate to the small- or medium-sized enterprise, it will be difficult if not impossible to achieve the other way round. People from big branded organizations are always attractive to small companies as they have a different skill set that could add value to a fast growing business. However, someone who has not had the benefits of a graduate trainee scheme will find it difficult to make the transition into that big brand.

Why is this so? Well, within the PLC, the multinational organization, the financial institution or the global player, it is likely that you will join as part of a graduate trainee scheme and you will go through carefully planned training where you will learn about the company, the role you will be fulfilling and the nature of the corporate structure of which you have become a part. You will become familiar with their language and their way of managing and working. You will be able to forge a career path here or in a similar company. The same is true for accountancy and legal jobs.

Be aware that certain companies have the reputation for delivering high quality people through their graduate trainee schemes and their subsequent integration into the organization. IBM employees used to be some of the most admired people around. Market leaders change so keep up to date with who is who and if you are ambitious, determined and ready to dedicate your all to the organization, target them because of what they will offer. To have a stint within some companies will open doors for you later in life so be clear that if you are aiming to create your own blue chip CV, you need to build it with years spent in blue chip organizations. If you have a more entrepreneurial mindset, building a blue chip CV will serve no purpose whatsoever so you need to consider what value you would gain from time spent in a corporate environment.

If you decide to join a small company that is entrepreneurially led where you are thrown in the deep end, you will develop your management style and your skills in a very different way. It is unlikely that there will be a structured training and development scheme. You will learn from people around you and have different kinds of responsibilities and decision-making in an often exciting, fast-moving environment. These may not always be attractive to the large corporate organizations, raising questions about your ability to fit into their culture.

There is nothing wrong with following either of these routes. Just be aware that they are different. And that the decision you make early in your career could close one of them off forever.

The best job for you

To track down the best job for you, you need to use all of those project management and research skills that you developed and perfected at university. Now you are going to use them to tackle the most important assignment you will have handled to date. It is called 'The best job for me'. Open up a file, either a physical paper/plastic file or a computer file or both. This is going to be the starting point for formulating the strategy that you will be following to get the best possible results. Before you leap into action, let's establish the goal. Ask yourself the following questions:

- Have I finished studying or do I want to go for a further qualification at this time?
- Am I going to go for another gap year?
- When do I want to start work?
- Where do I want to live?
- Where do I NOT want to live?
- Will I consider moving abroad?
- Are there any jobs I absolutely will not consider doing?
- How much money do I need to earn?

This job search might be the easiest task you have ever undertaken. You might be offered the first job that you apply for and you might decide to accept it. Equally, you might have to persevere and apply for hundreds of jobs, attend dozens of interviews and become an expert on the different kinds of assessment centres. Whatever you do, don't compromise about what you want to do as once you have started work, you are likely to stay there for a while and to keep at it. The best way to be sure that you are aiming for the right job is to pursue a broad range of options. You can do this via a number of means:

- University career services
- Graduate recruitment fairs
- Advertisements in newspapers and magazines
- Internet job sites and corporate recruitment pages
- Networking through friends and family
- Looking at the career paths of graduates in previous years.

Practicalities to consider

When you go into your job search, remember how hard you have worked to get to where you are today. Think of all of the obstacles you have overcome and all of the challenges you have faced to get to this point. This is the culmination of years of effort, work and expense. Determination, focus and motivation will get you to the next stage. You need to go out there to find the right job for you and you need to make it happen by uncovering as many possibilities as you can. Your unique skills and your unique personality will flourish in the right place so make sure you find it.

Following the stratagems in this book will help make sure that you take the element of chance out of your job. Be sure that what you are doing is a positive choice and is absolutely what you want to do, not what you have ended up doing.

The challenge you will face is how to open up career possibilities. How can you open up choices if you don't even know they exist? How irritating is it to be asked as a teenager or new graduate what it is you want to do when you start work? How on earth can you know, unless you are one of the 8% with a clear vocation or unless you have a superb careers service that has given you a comprehensive insight into the world of work?

To broaden your horizons, move outside the known and the comfortable. Research shows that many people follow their parents or their siblings into similar roles. Despite the vast possibilities that there are in the world, it seems that we do little to explore them. Make a conscious decision now to aspire to more and to be ambitious.

How are you practically going to achieve this? Ideas to find out more could include:

- Roaming the Internet
- Talking to people – friends, relatives, advisers and those you admire in business
- Exploring job boards
- Visiting careers fairs
- Reading a broad selection of newspapers
- Buying and reading magazines and trade press or journals.

Facing the financial music

Whenever you make a change in careers or consider the start of a brand new one, there will be a financial impact, either positive or negative. If you have a gap between jobs, there could be cash flow implications that could cause you anxiety and could impact on the confidence you portray at job interviews. In order to avoid this, the best way forward is to face the financial music and work out exactly where you stand. To get the best advice I could on this I spoke to Kevin Johnson to discuss the financial impact that being out of work can have. Based on the assumption that the money you are paid is for the work that you do, it follows that when that financial security disappears, then anxiety, worry, desperation or panic can ensue, wondering about the mortgage, the supermarket bills, the credit card bills and the utility bills, never mind the realization that the holiday in the Caribbean has just disappeared over the horizon. Kevin believes in facing up to those concerns and worries. He believes you need to assess exactly what your financial situation is as you need to be on top of all of the financial facts in order to make the right kind of career decisions. You need to know whether you can afford to take a pay cut if you are considering changing career direction. You need to know what impact there would be if your company did not pay the bonus that is on offer.

The 'Kevin Johnson personal business plan'

To complement the job seeking process, produce your own financial plan. In order to do this you will need to:

- Create a personal balance sheet
- Create a cash emergency fund
- Look at your levels of protection, e.g. insurance policies
- Identify your 'personal worth' – i.e. how much will someone pay you?
- Establish new financial plans to take control of your future and build your wealth for a secure and comfortable future.

Let's deal with these in a little more detail one by one:

Create a personal balance sheet

When you lose your job or are contemplating a change in job, a useful and usually reassuring exercise is to create a personal balance sheet. As Kevin says, you wouldn't run a business without one so why run yourself and your family this way?

You may have many assets but not be aware of all of them and certainly not their value. Take the time to review everything that you have. Start with a list of your assets and know exactly what you have, for example:

- The equity in your house, which is its value less outstanding mortgage
- Endowment policies taken out to repay your mortgage
- Bank and building society deposits.
- A car
- ISAs and PEPs
- Shares and share options

- Insurance policies
- Child benefit
- Premium bonds
- Pensions, personal and from previous employers
- Antiques and collectables
- State pension.

Also list your possible liabilities, such as:

- Mortgage
- Credit cards
- Student loans
- Overdraft and loans
- School fees
- Insurance policies.

Once you have quantified the situation you will have a much improved understanding of your finances and have the foundation from which to continue building your wealth. You may feel your balance sheet needs to be made more liquid to manage your short-term commitments or you may wish to change your investments to meet your new attitude to risk. Whatever the outcome, you will learn a great deal. Kevin advocates facing demons and resisting any effort to bury your head in the sand. Knowing where you stand financially is much better than living with the gnawing anxiety of where you think you might be.

Create a cash emergency fund

If you lose your job or decide to start a new venture it is vital to be able to manage your family finances until income returns.

The first important step is to analyse your expenditure. It's surprising how much is spent on non-essentials. I didn't like to own up to Kevin just where I stand on this one. However, I am sure we all have different definitions of the word 'essential'. Like a business that has to conserve cash and operate on a tight budget, Kevin tells us to cut out capital and exceptional expenditure. If you can take a payment holiday on savings plans it may be helpful to keep your money in cash form rather than tie it up over the medium to long term. However, before you embark on anything like this, make sure that you always take independent advice.

It is surprising how little you need to cover the bare essentials and once you have established exactly what this is, try to see that you have the cash to cover this level of expenditure for at least three months.

Protection

When you are employed it is usual for employers to provide varying forms of protection such as Life and Critical Illness Assurance and private medical provisions. Once you are no longer employed these benefits cease. Whilst the conservation of cash is key to managing the transition back to work, the loss of life or medical cover to a family should seriously be considered and, again, independent advice sought before you do anything.

Identify your 'worth'

I was curious to know why Kevin was so rigorous in personal financial management. He told me that it all stemmed from a time when he first became aware of the money someone would spend to employ him. He had been made redundant and had found an interim role with a private company manufacturing and marketing collectable giftware. Obviously in his previous roles he knew what salary he had been paid and the benefits package that went with it but he had never calculated it on a daily rate. He said that on returning from the first day in the interim role, he recalled thinking that for the first time in his career he had been paid for a day's work and that he was returning the following day to earn the same amount of money. The realization dawned on Kevin that he had to earn his money daily and each day's performance was critical to his being retained. He says that he promised himself that even if he were to revert to being salaried, he would always retain this self-employed philosophy. His perspective also changed so that instead of thinking as if he was working for the company, he felt he was working for himself. He realized that he was as good as the last day's achievements and no-one owed him a living.

Establish new financial plans

Once you are back to receiving an income you should build on your experience of the disappearance of the monthly pay cheque and the change of perspective that it brought with it.

You should have already built your balance sheet which will tell you your net worth. You should then decide your or your family's financial objectives and develop investment and protection strategies to achieve your goals. This is the way a business normally develops its plans but so often this process is neglected by individuals who ironically perform this task for their business but fail to do it for their family's future. Establish new financial plans to take control of your life and build your wealth so you can enjoy a secure and comfortable future. While you are actively job seeking, you will achieve greater confidence if you know exactly where you stand financially. You will know if you need to compromise your career aspirations for now in order to gain an income in the short term or if you can afford to keep on looking. You will negotiate a better package with your new employer because you will know exactly what parameters you are working within.

Thinking of starting your own business?

Are you attracted by the dream of running your own business? In the entrepreneurial business environment of the 21st century, the job for life with the gilt-edged pension is a rare commodity so running your own business is comparatively not as risky as it used to be.

Ensure that you make the time to consider whether or not running your own business is really for you. Is it a dream or can it be a reality? So many people look back at their careers and regret that they never took the chance to break away from being a wage slave. They read the *Sunday Times* Rich List and wistfully wonder if that could have been them. If this is what you think, then make a decision about it now and don't let it be a regret for your old age. Bring the dream into sharper focus by homing in on the details: the idea, the business plan, your experience.

Ask yourself the hard questions:

1 **Company structure**
   Who owns the equity?
   How will you structure the board?
2 **People**
   How many people do you need?
   What will the management structure look like?
   Who will be responsible for what?
   What skills are critical for the first few months?
   How will decisions be made?
3 **Finance and planning**
   Where is the initial investment coming from and how will you fund it?

Have you explored the options for funding? For example, venture capital, external funders, business angels, bank loan, remortgaging the house?

What is the three-year plan for growth?

What is a realistic target for year 1, year 2 and year 3?

4 **Markets and customers**

Define your product

What is your market?

Who are your customers?

Who are your competitors?

5 **Selling the business**

What is the 'exit' strategy? Will you sell it on or will you run it forever?

Talk through your plans and your ideas with someone whose opinion you value and who has achieved business success themselves. See what the plan looks like when it is exposed to the harsh light of day.

When you run your own business, the buck stops with you. You are the person who puts the energy into the business and makes things happen. A huge percentage of new businesses fail within the first 12 months, and this rises even more steeply within five years of starting up. You need vision, determination and the confidence to get through – good luck.

For further help and information on starting out on this path, see the following websites and books:

www.beermat.biz/
www.flyingstartups.com
www.businesslink.gov.uk
www.startups.co.uk/

1   Ashton, Robert, *The Entrepreneur's Book of Checklists: 1000 tips to help you start and grow your business* (£12.99, Prentice-Hall, September 2004)

2   Barrow, Colin, *Starting a Business For Dummies* (£15.99, Wiley, June 2004)

3   Barrow, Colin & Tracy, John, *Understanding Business Accounting For Dummies* (£16.99, Wiley, September 2004)

4   Branson, Sir Richard, *Losing My Virginity: The Autobiography* (£9.99, Virgin Books, June 2005)

5   Dearlove, Des, *Business the Richard Branson Way: 10 secrets of the world's greatest brand builder*, 3rd edition (£9.99, Capstone, March 2007)

6   Hashemi, Sahar, *Anyone Can Do It: Building Coffee Republic From Our Kitchen Table: 57 Real-life Laws on Entrepreneurship*, 2nd edition (£8.99, Capstone, February 2007)

7   Robbins, Anthony, *Awaken the Giant Within: How to take immediate control of your mental, emotional, physical and financial life* (£10.99, Pocket Books, June 2001)

8   Southon, Mike & West, Chris, *The Beermat Entrepreneur: Turn your idea into a great business* (£12.99, Prentice-Hall, October 2005)

9   Summers, Heather & Watson, Anne, *The Book of Luck: Brilliant ideas for creating your own success and making life go your way* (£7.99, Capstone, April 2006)

10   Webb, Martin, *Make Your First Million: Ditch the 9–5 and start the business of your dreams* (£12.99, Capstone, April 2007).

The right job for you

So, what does your ideal job look like? Before you begin to formulate your job strategy, make sure you think about the things you enjoy and what you like doing, putting them in a work or a business context. Use a sheet or paper or the worksheet overleaf to start identifying and listing the vital elements of your life that are the most important to you. This way you will be sure that you are moving in a direction which fits with your broader life goals.

Next, find three people whose opinions you value and ask them to tell you what they think you are good at and add this to the table. The external view is one that you will find encourages you as you will gain something unexpected from this objective viewpoint. It can also be quite challenging as you will have cause to reflect on the opinions of others. They might identify something about you that you were completely unaware of. It could be something good and it might be something bad. If you didn't know about it then it is a blindspot and this blindspot could cause you problems in job seeking situations – knowing about it in advance is a real advantage.

The strengths that others identify that you might not have been aware of may flag up previously untapped areas for personal growth and may cause you to think differently about the scope that you have.

What I like doing:	What I don't like doing:
1.	1.
2.	2.
3.	3.
4.	4.
5.	5.
What I am good at:	**What I am bad at and refuse to do:**
1.	1.
2.	2.
3.	3.
4.	4.
5.	5.

What do other people think I am good at?
1.
2.
3.

Jane Chapman's 'Who are you really?' exercise

Before you start to fill this in, start thinking of occasions when you enjoy yourself, times when you most enjoy what you are doing. Put this in a work context as we are focusing on what is important to you in your work and your career. Of course, you can do it again thinking about your personal life to apply the microscope to how you spend your free time.

- Take away any constraints and imagine six occasions and events when you were thoroughly happy, thoroughly at ease and caught up in the enjoyment of the event.
- Having thought of these events, now look at them with different eyes. This is to help you identify the situation or context which you were enjoying, e.g. a meeting with a like-minded colleague or a visit to a customer or being part of a team for an exciting project. Look at these situations as though you were a camera operator. See the events as though they were unfolding in front of you and look at the person that is you objectively. What do you see?
- Now look closer and hear what you are saying and see what you are doing. What words are you using and what is the tone and the pitch of your voice? How are you behaving?
- Look even closer and work out what you are thinking and feeling inside.

Now write it all down in the chart overleaf. If you need to, use extra paper. Get it all down about exactly what was going on during these six key occasions in your life. Although most of the situations should be work-related it may be helpful to include a couple of non-work examples to increase the possibility of spotting useful themes.

	What the video sees	What I am saying and doing	What I am thinking and feeling inside
Event number 1			
Event number 2			
Event number 3			
Event number 4			
Event number 5			
Event number 6			

Who are you really?

Now that you have finished, look at the three columns and find the consistencies. Where are the common threads?

- Is it when you are talking or when you are listening?
- Is it when you are acting or when you are reflecting?
- Is it when you are solving problems and finding ways forward or is it when you are sitting in a calm, ordered environment with no crises?
- Is it an environment with lots of people present, just a few or just yourself?

Look at all of this carefully and find out what the common denominators are. You should have now defined the critical qualities of enjoyment in a job and you can evaluate your current role against them.

Here's an example of what it could look like:

	What the video sees	What I am saying and doing	What I am thinking and feeling inside
Event number 1	Active participant in a management meeting. Good team player – helps the meeting along with ideas and chat.	I am talking a lot and probably not listening as much as I could. I am filling in all of the silences and being a good leader.	I love the energy I get from being part of the team and working with others. I feel more confident and think I will be more successful when I am in front of customers.
Event number 2	A competent exhibitor at an international exhibition. Making the most of opportunities.	I am stopping people passing by and initiating a lot of conversations with strangers.	I love the action and the pace. I feel on a high because I am meeting so many new people. I feel optimistic that I am getting things right.
Event number 3	A confident salesperson talking to a customer and making a good presentation.	I am using all of my sales materials and skills to close a sale. Maybe I am not letting the customer talk as much as they should.	I feel an adrenalin rush and like the feeling that I may close a sale. I feel confident and optimistic that I will win it, even if I don't.
Event number 4	A manager is meeting with a team member to give feedback on performance.	I am meeting with a field sales person to discuss performance. I am using charts and graphs to make my point and I am being quite direct in my opinions.	I am feeling a bit awkward about this. I don't like giving bad news and I could be more forceful.
Event number 5	A group of people attending a training course about finance for non-financial managers.	I am alert, active and making sure that people know I am there.	I am a bit bored and keep catching myself day dreaming and drifting.
Event number 6	A busy gym after work with lots of people working away on their fitness programmes.	I am here for one of my three visits per week. Busy getting on with it and chatting to friends who are there.	I feel involved and included, liking the buzz and the companionship.

The common threads of this example are that we have someone who loves being part of the crowd, working in a fast-paced environment and engaging in constant interaction with others. This person is more action orientated than reflective and seems to operate at their best in a team environment. They have already identified as part of the process that talking is their preferred option, rather than listening. Any role should therefore be one that is customer-focused, part of a large team and one that requires an intuitive and fast response, rather than a well thought through and academic reaction. A sales role would be ideal, or a teacher: anything that means they will be surrounded by people and with constant external stimuli.

Identify your skills and experience

It is also important to work out what experience and skills you have already, what personal attributes you have that add a unique quality to the job that you do, and what environment you thrive in. Work these things out before you begin your job search and you will be able to recognize the right job when you find it. Not only that, you will avoid blind alleys and wasting time looking at jobs that will be wrong for you. Now is the time to recognize what skill gaps you might have and start to take steps to bridge them. If, for example, you don't have a degree and this is proving to be a barrier for you in your career development, explore whether or not you want to embark on some kind of degree course. You could have a look at courses in the Open University or you could consider bypassing a first degree and going straight for an MBA. There are a great deal of flexible learning options so decide what it is that you lack and consider how far you are prepared to go to address them. You can then include this study programme on your CV and demonstrate that you are keen to develop and to learn.

Your ideal job is likely to be one where you are using the skills and behaviours you enjoy, with the right sort of people, in the right sort of environment.

Fill in the chart opposite to help you identify the skills that you have and the ones that you would like to develop. Remember:

- Include hard skills – computer programming, forecasting, buying, merchandising, budget planning, languages, software knowledge, coaching, public speaking, legal, technical, driving, writing, digging, nursing.
- And include soft skills – relationship building, listening, communicating, managing people, conflict resolving.
- What are the core skills you want to use?

- what are the specialist skills you want to use?

When describing your ideal job, you can include skills you don't currently have but that you are developing or hoping to develop.

	Hard skills I have now	Hard skills I want to develop	Soft skills I have now	Soft skills I want to develop
1.				
2.				
3.				
4.				
5.				
6.				
7.				
8.				
9.				
10.				

You can use this chart to focus on how you can develop in your existing role or use it to work out what you need to work on and develop to move into the kind of role that is more appealing.

People and environment

Now think about the people who are (or were) in your orbit at work or university, and who can have an impact on your working day. This will include your colleagues, customers, boss, managers, suppliers and staff.

- What are they like?
- How would you describe them?
- How would you recognize them?
- What do you talk to them about?
- What do they say about you?
- What do you have in common?
- Where is there irritation or a source of conflict?
- Where do you think you will operate best?

Be honest with yourself and decide if you want to relocate or if you are happy with where you are now. Perhaps you like the town where you went to university. Maybe relocation is not an option because of your children's education or your partner's career. Whatever it is, take the time to work out what is right for you so that you get to the place where you want to be, working the hours that suit you and in the culture that matches your values. So what do you want?

- Local, national, international or global?
- Which industry sector, e.g. telecoms, public sector, health care or high tech?
- What working conditions – full or part-time, flexible, working from home or commuting?
- What organizational culture and values are you looking for?
- What working style do you prefer? (e.g. research lab or high-paced media, etc).
- What pay and benefits do you expect?

List the elements of your ideal job:

Skills and behaviours	People	Environment

Now rate your current or recent job against your ideal job. If your current job gives you satisfaction in less than five areas, is it time to move on, or at least to change the scope of your current role?

Jane Chapman, Development Consultant, Financial Services, says:

Remember that every job has bits that we don't enjoy. However, no more than 20% should be a pain to do. Someone who has a job that is sheer unadulterated and unalloyed pleasure 100% of the time is either hugely fortunate or lying. Life is about balance so make sure the balance is right for you.

CHAPTER 2

CRAFTING THE PERFECT CV

RESULT: THE PERFECT MARKETING TOOL

You are unique

Your CV reflects the person that you are with all of your unique skills, experience, qualifications, character and achievements. No-one else will have a CV that is the same as yours. This is you, only you. That is why it is so important to spend the time you need to get it right and to be sure that when you have finished you are satisfied that it matches who you think you are. However, you need to remember that this document will be two or three pages long. It cannot possibly be the ultimate and definitive version of who you are. It is one version and needs constant fine-tuning, redefining and repositioning. Bearing that in mind, how do you go about creating it?

The five stages of life

There are five key categories of people who will be assessing their experience and wondering how to make it accurate and exciting.

These key categories are:

The graduate. At this stage of life, academic and theoretical knowledge far outweighs experience. The challenge here is to make the most of the life experiences that you have to date and from them to create a compelling story that shows your potential. You need to include your holiday jobs, voluntary work, gap year experience, jury service, dissertation-writing, clubs you joined and draw from that the life lessons and the skills that you have so a potential employer will be able to see what you are capable of.

The second jobber. By now you have experience to draw on and you can point to achievements within a corporate and business environment that show you are building a career on solid foundations. You need to highlight the key learnings in your role and the self-knowledge that came with it. You will be demonstrating a maturity of thought that excites the reader.

The step changer. You are now established in your career and you are looking for advancement, either in your chosen field or branching out in a new direction. You may be reinventing yourself and need to ensure that you position yourself appropriately

Third lifer/redundant executive. You are job seeking because of where life has led you and you are facing difficult choices. You need to assess how marketable you are, you may be overqualified and you might want to do something different. You will need to keep an open mind and make sure that your CV reflects the flexibility and diversity of your attitude and experience.

The return-to-worker. You don't fit the mould and you are having to make major adjustments to re-enter the conventional job market. You might be returning to work after an absence where you looked after children or cared for others; you might have left the armed forces and are re-entering civilian life. You could be re-entering the UK after time overseas. Your challenge is to shape and mould your experiences and achievements so that they are relevant to the job market that you want to enter.

The perfect CV

The preparation of the perfect CV is the most essential item for any job search or life change. This will be your personal calling card and will be your own brochure, the synopsis of who you are and the essence of you. It will contain the information that you want other people to know about you. When someone reads it, they will instantly get a clear picture of your experience, your education, your achievements and an idea about the talents you would bring to another organization. Just one, two or three pages will give someone all of the information that they may need to make the decision whether or not they want to meet you. The most important document that you will have in the course of this search is the perfectly crafted CV. Even better, while you are working on creating this wonderful document, you will have the opportunity to reflect on who you are, what you have achieved and where you are going. It will allow you to think about what you enjoyed along the way and what you didn't. You can think about tasks you excelled at and tasks you struggled with. It is the chance to evaluate and reflect so let's make sure you make the most of it.

Before you begin, first of all recognize that the perfect CV does not exist. It is a myth that has been perpetrated by employers, recruiters and people who believe that they know better than anyone. All that exists around the perfect CV is a plethora of opinions and prejudices. Your task is to come up with a solution that you can use for a number of situations so you will have to recognize before you begin that you need not one but two or more versions of the same document. A generic CV will work if you just want to give people the bare facts about who you are. It won't do as part of a carefully thought through application for a specific job. Flexibility is the name of the game and it has to come from you. The perfect CV for your purposes is going to be a CV that exists in several formats and is regularly updated, depending on what you intend to use it for. Let's make sure that you have a portfolio of CVs to meet every eventuality, every prejudice and every situation.

No shortcuts

Never be tempted to rush out a CV to someone just because they are in a hurry and they are pushing you to give them what they want. As soon as you send out a CV that has been hastily prepared and thrown together, it will be there in black and white for all to see. It will be forgotten that you did it in an hour late at night because the head-hunter needed to find out more about you. You will be remembered for a poorly thought through document and it will be the only example that anyone has of your quality of work. You would not send out a draft copy of something to a customer so don't think that it can ever be right to rush out a CV. There is only one way to do a CV and that is properly. If you are put under pressure to deliver a CV, offer to have a telephone conversation to describe your career. Failing that, stay up all night and get it perfect. If you are reviewing an existing CV, please don't be lazy – you can't update a CV by just inserting your new job. You need to review it radically. That CV was written when you were working for someone else and the tone will reflect it.

The one that is too thin

One CV you need in your portfolio is the analytical and objective 'snapshot' CV that is short, sharp, and to the point. This CV will exclude anything that could reveal the inner you. It will be a maximum of two pages and, if you are feeling particularly word-shy, you could even get it onto one page. This will work marvellously as your terse 'bare facts' CV. It is one that can be included in tender documents or proffered when you are unsure of the recruitment situation you are approaching. Use this for the brisk no nonsense, no frills, facts-only situations when your audience is likely to be totally disinterested in your hobbies, your family, your interests, your passions, your ambitions or your values. This works well as your introduction to an unknown situation. Your 'bare facts' CV will not set off any possible prejudices in your readership. You won't annoy anyone with your use of English as it is all just factual. This is just the scaled down essentials of who you are. Remember, however, that this CV has its limitations. It won't irritate or jar but equally it won't engage. It won't work for a specific advertisement where there are specific skills and experience required of the successful candidate.

The one that is too fat

A CV that I often see is the one that is pages long and gives every detail of someone's life and experience. They have put everything in there, every detail about every job, every achievement, every success and every detail of their life. It is as though the reader will want to know every element of the candidate's life and have to work out for themselves what is relevant for the job that could be on offer. This CV gives a detailed, technicolour picture that the candidate naively believes will help me to make a positive decision about their future. This is the confident, too fat CV – the no-holds-barred view of their life where they have let down their guard, opening up everything about them. Unfortunately, there are not many situations when anyone is sufficiently interested to read this mini biography. No-one has the time to sift through such a pile of information. The recipient will form adverse conclusions about the lack of clarity of thought and the inability to be incisive and concise. This kind of CV is only about the person and not about the proposed role. It shows no reflection on how the experiences could be tempered or moulded to new demands and it will be consigned to the reject pile.

The one that is just right

The one that is just right is the one that is less cryptic than the too thin CV and less open than the too fat CV. This is the CV that sits neatly in the middle. It contains all of the facts that anyone could possibly want and at the same time is quite revealing. It explores and develops the facts, allowing the reader to see just what you can lay claim to in terms of achievements in specific roles. It is professional, objective and warm in its tone. It will also be intelligent, it will reflect the experience you have that is relevant for this specific role and it will look as though it has been specifically tailored. In addition, it will show the occasional tantalizing glimpse of the real you and it will lure people into wanting to know more about you, your style and your ambitions. It will arouse some curiosity in the reader and it will leave them wondering about how you managed to achieve certain successes and why you made certain career moves. In short, it will mean that the reader wants to meet you to find out more. This is the objective of any CV and is the measure of its success.

The right one for you

When you are preparing your CV, it might be perfectly clear to you that you are seeking a specific role in one type of organization. You might be a teacher, an accountant, an engineer, a nurse, an operational research scientist or a graphic artist, and you might be seeking a similar role in another organization. If you have this total clarity about your next move, then it is easier to focus on the skills, experience and achievements that you need to highlight. However, you may well be someone with a number of career options open to you and your CV needs to make it clear which path it is you want to follow. In this case, you might need a different CV for each eventuality. I know someone who is a qualified medical doctor, a psychiatrist and an international tax specialist. He probably has three CVs where he emphasizes different areas.

Equally there are many people with strong technical, scientific or engineering backgrounds who have moved into sales. They could move easily into either a sales or a technical discipline so the CV needs to make explicit what it is they are seeking. It is very important that the CV reflects very clearly what your intentions are. If you want an engineering role, concentrate on those aspects of your career and your achievements. If you want a sales role, give all of the data that demonstrates your ability to develop and grow accounts. Just do not mix them up, hoping that a prospective employer will be able to work it out for themselves. The most dangerous thing a job seeker can do it to make assumptions either about the level of interest a reader has in their CV or the level of intelligence they are applying to reading it. Be clear about who you are, what you are good at and what you are aspiring to. Make it easy for the reader so that when I, a simple-minded recruitment consultant, pick up your CV, I will understand what you can do and what you want out of life. Above and beyond anything else, make sure I am interested enough to want to meet you.

Creating a career data bank

Before you begin to think about style, format, phrases and the way you will structure your CV, you need to collect the data that you will be using. The format will come later. Now is your opportunity to rack your brains and remember everywhere you have been, what you did when you were there and what you achieved. If you can't remember specific dates, then find out. Ask your mother, ask your partner, find old diaries, look at certificates, hunt out old salary slips, P45s, P60s and anything else that you have in a box under the bed or in the attic that will refresh your memory of your past. This is your opportunity to remember things you had forgotten. You may have skills that you learnt a few years ago that are not relevant in your current role but which would be highly attractive to a new employer. Give yourself the time and the space to go back over your past and bring everything to the front of your mind. Use the following charts to start sketching out the framework of fact that will form the backbone of your CV. This exercise will also ensure that what you are putting on your CV will be accurate – you will know the grades of your exams and you will get all of the dates right for your previous jobs.

PERSONAL	
Name	
Address	
Home telephone number	
Office telephone number	
Mobile telephone number	
Date of birth (if you want)	
Age (if you want)	
Marital status (Single/married/separated/divorced/ cohabiting. No adjectives or adverbs please – no 'happily' no 'wonderful' or 'blissful'!)	
Children (Ages only. No names, no adjectives.)	
EDUCATION	
University – name and dates attended	
Technical college – name and dates attended	
Open University – dates attended	
Secondary school – name and dates attended	
Primary school – name and dates attended	
Degree	
GNVQ	
NVQ	
A/A2 levels – subjects and grades	

AS levels – subjects and grades	
GCSE – subjects and grades	
Professional qualifications	
TRAINING	
Courses undertaken, starting with the most recent	
1.	
2.	
3.	
4.	
5.	
6.	
Career Start with the most recent and work backwards. The impact you want to make is what you have been doing in the past month, not what you were doing when you were 21.	
Most recent company Brief description of it: market, turnover, products, no. of employees, location. Just because you know all about it does not mean that I will.	
Your job title Reporting to?	

Key achievements while there (give me the highlights! What are you most proud of? What will you be remembered for?):
  1.
  2.
  3.
  4.
  5.
  6.
  7.
Come on – keep going! You did more than that!
  8.
  9.
  10.	

Company before that Brief description of it: market, turnover, products, no. of employees, location.	
Your job title Reporting to?	

Key achievements while there (we are not going for quite as much detail as the first job but still focusing on the value that you added to the business):
  1.
  2.
  3.
  4.
  5.
  6.	

Company before that Brief description of it: market, turnover, products, no. of employees, location.	
Your job title Reporting to?	

Key achievements while there:
  1.
  2.
  3.	

Company before that Brief description of it: market, turnover, products, no. of employees, location.	
Your job title Reporting to?	
Key achievements while there: 1. 2. 3.	
Holiday jobs, part-time jobs, work experience (If you are a recent graduate, you will want to include these to show that you haven't spent every holiday on a beach or at music festivals.)	
Leisure pursuits (You probably won't be including this on your CV but you will need to have thought about it just in case you are asked the question at interview. Also, if you are filling in an online application, you may be asked abour this so let's be prepared).	
Anything else we have missed out? (Publications, claims to fame, awards, offices held, club treasurer, part-time counsellor, charity work?)	

Remember that at interview you are going to be challenged on what you claim on your CV. This might be a direct question about when you were National Sales Manager, asking you about the number of accounts that you handled, how much they grew when you were managing them and asking you to highlight a specific account and what you did to grow it. You may not include this on your CV but make sure that you have those specific examples and case studies at the front of your mind so that you are ready to substantiate the claims that you are making.

Achievement – what you claim in your CV, e.g. profit growth, change in systems, team building, cross-cultural growth, new product development, operational excellence, financial controls, management of people, logistics, systems, procedures, processes	A specific example or case study to justify it
1.	
2.	
3.	
4.	
5.	
6.	
7.	
8.	
9.	
10.	

General rules for creating your 'perfect' CV

Before you launch yourself enthusiastically into the task of writing your CV, let's explore the common mistakes that people make when they are creating their CV.

Martine Robins, European Human Resources Director, Cookson Electronics, says:

In order to have a credible CV you need to:
- *Map events in your career*
- *Give highlights not detail*

You pick up the language in a CV – you're looking for it to be proactive and dynamic. The CV needs to whet the appetite of the reader. At interview this will be qualified and will be focused on in more detail. The CV itself needs to be well laid out with not too much information, yet not be too sparse. You need to show that you have thought about the key points in your career and show that you are someone who is in tune with what has gone on in your career and savvy enough to portray it. If you have had a bad experience, include it in your CV.

Truth – the golden rule

Whatever you put in your CV, make sure it is the truth. Leave out all inventions and fabrications. Don't be tempted to stretch the truth and lay claim to something that you haven't got and that you never did. Embellishing CVs takes many forms and the most common lie is the claim to a qualification that you don't have. Be aware that, eventually, you will be found out and then not only will you then lose your job, but your reputation will be irreparably damaged. Look at high-profile examples of people who have fallen into the trap of overstating their case:

- Alison Ryan was sacked before she even started as Head of PR for Manchester United in 2000 when she was caught out in a lie about her degree.
- Marilee Jones, dean of admissions of Massachusetts Institute of Technology (MIT) lied about her qualifications in 1979 when she applied for a secretarial job. The lie was uncovered in 2007, 28 years after her original false claims. She was forced to resign and her reputation is in tatters.

Another common CV lie is to omit a job and pretend you were never there. This may be because you only stayed there a short time and you don't think it counts. People can check out your employment record and it is much harder to explain away a lie than it is to justify why you joined a company and it did not work out.

Maintain your integrity and you will have nothing to fear.

Technology to help you

Many of the job boards you will visit will have a CV format that you can look at and adapt. Remember that the key to success is constant reinvention of who you are and how your skills can be applied in different situations. The careers page on corporate websites may have a CV format for you to follow and the websites of many head-hunters have tips on how they like to see CVs presented. Look at all of them and do so with a critical eye. You know what you need to do to ensure that you put yourself forward in the best possible light. Don't be deflected by others. Maintain your focus and yet always be open to new possibilities.

Do you want to update your CV electronically? Clare Howard of e-coaches cordially invites all of you to register at www.i-portfolio.co.uk where you can create your free i-portfolio to keep your career data all in one place, and use it as building blocks for creating your CV time and time again. You can also access more toolkit tests to help you find out about yourself, and explore career and training options.

Updating your CV

Having got your CV into a shape that you are satisfied with, don't rest on your laurels. You need to keep reviewing it and updating it. Your career is dynamic and your learning opportunities are continuous. The CV will quickly cease to reflect all of your achievements so revisit and update it. This way you will be sure that it is always ready for the opportunities that are awaiting you.

Nadine Jones, Head of Human Resources, Baugur says:
Update your CV regularly – I would recommend reviewing your CV every time you apply for a role. The analogy here is to view your CV like your passport – you need to know where it is and be ready to 'travel' – most of us will check before we travel – how will I get to and from the airport, do I need vaccinations, etc.; yet I've met many candidates who think it's adequate to subject a recruiter to a dusty dog-eared copy of a CV that was (if at all) updated in five minutes the night before it was sent! If you view your CV in the same way as your passport and invest time in tailoring your CV and application to the role your chances of success are much higher.

The e-mail address

One of the first things you will be showing a prospective employer is your e-mail address. It is part of your identity, just like your name, your mobile telephone number and your home address. It is the first thing that someone like me will read when it appears in my in box. The first line of contact from me would be anne@executive-focus.co.uk – nothing wrong with that, is there? Now have a look at your e-mail address and consider what it says about you. Is it one of those zany addresses that make all of your friends laugh? Believe me, drunkstudent@email.com or partygoer@email.com may bring the house down with your mates in the pub but it will cut no ice with a future employer. Give yourself a professional image and get a boring e-mail address that has your name in it.

Perhaps you haven't bothered to get a private e-mail address and you use your girlfriend's, your boyfriend's, your mother's or your flatmate's? It is strangely unsettling to find that an e-mail from Jane Fletcher is actually from her husband George. It sits in my in box looking like someone else. What does this tell me about you before I even begin? Are you so far behind in the technological age that you haven't mastered the art of having your own e-mail address? Or are you just too lazy to get one? Whichever it is, it is the wrong message to someone who is going to help you get the next job. Go on, sign up for an e-mail account and keep it for the job search.

Another major faux pas is to apply for a job using your current work e-mail address. Please don't do this. Firstly it isn't secure, it certainly isn't private and moreover, you are giving a prospective employer the impression that you are job-hunting in office time. Whether you are or you are not, there is no need to advertise it, so get that private address out and use it! Keep your work e-mail address off your CV and never be tempted to use it.

Spelling

A recent report from the BBC showed that poor spelling on CVs is a major flaw for most job hunters. Research carried out by the Recruitment and Employment Confederation found that:

'47% of all CVs received by agencies contained mistakes. Applicants aged between 21 and 25 were found to have made the most mistakes while 70% of firms said that female applicants were less error-prone than their male counterparts. Frequent mistakes included misspelling of the words curriculum vitae, liaison, role and personal as well as the incorrect use of capital letters.'

My own experience is that the inability to spell cuts across all ages and all management levels. I don't care why people can't spell, whether it is because they rely too heavily on spell check, or whether it is a consequence of failures in the school system; all I care about is that, when I receive a CV, it has to be 100% accurate. Nothing else will do. When I am looking at a pile of pristine CVs that are well crafted, why should I make allowances for the fact that your CV has a typo? I will reach the conclusion that you have poor attention to detail and that, if you can't get your own CV right, then you certainly won't be able to produce work for an employer with the requisite detail. That may be unfair and taking things too far but this is the harsh reality of the job-hunting world. Every recruitment person I met mentioned the need for accuracy in the CV. Not a single one was prepared to make allowances and let a single mistake slip through.

Therefore to get your CV right you must:

- Spell check it
- Print it off and read it through. Read what is there and not what you think is there
- Get a good speller to read it through for you
- Get another good speller to check it again.

Nadine Jones, Head of Human Resources, Baugur, says:

Spell check – it's an automatic function and so many candidates don't switch it on. Check, double check and check again before hitting the send button. An e-mail approach is no excuse for a lazy application. Do remember you're not texting and write words out in full – the Internet dating approach will turn off most recruiters!

Commonly misspelt words on CVs – but remember that any word is vulnerable to misuse!

- Acclaimed
- Accommodation
- Accustomed
- Driving licence
- Enthusiastic
- Excited
- Implement
- Independent
- Innovative
- Liaise
- Occasional
- Practice (noun)/Practise (verb)

- Principle/principal
- Professional
- Separate
- Success

Photo

Why would you want to put a photo on your CV? Even if you are totally confident about the way you look and you are happy to have a photo as part of the assessment process, reflect on how it might be used. Remember that by including it you are giving away a lot of information about yourself that may detract from an objective decision being made about you. The colour of your skin, your hair, your weight and your eyes are all there for someone to think that you remind them of someone they didn't like or feed their prejudices, unconscious or otherwise, in another way.

Your objective is to encourage someone to meet you based on your qualifications, your experience and the brilliant presentation you have made about the impact you could have in this new job. Why jeopardize it with superfluous and potentially damaging information?

If you still want to put it on, remember also that if you are e-mailing it may not get through a company's firewall. Given that we are doing our best to make life simple and avoid potential problems, maybe this isn't such a smart idea?

Desperately trying to find something on the plus side, if you have been head-hunted and you are meeting for an interview in a hotel lobby or coffee shop, the fact that you have included your photo will help you to be recognized.

And the public sector view?

Rachel Hannan, Director, Gatenby Sanderson, says:

Just don't do it. Don't put them on the CV as it is just not adding anything. What you look like is just not what we want to know. You are inviting us to form a subjective opinion about you. Given that the public sector in particular invests time, energy and money in making the process as fair and unbiased as possible, why would you ask someone to blow all of this out of the water by showing them what you look like and tapping into everyone's personal prejudices and biases about appearance – fat, thin, short hair, long hair, beard, moustache, freckles, glasses, big ears, make-up – see just how much you are giving away when you don't need to? Keep the photo for your passport or for giving to your granny at Christmas. Don't put it on your CV.

The leisure pursuit blacklist

Every recruitment person I have met agrees on the topic of leisure pursuits on a CV – they are not needed and they are not wanted. They supply information that is not relevant to the job application and it exposes you to the prejudices and dislikes of the reader. You might be asked about your interests at interview so you need to be prepared for the question but the best advice is not to include it on the CV. However, if you decide that you still want to go ahead and include them on your CV or if you are asked to include it on an application form, let's be clear about what you cannot include:

1. Socializing

What does this mean? That you go to the pub with your friends and play darts? That you talk to people in the supermarket queue? Or does it mean that you go out on a Saturday night and hit the club scene? What will a potential employer learn about you from this? They need to be able to make a swift mental calculation about the value that this might add to the work place. If you want to emphasize that you are naturally extroverted and you enjoy activities that include others and that you are an excellent team player, then the word socializing is too vague and open to misinterpretation. Why not subtly include references to the results of your socializing as part of the 'Skills' section on your CV? This could be successes in the Duke of Edinburgh Award scheme, your recent walk-on role in an amateur dramatic production, your successes as a salesperson. The best way to demonstrate your social skills is to show what the outcome of those social skills has been.

2. Reading

Any job you apply for will bring with it a requirement to read so stating that you can read is not going to impress anyone. What will impress the reader is an indication that the reading you are doing will be adding to your knowledge and your skills at work. You might want to describe the kind of reading that you do if it is constructive and purposeful. This can be newspapers, (indicating a keen interest in political affairs), biographies, books on a particular interesting theme or topic or books that show you up in a good, or relevant, light. You could indicate that you read business books or books for personal development. Only include them if it is true and don't include anything that could be considered to be trash. Now is not the time to admit to an enthusiasm for romantic fiction, gruesome horror stories or Harry Potter.

3. Support a football team

This can work for you and it can work against you. Your dedicated support for Manchester United, manifested by a season ticket you have held for nine years will strike a chord if your CV is being read by someone who is keen on football or a fellow supporter. However, what happens if you come up against someone who either hates football or hates your team? Then you really do have a problem as you have given them a reason to dislike you before they have even met you. A candidate wrote proudly in his CV that he was a supporter of 'the mighty Celtic'. He was applying for the role of Managing Director of a business in Scotland where he would be managing a workforce with divided football loyalties, split between Rangers and Celtic. He was discounted as a potential candidate as I worried about his ability to keep his obviously strong feelings of support for a club out of the workplace. Those two words, 'mighty Celtic', cost him dearly.

4. Spending time with my family

You would be astonished at the number of people who include this as a leisure pursuit. Surely it is a statement of the obvious? People are expected to work and they are expected to enjoy the company of their family and friends. Do not include it as though it is something that is unusual or different.

5. Weird and wonderful hobbies

Be careful about what you own up to in the form of unusual hobbies as they may disclose more about you than you may realize. People will draw their own conclusions about you, drawing on their own prejudices and experiences, and so you need to be sure that what you are disclosing is relevant and is adding value to the CV. If you spend the weekend watching birds or train spotting, keep it to yourself, unless you are applying for a job with the RSPB, the Wildlife Trust or GNER.

6. Television

If you want to be a runner in a television studio, by all means include the fact that you are a telly addict on your CV. Broadcast your knowledge of reality TV shows, soaps and long-running series. For any other job you will be giving the impression that you are a couch potato so don't do it.

7. Controversial hobbies

The CV is not the place to disclose your political allegiances and your membership of a political party. It could be very tricky to own up to being a member of the Countryside Alliance or the Anti Hunt lobby. This may not win you friends and it serves no purpose to tell complete strangers what your values are when they have no bearing on the job you want to do.

Rob Walker, Senior Consultant Gaulter Russell and his 'CV 10 Commandments':

1   *Don't put your picture on your CV – it's rarely pretty and will ensure you become an object of derision at the recruitment company.*

2   *Do try and keep your CV to three pages maximum – remember you are one of a cast of hundreds and as much as we would love to read about your holidays and personal interests, we don't have the time.*

3   *Don't lie about your salary – we WILL find out! (Every recruiter has a story about the candidate fired on day one for lying about earnings and thus securing themselves a better package!)*

4   *Likewise those three jobs you didn't stick around in. Tell your recruitment consultant and let them advise on how to position your somewhat erratic career.*

5   *Unusual hobbies are best kept to yourself – see Commandment 1).*

6   *Ensure your mobile phone answer machine message projects a suitable image. 'Yo! Dude, leave me a message!' in a gangster rap style may not secure you that interview!*

7   *'I' versus 'We'. Selling yourself is expected – blatant dishonesty isn't. Make sure the successes you claim as your own are indeed yours and not actually a team effort – or worse: someone else's. Again, we will find out (most of the time …).*

8   *Attention to detail – spell check exists on your computer for a reason. Spelling 'education' incorrectly is unlikely to enhance your employment prospects.*

9 *Likewise, the covering letter. Try to get the recruiting manager / consultant's name right – it's a good start! What's more, make sure you put the right application in the right envelope / e-mail – failure to do this will have you filed in the recycle bin quicker than you can say ...*

10 *Don't engage in rude, offensive or 'witty' banter with your recruitment consultant after yet another rejection. Telling me I'm an 'ignorant, heartless ***** who doesn't know the first thing about recruitment' is, whilst possibly true, unlikely to make me look upon you more favourably the next time.*

Rachel Hannan is adamant that she will not ask any candidate for information about their social life as this is something that could be used subjectively to influence an application. Bearing in mind that fairness, openness and transparency are the critical objectives in best practice recruitment, hopefully across all sectors but most definitely within the public sector, Rachel believes that it is wrong to use information about social life in the work situation. She gave the example of a working woman who has a full-time job and a young family. It is highly likely that at weekends she is engrossed in running her home and focusing on her children rather than spending the day on the golf course or climbing crags in Scotland. It is wrong, therefore, that she should be placed at a disadvantage to someone who does not have those family responsibilities or should be considered to be a less rounded person because she does not have a portfolio of eclectic leisure pursuits.

How old are you?

In the UK it would seem that everyone can breathe more easily because it is illegal to discriminate on the basis of age. Job advertisements can no longer use age as one of the criteria for the job. Vocabulary that also indicates an age bias is now outlawed so we will no longer see phrases like 'young graduates', 'youthful energy', 'mature gravitas' or other vocabulary that shows the employer is targeting a certain sector of the population. This means that you can leave your date of birth off your CV and not worry if you are 22 or 58 as your application will be treated in the same way.

The reality of this is that it is still possible to filter candidates out on the basis of their age as a swift calculation based on the dates in your CV will soon give a fairly accurate indication of how old you are. This may not matter and the employer may genuinely be someone who just wants the best person for the job and does not care if they are old or young. However, there will still be people who will have their own prejudices and opinions on employing someone who at first glance might be too young or old for the role. Age discriminators still exist – they have just been driven underground. Although it is perfectly legal not to put your age on a CV and no-one can ask you how old you are, you might like to think whether this is something that you choose to ignore and decide to provide that information. If you are a graduate, what harm can there be in letting someone know your exact date of birth? Does it matter? If you are over 50, it might look as though you consider age to be an issue and that you have something to hide. Look at each application you make and decide on your age policy.

This invisible discrimination is hard to identify and hard to prove. You can therefore decide to make it your life's mission to challenge people under the provisions of employment legislation, becoming a pioneer and potentially a creator of new case law, selflessly sacrificing yourself for the benefit of others. More realistically, you can take steps to challenge this prejudice by minimizing its impact through your own skill.

What are the invisible prejudices that older people face? Why is it that some people are reluctant to employ the over-50s? Perhaps they think that everyone over 50 is slightly over the hill, not as ambitious as they used to be and looking for an easy ride. The harsh reality is that most people are facing escalating costs in educating their children. They are looking at holes in their pension funds so they are sharply aware of the need to work harder and longer. Improved standards of living and a conscious need to live a healthy lifestyle probably mean that they are in fact fitter and more motivated than many younger people. However, they are fighting perceptions rather than facts so it is up to you to alter those perceptions by how you present yourself, and find your way round these invisible barriers.

Let's look at what you might be facing:

'We need highly ambitious people.'

Inference: You have probably paid off your mortgage, got your children through education and you are not as fired up as someone with a young family and big financial outgoings.

Solution: If you have a young family, put their ages on the CV so people can see that you are under pressure. A 55-year-old with three children under 18 is going to work for a long time yet! Use words in your CV that spell out this aspiration to achieve rather than complacency at what has gone before.

'We need flexible and adaptable people.'

Inference: You are probably set in your ways and reluctant to change.

Solution: Point out the number of roles that you have had and the number of cultures you have worked within. Spell out how adaptable and resourceful you are. Find a way of showing your skills with new technologies.

'We need high energy people.'

Inference: You are probably not as fit as younger people and therefore you won't have the resilience for the demands of the job.

Solution: Include a section of leisure pursuits and make sure that it includes your successes in running marathons, your 30-mile commute to work on a cycle and your participation in adrenalin sports. All of these are implicitly telling the reader that you are not overweight and unfit but that you are probably more toned than some of the 30-year-olds who are applying. If you cannot claim this level of physical fitness, get yourself a pair of trainers and start now.

'Our business is young and therefore we need people who will fit.'

Inference: A team needs people who are all alike.

Solution: Point to something in your track record that shows you have worked with old and young alike.

Style – find the right font

Opinions differ on what style the CV should have and what length it should be. There is definitely not a style or type of CV that will be universally accepted and applauded. However, certain rules are agreed on by all. Staring at a blank page, wondering how to create that perfect CV, is as tough for the new graduate as it is for the recently redundant senior executive. Use these tips, ideas, thoughts and rules to formulate a series of CVs that will see you through to the perfect job.

First of all, let's make sure we don't have a triumph of style over content. Take a tip from universities who insist on essays being presented in Times New Roman typeface, size 12 point. They can't all be wrong. Unless you are deliberately demonstrating your prowess in some obscure font with amazing graphs and charts, don't stand out; be professional. If you are applying for a role that is creative, perhaps in advertising or in the graphics industry, you can use the CV as an opportunity to show your creative skills. However, for most positions, stick to the tried and the tested.

Before you even touch the keyboard, remember that a CV needs to be written in lower case. Why is this? The answer is very simple, it is easy to read. That's why all printed matter we read – newspapers, magazines, books – observe this convention. The objective you have is to get people to read the CV, so let's make it easy for them. On average, between five and ten per cent of CVs that are sent to me come in capital letters. PLEASE DON'T SHOUT AT ME. Talk nicely and go for lower case. Another practical point is that spell check doesn't work on capital letters. I recently had an application from someone who had written his CV completely in upper case and there were 53 spelling errors in it. Spectacular. He was a candidate for the *Guinness Book of Records* but for all the wrong reasons.

In terms of format for the CV, this is a question of personal choice. The Internet and Microsoft, etc. offer a number of possible versions and, so long as they are clear and enhance the reading experience, feel free to go for whatever you prefer. In fact, have a number of versions and keep playing about with the format. There is not a perfect solution, remember, so keep changing it.

Job sites such as monster.co.uk and totaljobs.com will provide you with possible formats. Whichever one you favour, it must be clear, easy to read and one that allows the reader to understand everything about you easily.

Clare Howard, Director of e-coaches.co.uk, says:

Remember to apply the 'So what?' litmus test to both your interview preparation and to your CV and accompanying letter. 'So what?' helps you think about the results and effects of your actions or claims to success. 'Responsible for a sales team of 20' doesn't actually tell me anything. 'Recruited, set targets, trained and coached a sales team of 20 over a period of 18 months so that we increased sales by 11% and introduced 2 new product lines …' gives me my answer to 'So what?'.

References

Unless you have specifically been asked to include a list of referees with your application, as is likely to be the case in the public sector, do not include the names of your referees on your CV. This is jumping the gun in recruitment terms as the taking up of formal references is the very last stage of the process. Your task is to make the CV as compelling and as interesting as you possibly can so that someone will want to meet you. If they like what they see, they may then check you out informally through your network. They are not likely to go to the people you list on a CV because, let's face it, you wouldn't have them on there if they were going to say anything other than marvellous things about you!

The devil is in the detail

Name, address and contact details

Now that we are agreed on that, let's go for the first words on the CV. Your name. The most important feature of the CV should be your name. It should not be 'CV' or 'Curriculum Vitae' or anything other than your name. This is who you are and it is what you want to highlight. It is what you want people to remember about you so place it in the centre, in a larger font and in bold. Directly underneath let's put the information that people will need in order to contact you – your address and telephone numbers, including mobile as well as work or home, (indicate which is which). Your e-mail address is vital as it is the fastest way to get in touch, so omit it at your peril.

Profile

It has become common practice to have a short synopsis, 'mission statement' style, at the top of your CV that describes who you are and gives a brief summary of the essence of who you are and what value you can add to an organization. This is your opportunity to make a powerful impact and to give a stunning first impression to the reader of your CV. It is a brilliant investment of your time to come up with a well thought through and positive synopsis of your skills and your capabilities. Take time to play around with it and possibly come up with a few options and different possibilities.

Here are a few examples of profile summaries that people have used in their CVs. Read them and see how you can apply the same principles to your own background.

Experienced Regional Operations Manager who achieves objectives. Wide range of experience across a large number of projects and services. Good interpersonal skills, motivation and team building, with an analytical and investigative approach to work. In-depth understanding of financial, commercial and contractual issues, with proven success in formulating and negotiating commercially sound solutions.

Finance Director with general management experience in both permanent and interim positions in various service and manufacturing businesses. With extensive experience in SME businesses, achievements include company rescue and growth, acquisitions and disposals, strategic planning and restructuring.

A highly motivated Senior Business Manager with experience of capital equipment and after-market sales, product and market development, procurement and supply chain gained within the capital sales and business-to-business distribution environments. A results-orientated leader who has successfully developed and implemented strategies for growth, with an emphasis on profitable customer service.

A dynamic and creative post-graduate with excellent management, interpersonal and communication skills. Experienced in providing high levels of customer service and has a firm understanding of sales, marketing, promotions and racecourse management. Has a bright personality and is experienced in working to tight deadlines and under pressure.

Results-driven CEO with a highly successful track record in consumer multi-national businesses and in providing services to the government/public sector. Direct experience in technology, consumer electronics and food and drink sectors. Significant experience in corporate restructuring, mergers and acquisitions.

An accomplished and successful professional with 21 years in the textile industry and proven record, including branded and private label businesses. Internationally experienced with a wealth of knowledge in all aspects of manufacturing from concept through to finished product. Good people management skills across a broad cultural spectrum.

Having a passion and a high level of commitment to achieving excellent product quality with a real understanding of the importance of quality deliveries on time.

I am an ambitious and enthusiastic supply chain professional with an energetic approach to work, ensuring continuous supply of quality products and services. I have 8 years' experience working within various industries. An excellent negotiator and team player, I excel in challenging environments where I enjoy being involved in determining the strategic direction of a company. I manage and reduce multi-million pound spends and stocks and budgets whilst maintaining service levels.

A broad-based and skilful commercially minded operations professional who uses his sound engineering experience to grow sales in a global environment. A consummate manufacturing operations professional who optimizes business processes and who focuses on profit, cash generation and sales growth by implementing global consistency in his strategic view of group operational performance.

These examples show you the way that other people approach writing their profile. It will get you started thinking about what you can write about yourself and how you would sum yourself up in less than 50 words. Each word must count so make sure that it conveys the right impression and has impact.

Imagine you are the recruitment consultant describing very briefly who you are to the client. What would they be saying? Think of yourself objectively and dispassionately. See yourself as others see you and take the third party view of who you are.

Beware the 'DSP'

Andrew Harley, Management Consultant, Aquarius, recounts the following tale:
A caring, meticulous and methodical HR Director had carefully set aside half a day to read through the CVs he had received in response to an advertisement he had placed to recruit a Managing Director for a subsidiary of a major PLC.

He read through each CV quickly and then settled down to read each one thoroughly, annotating each CV with reasons why he was going to invite them to interview or not. He was not a great fan of the carefully crafted synopsis at the top of a CV so his brow furrowed when he read 'dynamic self-starter' as an opening phrase. By the time he read 'dynamic self-starter' 15 times in the pile of CVs, this punctilious and professional man started to scribble 'Prat!' at the side.

The advice, therefore, is to steer well away from these meaningless phrases, culled from newspaper advertisements that have been drafted by the semi-literate. What does it mean? This empty phrase had no relevance in this situation where it is assumed that you can manage to get yourself out of bed in the morning and turn up for work. Don't be a dynamic self-starting prat – be true to yourself and who you are.

Make sure that you do not fall into the trap of coming out with platitudes, clichés or hackneyed phrases. Your starting point could be your title: 'An operations director', 'A marketing executive', 'A board-level logistics professional', 'A first-class hotelier'. Don't fall into the trap of using someone else's words or phrases. This is one piece of your CV that you cannot cut and paste from elsewhere. You are unique and this profile needs to reflect that so make it a compelling description that summarizes your key attributes.

Remember that your CV will be carefully read by the person who is going to interview you so be sure that you have been open and truthful and that you are ready to be challenged about any claims that you may have made.

Martine Robins, European Human Resources Director, Cookson Electronics, says:
During the course of the interview I will quote a bit from the CV. The response from the candidate should be automatic rather than having to think through what is on the CV. I am looking for overselling on CVs. Lying is a recent phenomenon and a major issue.

You can create an overall impression by the language that you use and the vocabulary that you favour.

Here is a list of words to avoid:

- Can't
- Comfort zone
- Comfortable
- Competent
- Criticize
- Cut
- Decrease
- Didn't
- Diminish
- Eventually
- Expected
- Fail
- Methodical
- Mild
- Negative
- Persevere
- Prudent
- Regret
- Responsibility
- Satisfied
- Sensible
- Steady
- Try
- Unassuming
- Underachieve
- Unfortunate
- Volatile
- We.

Instead, choose the following:

- Accountable
- Achieve
- Achievement
- Curious
- Develop
- Dramatic
- Effective
- Energy

- Enthusiasm
- Exceeded
- Excel
- Illustrate
- Improve
- Increase
- Initiate
- Inspire
- Inventive
- Launch
- Optimistic
- Pace
- Passion
- Perform
- Plan
- Promote
- Resolve
- Secure
- Solve
- Team.

Describe the company

Just because you are only too familiar with the organization that you work for, knowing where it is based, what it does and how many people work there, don't assume that everyone else knows about it. You need to put in a short description of who they are so that the reader can gauge the scope, the markets, the products and the style of the organization.

It isn't good enough just to put down the name of the company. For example, what do you know about the following?

- AP UK LTD, West Midlands
- Inter-Alliance, London
- Neopost Ltd.
- Morgans Ltd, Bath
- Betfair.com – London
- Adidas UK Ltd
- Fisher Scientific International Inc.

Wouldn't you be happier to know where they are based, how big they are and what they do?

Compare that with:

1 MFI UK Limited is Europe's largest furniture manufacturer and retailer. Its UK operations have two manufacturing sites in Howden and Runcorn, and a central warehousing and distribution centre based in Northampton.

2 Capita Group plc is a Listed UK FTSE 100 company with revenue of c£1.4bn and capitalized at c£2.5bn. Capita is one of the largest and fastest growing professional support services companies in the UK. Specializing in outsourcing in IT, business process outsourcing and call centres in central & local government, and also in the insurance and life & pensions markets.

3 American Bureau of Shipping – Group Division. Blue chip American multinational with offices worldwide, specializing in shipping classification and general engineering consultancy. Worldwide turnover $250m.

4 Sherwood Group Plc Nottingham, now Intimas Group Plc. International brand and suppliers of ladies' lingerie, swimwear and nightwear to major high-street store groups. Annual wholesale turnover in excess of £25 million.

5 Linpac Plastics Ltd, Leeds 1997–2000. One of the largest privately-owned businesses in the UK with a turnover of £1bn from global production and sales of plastic food packaging.

6 NCH Europe. European HQ of NCH Corporation, manufacturer and distributor of chemicals for the maintenance industry. European turnover $250 million. Operating in 25 countries with total direct sales force of over 2000 reps.

An explanation, however brief, sets the context and demonstrates that you are already thinking like someone outside the company. You are not assuming that the activity in your world is bound to be familiar to all. Now take the time to write a brief description of every company you have ever worked for. If you want a shortcut, go to the company website and use their words.

Achievements and responsibilities

All of the recruitment insiders are unanimous in their view that the CV must be achievement driven. Achievements are not the same as responsibilities. Do not confuse the two. This is not your opportunity to take your job description and put it in your CV and think that it will work. Just because you were responsible for something does not mean to say that you achieved it. You may have underperformed, overperformed, hit the target bang-on or made a complete hash of it. What the reader wants to know is what you actually did. More than this, the reader wants to know how relevant this is to their company, the role they are recruiting for and their culture. What value are you going to add? A simple list of responsibilities won't begin to address this.

Look at the following, for example:

Achievements/responsibilities

- Main responsibility to ensure that the contract was delivered on time within budget. The contract was worth £176m over five years, with capital expenditure during the implementation in the region of £47m.
- Financial management of change control process, ensuring that each contractual change is impact assessed, with changes charged back to client over life of contract, but importantly whether we could deliver operationally, and that the contract profitability was improved and revenue increased by £9m.
- Introduction of monthly internal reporting procedures for group reporting requirements, devolving and managing budgets to newly installed operations team, and recruitment of new finance team.
- Part of a management team of four directors, responsible for implementing operational model, with workforce of over 1200 staff on a greenfield operation, the modelling of staff levels during the period of ramping up the operation, and ensuring that the logistics of recruiting over 900 staff within three months was properly managed both financially and operationally.
- Operational responsibility during a period of handover between Operations Directors, and recruitment of successor.

This is subtitled as 'achievements/responsibilities' but in fact it is a large 'to do' list. It should be totally rewritten to reflect what actually was done.

And again:

- Project manage the relocation of the company's premises.
- Strategic and day-to-day operational management to maximize sales and profitability; P&L responsibility; business planning and forecasting.
- Sales and marketing, including designing and marketing a new website.
- Staff recruitment, training, motivation and management.
- Manage standards and operational controls.
- Establish customer profile and adapt product range to match.
- Drive effective customer service to ensure customer satisfaction and loyalty.
- Performance management and productivity analysis.

This is a description of what needed to be done. But how was it done? Where are the statistics, the data to demonstrate how these things were achieved? Numbers need to be attached to this to answer the question, 'So what?'.

Responsible for motivating, training and developing a team of six sales executives towards an on target performance. My sales team covered a geographical area in the north-east of England from Bradford to Newcastle-upon-Tyne.

This one is just crying out for a bit more time and attention. What did the team do? What did they actually sell? Was it an 'on-target performance' or did they miss? How did this team measure up against the other teams in the country? Did they win sales competitions or were they at the bottom of the pile?

So what exactly could achievements look like? You have already set these out in your career databank form. Check now that they are crisp and definitive, because they need to be. Look at the list below and see how each one is something that could be backed up. At interview this will be an invitation to recount your triumphs and successes. Martine Robins will pick on one of these and ask you to elaborate. You are not going into the detail of who, how and where precisely, you are setting it down as an incontrovertible fact. Remember too that these need to be linked very closely to the demands of the job that you are applying for. One size does not fit all.

- Increased sales from a to b.

- Grew the business 100% by opening two new coffee shops in 12 months.
- Delivered profitable growth of restaurant by operating in a fast paced, team orientated, rewarding environment.
- Designed and implemented a new computer system across the organization.
- Redesigned the company website and improved its visibility on the web
- Added on x number of new business accounts and achieving 112% against forecasts and budget.
- Launched three new products generating operating profits in year 1.
- Built a strong team with increased focus and delivery of objectives.
- Aided the founding shareholders in a £22m buy-out of venture capital investors.
- Refinanced the business, increasing borrowing facilities to allow further expansion.
- Company income increased by 100% p.a. with a vastly more efficient cost base.
- Reduced monthly cash burn from $3m to break even.
- Successfully led negotiations to merge group with UK plc in order to maximize shareholder returns in a very difficult trading market.
- Implemented new compensation and benefits structures and agreements (including extensive regional and national union negotiations) linked to driving and achieving corporate business strategy.
- Achieved HR, facilities and IT integration, substantially under budget and ahead of deadlines.
- Developed a unique culture supported by a vision, mission and values translated and implemented across the organization.
- Established new distributors in previously untouched markets.
- Won National Sales Award for best six-monthly performer.
- Developed new marketing materials and increased products awareness by organizing eye-catching stands at trade exhibitions.
- Increased sales through improved customer service by running staff training courses and by introducing an incentive plan of 'employee of the month'.

Time to get started: template CVs

Having spent all of this time thinking about where you can go wrong in writing your CV and having reflected on all of the skills that you have and need to incorporate in the document itself, now is the time to start writing it. If the content itself is strong, the format you use should make it easier to read and more attractive to the reader. Simplicity and clarity are the order of the day. If you have a good eye for presentation and style, then you may like to put together your own format. If you need something to get you started, you might want to try out one of the following formats to see what they look like. I am not saying that these are the right way to do a CV. They are one of a number of options that you can use. If you don't like any of these, the Internet is an excellent provider of potential formats. If you Google 'CV format' you will get almost three million hits. Have a look and see what works for you. Meanwhile, look at the following formats and put your data into one or all of them.

Template no. 1:

Home address	Tel no (m)	
	Tel no (w)	
	Tel no (h)	
	E-mail address	

Your name

Summary	Who you are	
Career history to date		
Latest company Achievements		
Company before that Achievements		
Company before that Achievements		
Company before that Achievements		
Company before that Achievements		
Education		
Professional training		
Professional memberships		
Interests	(If you insist)	
Date of birth	(if you want)	**Marital status**

Template no. 2:

Your Name
Your address and post code all in one long line
Your telephone numbers and your e-mail address all in one line

A three line summary of who you are, all written in the third person.

CAREER

Nov 2003 – date   Latest role, company name and brief description
- Developed, etc.
- Achieved, etc.
- Grew, etc.
- Achievement
- Achievement
- Achievement
- Achievement
- Achievement

Dec 1996 – Oct 2002   Job title and company description
- Developed, etc.
- Achieved, etc.
- Grew, etc.
- Achievement
- Achievement
- Achievement
- Achievement
- Achievement

Nov 1995 – Nov 1996   Job title and company description
- Developed, etc.
- Achieved, etc.
- Grew, etc.
- Achievement

Jan 1991 – Oct 1995   Job title and company description
- Developed, etc.
- Achieved, etc.
- Grew, etc.
- Achievement

Qualifications:

Personal

| Age | Marital status | children |

Template no. 3:

YOUR NAME

Address · Street name and number · Town · County · Postcode
Home tel no · Mobile · E-mail address
Marital status · Nationality

JOB TITLE

PROFILE

The synopsis of who you are, what you have achieved and where you are going.

Career history summary
Date	**Company name and job tile (most recent)**
Date	**Company name and job title**
Date	**Company name and job title**

EDUCATION
Qualification gained
Years studied
From – to
Name of institute
Qualification gained
Years studied
Name of college
Qualification gained
Years studied
Name of school

TECHNICAL EXPERTISE
Provide a bullet point guide to the technical skills you possess and those you have been trained in.
-
-
-

DETAILED CAREER HISTORY
Company
Job title
Short description of company
Dates worked
Outline a description of your key achievements:

Company
Job title
Dates worked
Outline a description of your key achievements

Company
Job title
Dates worked
Outline a description of your achievements

REFERENCES   **Referees available on request.**

The 'CV to-don't list' by Gareth James, Director, People Plus Ltd:

1 DON'T turn up with a CV that you haven't written yourself. CVs that are clearly produced by an outplacement company, styled into their format with all individuality squeezed out are out. Your CV is an extension of your personality and therefore needs to be written by you, however much help you've had.

2 DON'T procrastinate. It needs to answer two questions very quickly: 'What are you?' That is to say, are you a marketing manager, a general manager, a technical manager, an operations manager? And 'Where do you fit in a company's organization structure, and why should I meet you?' If the CV does not answer this in the first half-page, then the recruiter will lose interest.

3 DON'T have inconsistencies in a CV. If you put something in your CV, you should be able to elaborate on it. If you lay claim to certain achievements, you need to talk with authority and knowledge. The facts should be at your fingertips. If you flounder and struggle to answer the questions, then the interviewer will be asking themselves if you truly did what you said you did.

4 DON'T include a photograph in your CV unless you want the recipient to make it part of his or her selection process. You may want to think about that one.

5 DON'T standardize your CV or accompanying letter, they should be personal and not processed. You need to demonstrate that this application is one you have thought about and you have looked at the requirements of the role and compared them with your own skills and experience. It can't be just a standard letter that you print out for everyone. When ploughing through a pile of CVs, it is the individual one that jumps out at a recruiter.

How not to do it – real examples

The CV of Mary Williams is a real one, with names changed to protect the guilty. It is a stream of consciousness, reading like a long, newsy letter home rather than a CV that is supposed to be selling the skills, experiences and successes of a top-flight manager. Work and personal life overlap. Grammar has gone to the four winds and its real crime is that it is personal, unstructured, lacking in focus and, more dangerous than anything else, shows that Mary thinks in a woolly and superficial way. How can you believe the business successes that she is laying claim to when the CV is so truly dreadful? Read it and then vow never, ever to write in such a way yourself.

Mary Jane Williams BSc (Hons)

2 Alfred Square
Lithington
RS12 4PQ
Tel: 0190 217 322
Mobile: 0751 1605 631
e-mail: mjwills@esf.com

Date of birth: 12 November 1963

Personal Background

Happily married – two lovely children, Michael aged 12 and Olivia aged 10

I have decided to take time out to be with my children more than I have been to date and I am therefore seeking a part time role that will still allow me to make an impact on a business

I have always been an optimistic and enthusiastic person with abundant energy to tackle new projects. I am a natural extravert and I consider one of my greatest strengths is my ability to get on with people and communicate well with them I have a fast mind and I can grasp complex and technical issues quickly. Although I am not a 'techie', I enjoy new technology and I love explaining it to people who do not share my skill base. I know how to work effectively across an organization and how to bring teams together..

My leisure pursuits are:
- family – spending a lot of time with the children. Playing an active role in the PTA
- Reading – as a keen reader, I am a member of a local book club to help me expand my horizons as I love reading.
- Working in the local community and helping in local charity shop as I love helping people
- keeping fit – gym, pilates, yoga and running.

Career Summary

I left school at 16 with 8 O levels and a determination to work my way to the top whilst earning a salary. My first job as an assistant with Marks and Spencer's showed me very quickly that a lack of qualifications would be a barrier to highly paid and interesting jobs. I therefore found a job with a company where they sent me on day release the local college where I first of all passed three 'A' levels and then sponsored me to do a sandwich course business studies degree.

After 2 years in the accounts department of Rethingtons, I worked in various other companies until I joined Remarche as a management consultant. In my 10 years at Accountants Partnership, I worked towards increasing my skill set and became a fellow of the IoD, a qualified accountant and a member of other influential networking organisations. I was on the career fast track with my organization and achieved three major promotions in a less than seven years, specialising in change management programmes for the public and private sectors. During this period I married and had two children, taking only six months maternity leave for each child.

I left Accounting Partnership to join the Indrico Corporation for 5 years in a consultancy role.. After this I was promoted to the board with special responsibilities for the Pacifc Rim

From Indrico I moved to Global Technology plc as an Executive (one of the 320 most senior people in the group). I joined just after they made two major acquisitions and spent 5 years with them starting as Head of Acquisitions Integration as well as having responsibility for the consultancy arm of the business. This meant that I spent a lot of time carrying out due diligence on potential acquisitions, which undertakes due diligence and integrations of companies acquired by them.

A more detailed description of my career, roles and achievements is given in the next five pages.

I will spare you the next five pages as they are all much in the same vein. This self-indulgent CV will get her nowhere. Whilst it might have been therapeutic for her to write it, it is not a riveting read for a stranger who is measuring her capabilities to do the job. The potential employer is not looking for a biographical 'stream of consciousness' but a crisp, objective and informative CV that gives a clear picture of skills, knowledge, experience and achievements.

The following CV is another 'to don't' CV. Read it and spot the way that it jars on the reader, leaving you indifferent to who he is and what he has done.

PETER WILLIAM ROBERTS FCA

PROFESSIONAL EXPERIENCE

October 1999 to July 2006
Finance Director and Company Secretary: Millington Internet Services Limited

Millington Internet Services is a privately owned business that operates throughout the UK. Customers range from small organizations to large industrial users. It has a market share of 23% and it is growing in profit by 21% per annum. Capital investment runs at 13% and R & D budget is an average of 7%

The current owners have decided to realise their investment and after a process lasting 10 months, a majority stake in the business has been sold to a VC.

Principal responsibilities of the role included:
> *introduction of financial / management reporting and control procedures*
> *preparation and continuing maintenance of business projections and plans*
> *working with the commercial team on the negotiation of individual customer contracts*
> *assisting the operational management of the business with performance appraisal and understanding the financial impact of their decisions*
> *provision of information to company directors and the UK investors.*

- Principal achievements include:
  development of a business model to facilitate the growth of the Atlantic business within the facilities available. Discussing this with directors / shareholders and achieving agreement as to the future development of the business
  following on from this securing additional funding from the shareholders to finance the entry into the residential market place
  negotiation of the termination of an outsourcing contract on a favourable cash flow basis with payment over three years
  working as a key member of the negotiating team in the securing of new customer contracts with particular emphasis on pricing and payment terms
  managing relationships with creditors, counterparties and sales agents in order to maximize payment terms and minimize working capital held as security deposits
  preparation of year end financial statements (both UK and US GAAP) and their agreement with the auditors
  negotiation and agreement of a new lease for the customer service centre to include favourable rent, break clauses and a rent free period
  development of the finance function to provide an added value service to the business units

PETER WILLIAM ROBERTS FCA

PROFESSIONAL EXPERIENCE CONTINUED

July 1996 to September 1999
Senior Manager: Maths Unlimited Accountants

My role was three-fold:

working with Maths Unlimited Accountants clients to improve their financial reporting procedures and structures

development and presentation of material on financial reporting for the Maths Unlimited Accountants offices within the Central Business Area. This was used for presentations to both staff and clients.

provision of technical advice to client facing partners and staff within the Central Business Area.

I spent a substantial amount of time advising clients on the possible impact of recently issued accounting standards on their financial reporting and future strategy.

I also advised on the acquisition and flotation of a number of businesses concentrating on accounting treatments and deal structures.

I developed and presented material introducing International Accounting Standards and outlining significant differences when compared to UK GAAP.

April 1990 to June 1996
Group Financial Controller: Corner Shop Ltd

In January 1991 Corner Shop Ltd had 250 stores and a group turnover of £91m. By June 1996 the group had significant DIY interests producing an annual turnover of £390 m.

I was directly responsible for the group finance team which comprised 4 staff. Additionally I had significant operational involvement through liaison with subsidiary companies and control of the group pension and payroll departments.

*   Some achievements during the period were:
introduction of financial discipline through management accounting and group budgetary control.

management of the group payroll department with the introduction of new systems and considerable change to work methods

introduction of treasury procedures to optimise the use of the group's free cash resources

---

PETER WILLIAM ROBERTS FCA

PROFESSIONAL EXPERIENCE CONTINUED

renegotiation of loan facilities
introduction and administration of a loan guarantee scheme for customers of the
group's wholesaling businesses
integration of acquisitions into the group reporting procedures
introduction of EPOS into the group including commercial negotiation and overall
project management
a group reorganization to achieve optimal VAT position and corporation tax.

September 1982 to March 1990
Brown & Co Accountants

I entered into a training contract in September 1982

All examinations were passed within three years at the first attempt.

Between July 1986 and July 1987 I was seconded to the National Audit Department
based in the Birmingham Office.

On my return to the Head Office I was appointed a manager within the business services
group.

I managed all services provided to a core group of 4 major businesses including audit,
taxation and investigation assignments.

Other responsibilities included the provision of management accounting and business
advisory services to SMEs

LEISURE INTERESTS

I particularly enjoy attending football matches and spending evenings socialising.

Day to day I take a keen interest in current affairs and business matters.

Peter Roberts' CV is dull. It is poorly set out and it does not engage the
reader. It is a tedious account of the facts of his career but it does not come
to life. The use of 'I' seems to give the impression that he is caught up in his
own world. The potential employer is looking for a critical analysis of skills,
not a reflection on how life has brought him to where he is today – and that
is what this looks like. There is no pace, no energy, no punchiness and no
sense of animation or interest.

PETER WILLIAM ROBERTS FCA

PERSONAL INFORMATION

ADDRESS: 23 Lobelia Avenus
Leathley
Leeds
LS29 4EB

TELEPHONE:
Home 01132 7897234
Mobile 07180 7897990

E-mail: peter@emailservices.co.uk

Date of birth: 23 July 1962

Marital status: Married with two children

Qualifications :

O Levels	**A Levels**
2 Grade A: Maths, Physics	2 Grade A: Maths, Physics
4 Grade B: Economics, French,	1 Grade C: Economics
Physical Science, Biology	
1 Grade C: English Literature	

Foundation Course In Accounting	**Professional Qualifications**
June 1982: Merit	PE1:May 1984
	PE2:July 1985

Now that you have got the templates to construct your CV and now that you have witnessed how badly it can go wrong by looking at these real examples of poor CVs, look at these examples of strong CVs that work well. Hopefully you will now be encouraged to review your CV, even if you are secretly pleased with yourself and you think that your CV is a bit of a winner. Cast an eye over it again and look to see what you might be doing to make it more powerful and for it to reflect your skills, your experience and your personality. While you are doing this, keep remembering that not everyone agrees on what a perfect CV looks like. Make sure that the CVs you construct are ones that you are pleased with. Ensure that they have been carefully crafted rather than hastily put together without due reflection and consideration. Allow the perfectionist in you to take over and keep playing with words, styles and layouts until you are happy with the outcome.

The CV 'dos' – how to do it well

- Do be sure that you have reflected long and hard about your achievements in your career to date
- Always tell the truth and be accurate
- Always make sure that your CV is geared towards the job you are applying for – one size does not fit all
- Be objective, use strong vocabulary and be interesting
- Set it out clearly in a legible font
- Make sure the spelling is 100% right
- Get someone to read it when you have finished and to tell you honestly what they think.

The first CV of Sophie Merridew is one that you can look at if you are a graduate and you do not have lots of job experience. You need to make sure that you remember everything you have achieved at school and university that is likely to impress an employer. This CV makes the most of what has happened at university and it includes all work experience, however menial. It describes the companies briefly and it is a CV that is straightforward and to the point. It excludes any zany elements that some people include in order to make themselves stand out. The objective of this CV is to impress someone as an eager graduate who wants a chance in the job market.

Sophie Olivia Merridew

Term time address
3 The Lilacs
Station Road
Nottingham
NS73 4BG

Home address
The Coach House
Westover Lane
Leicester
LS21 53PQ

E-mail: smerridew@email.com
Tel (M): 07295 732471
Tel (H): 07966 3232167
Date of Birth: 11/07/1984

PROFILE

I am a hard working, ambitious and determined individual who has good interpersonal skills. I can work well on my own as well as excelling within a team. I am an effective communicator, confident and quick to learn.

EDUCATION

Sept 2003 – 2007 University of Nottingham
BA (Hons) Business Studies
Graduated July 2007 with 2:1 Hons
 Modules included:
 Industrial Relations, Human Resource Management, International Business Analysis, Managing Finance, Microsoft applications, including Excel, Marketing, Operations and Business Systems Management.
 Business Statistics and Decision Making, Global markets, International Brand Development, Management and Organisational Behaviour, Political Economy of Work, Understanding Financial Accounting.
 I completed a dissertation on the development of three global brands and travelled to Switzerland to interview the Marketing Manager of a major confectionery company.

Sept 2001 – Sept 2003 Queen Elizabeth's Grammar School, Leicester

A Level: Business Studies B
 History C
 French B

Sept 1996 – Sept 2001 Leicester Technology College.

10 GCSEs at C or above including Maths, English and French.

WORK EXPERIENCE

Oct 2006 – Current, Pizza Dynamic Restaurants, Nottingham
Front of House Staff (part time)
 Pizza Dynamic is a UK chain of restaurants with the strongest of reputations for serving high quality Italian food.

As the restaurant is often at its full capacity I have to be able to remain 100% customer focused. I have therefore been able to develop my customer service skills but also learn resource planning which is essential within the restaurant.

Working at Pizza Dynamic has helped my team working skills whilst still working effectively independently.

May 2006 – Sept 2006, The Redoubtable Friend, Nottingham
Front of House Staff (full time)

The Redoubtable Friend is one of the busiest pubs/restaurants in a new and prestigious retail development in Nottingham.

I worked at The Redoubtable Friend during the summer months when trading was at its peak during the busy summer period. I learnt to work under pressure and to resolve problems quickly while remaining customer orientated.

Resource planning was vital in making sure the restaurant was prepared each day for the various events.

Oct 2006 – May 2006, Charlotte International Hotel, Nottingham
Breakfast Staff, (part time)

The Charlotte Hotel in Bristol is one of the top hotels in the country and recognized for having exceptional high quality customer service.

Being able to motivate myself and work on my own was imperative as I had the responsibility of looking after my own section of the restaurant, ensuring that the clientele received a positive customer experience.

May 2006 – Jack Wills, Richmond Surrey
Sales Assistant (part time)

Jack Wills is a fast growing, up-market brand with an established Internet presence.

I was given a four week induction programme, focusing on customer service, stock control and problem solving.

VOLUNTARY WORK

I am part of the volunteer scheme at university, which helps communities in and around Nottingham. I am an active fundraiser for a children's charity and in my final year I was a committee member for the rag week ball.

SKILLS

I am a fluent French speaker and I am a very confident IT user. I am a touch typist and am familiar with all Microsoft applications, particularly Power Point and Excel. At school I participated in the Duke of Edinburgh Awards scheme and achieved Gold Medal status.

INTERESTS

I am interested in current affairs and read a daily broadsheet newspaper.

I am interested in food and wine and am a competent cook. I am currently attending a Wine Society course

I was a member of the university hockey team as well as a member of the university women's running club

I play the piano and the guitar and enjoy live music in all its forms.

References available on request

The next CV of William Marriott is one that shows someone who has thought about what they have done and then ensured that it appears in the CV very clearly labelled as an achievement. The CV is interesting and it sets out short but comprehensive descriptions of the companies he has worked for. Nothing has been taken for granted. When you finish reading his CV you have a good idea of what he has been doing in his career and you begin to get a feel for what he is good at. He has included words like 'pioneered' and 'creative' so you get the sense of someone who is adding value to the role. The length of time he has been with his companies is a clear demonstration of loyalty and you begin to speculate that he is job hunting because he wants the next promotion.

The CV is one that does not fit into a standard CV format so it looks like something he has created himself so it has a very 'genuine' feel to it. It gives all of the data that you need. This CV would be put into the 'Yes' pile – mission accomplished.

William Marriott
115 Weatherstone Way, Ambridge, Borsetshire, BO16 8BU
Tel: 01379 7665341 Mobile: 07777 5588342 E-mail: wmarriott@email.com
British   Married with 2 children aged 4 and 2

A strong team player who has a track record of successful management in a dynamic and competitive marketplace. People orientated, energetic, goal driven and ambitious with an ability to bring creative flair to a broad product portfolio in a highly commercial way.

CAREER HISTORY:

July 2003 to date: Womenswear Buyer, Major Catalogue Company Ltd

Major Catalogue Company Limited is one of the UK's leading direct home shopping company, operating over 12 successful catalogue brands. Turnover in 2006 was £3.8 billion with high operating profit levels.

- Achievements included:

  Created and developed a 'younger' product range in order to appeal to a newly targeted customer base (35 – 45 yrs old). Now grown the department into one of the most profitable areas of the business.

  Successfully manage a designated team that supports the buying function. 1x Assistant buyer, 1 x QC, 1x Packaging Tech, 2x Merchandisers.

  Directly source own brand product from markets such as Pakistan, Cambodia, India, Malaysia, Hong Kong and China.

  Work with major brands in order to give a fully rounded product offer.

  Pioneered the planning, selection and marketing of online 'exclusive' product for the Internet selling sites. Also work closely with e-business in order to develop strategies in order to get existing product 'working harder'.

  Involved with internal supply base projects in order to fully utilize resources available from existing supply base and highlight potential supply base opportunities with new markets.

March 2001 to July 2003: Womenswear Category Manager – UK / Benelux Sportswear UK Ltd

Sportswear UK is global leader in the sporting goods industry with sports brands built on a passion for competition and a sporting lifestyle. Turnover in 2003 was around 1.9 billion and the business was highly profitable.

Achievements included:

Developed a product range, product cost and retail price strategy and product briefs to meet the needs of Benelux.

Worked with key sales personnel to ensure that top quality major account presentations were implemented to high quality standards.

Conducted strategic overview of the market place, identifying relevant trends and accommodating them within regional product development plans.

Used product sell-in and sell-through information to maintain tighter merchandising controls and warehouse levels.

Through effective use of management controls, ensured all products were available on time, in the correct quality in order to meet customer demand. Ensured excess stock levels ran at absolute minimum.

Prepared and delivered comprehensive and original account marketing plans for each season.

July 1997 to March 2001: Womenswear Buyer, Home Shopping Company

Home Shopping Company Home Retail Group is the UK's leading home and general merchandise retailer with sales of over £2.78 billion in 2001. It sells products under two distinctive and complementary retail brands.

Achievements included:

Managed the analytical planning, merchandise selection, product development, sourcing and negotiating of over 50 pages of the women's product offer. Ranges included women's branded and own-branded sportswear, outerwear and leathers.

Led the planning and selection of these ranges for all other channels to market within the Home Shopping portfolio. Also delivered results from all leaflet and marketing activity.

Direct sourcing worldwide including Far East, India, Vietnam and Europe.

Significant impact on bottom line profitability through negotiating RTM agreements, improved retrospective discounts and contributions from suppliers to feature in the catalogue.

Responsible for the European Purchasing i.e. common lines which Home Shopping Company can run along sister companies in France, Belgium and Denmark.

An academic CV is always slightly different, needing to demonstrate that not only do you have the requisite academic skills, that you are a good presenter, an excellent team player and a life-long learner but also that you have the empathy with younger people to help them learn and develop. Whilst you still need to demonstrate your achievements, perhaps your tone should not be as brisk and as impersonal.

Here's an example for you to consider:

	Tel : 012943 779736
Address	Mobile tel: 074698 561321
Address	E-mail: janesmith@email.co.uk

Jane Smith

Personal Profile: Age 49, married, 2 sons, clean driving licence

I am an energetic and expressive person, keen to participate fully in my working environment. I expect high standards but temper this with sensitivity to the demands placed on others, students and colleagues alike. I am a dedicated teacher, able to work in and direct teams and passionate about the effective teaching of languages to my students. I enjoy excellent working relationships with my colleagues and believe I have developed a range of skills to support and motivate them, but at the same time managing and delegating even-handedly.

Since graduating I have worked almost continuously in education, in a number of different fields. My experience encompasses teaching EFL in Portugal, and Spanish and French in Comprehensive, Sixth Form and Tertiary education. Teaching has always been my vocation and I have taken on a variety of projects throughout my professional life, thus providing me with continuous stimulation and at the same time ensuring my own professional development. I enjoy being in the classroom and believe that the strategies I use are not only effective but also bring a sense of achievement, injecting fun into the learning process. The challenges I have met in my experience as a language teacher have given me the confidence to experiment and adapt as necessary; I enjoy presenting students with similar challenges. I have derived great satisfaction from living abroad and actively using my foreign languages. This commitment and pleasure is something I have always conveyed to students, whilst also helping them to achieve their full potential. I am an ambitious professional, constantly seeking new challenges and establishing new goals.

Present Position

Lecturer in Modern Languages
Xyz College,
A place

1989 – date: Subject leader in French
(5 years as 0.6 Associate lecturer, full-time since 1996)

Additional responsibility: 1999 – 2002 Senior Tutor for the Faculty of Creative and Performing Arts

Principal achievements:

- Increased participation of post 16 students in French (from an average of 20 mainstream students in 1988 to 100 in 2002)
- Introduction of a variety of new French courses into the College curriculum: International Baccalaureate (ab initio), GNVQ languages option, BND languages option, new GCSE specifications in French (1997), Curriculum 2000 (AS & A2 French), OxOCN accreditation in Modern Languages (French, Spanish, German)
- Increased uptake of French evening classes (currently an average of 70 students study on beginners, intermediate, advanced courses)

- Examination Results commended by The Principalship (insert)
- 1993 – 1998 established and led exchange visit between the College and Poitiers
- 2001 & 2002 organized and led cultural visit to the Loire
- Grade 1 awarded in all internal teaching observations
- Responsible for the College Access course to HE in Humanities submission (accredited by Borsetshire Open College Network). I co-ordinated the unitized submission, which included a modern languages option and Key Skills, and constituted a 100-plus page document

Personal achievements:

Successful completion of a Masters Degree in Education, 1989

Successful completion of final honours module in French language, 1993, University (distinction)

Responsibilities as Lecturer in Modern Languages (subject leader in French)

- Co-ordinate delivery of all French courses, mainstream and evening
- Implement curriculum changes
- Manage the French budget
- Organize the purchase and collation of appropriate resources
- Support 2 part-time French tutors
- Hold regular team meetings
- Advise on methodology
- Involve students in appropriate visits and/ or day courses
- Check all examination entries
- Conduct oral examination assessment
- Assess written coursework
- Devise assignment-based assessment (GNVQ & BND) and liaise with the departments serviced
- Compile internal examination papers
- Appraise and assess training needs of part-time tutors
- Report to Head of Faculty: Languages and Communication
- Assist in the marketing of all French courses: via feeder school visits, College and departmental brochures, Open Evenings
- Work alongside other modern language lecturers to discuss: policies common to all, ICT developments, technical support
- Attend Modern Languages Panel (between the College and local feeder schools)
- Contribute to the College's Quality Assurance System: collect student evaluation questionnaires, complete subject evaluation forms, form an action plan

I have also been involved in the delivery of courses run by the German Department (GCSE and GNVQ, for 4 years, approximately)

Responsibilities as Senior Tutor

- Oversee delivery of College Tutorial Programme to 150 students
- Support the work of 8 group tutors within the Faculty of Creative and Performing Arts
- Advise students on AS and A2 programme combinations
- Hold twice-termly team meetings: Senior Tutor and Personal tutors
- Interview students re. issues arising from the group tutorial: attendance, personal and academic support, HE and careers advice
- Liaise with appropriate agencies: learning support, careers guidance, student counselling
- Liaise with parents, establishing a good communication network with them
- Report to Head of Faculty of Creative and Performing Arts, attend monthly review meetings, compile bi-annual report
- Attend termly senior tutor meetings to share good practice
- Advise on procedures as seen appropriate
- Update College database): course data, personal data

History of Previous Employment

1983 – 1988	Part-time teacher of Spanish and Communication Skills, Further and Community Education, Berkshire
1978 – 1983	Teacher of French and Spanish (all courses to A level), VIth Form College
1978 – 1984	Teacher of EFL in Lisbon, Portugal (for the British Council and private academies)
1974 – 1977	Teacher of French and Spanish, High School, Scotland

Qualifications

M.A. (Education), 1990 – 1992, University

Module in French Language, 1993, University (Distinction)

B.A. Honours Spanish (with French and Portuguese) II2
University of Leeds 1970 – 1973
PGCE, University of Liverpool, 1974
French A Level, Grade A, 1970
Spanish A level, Grade A, 1970
English Literature A level, Grade A, 1970
10 O levels 1968

Interests   Literature, theatre, amateur dramatics, friendship, voluntary worker, cookery, family activities, tennis, active member of local gym

References   Available on request

Saving the file

And finally, having now finished drafting your CV, you need to save it onto your computer. Now is the time to call it something memorable and I can tell you emphatically that 'CV' just won't do it. If you are going to be sending this CV off to a potential employer, you are hoping that they will either save it onto their own computer or forward it to someone else or, even better, both. The title of the document is what will appear on their screen so it needs to be something like 'Anne Watson CV 29 June 2007'. Failure to call it the right name can lead to terrible blunders. If you call it 'CV', it will end up in a Word folder and be destined never to be opened as there is nothing there that identifies it as being yours. If you have been lazy and if you send a CV entitled 'CV general', I will know that you haven't bothered tailoring this CV to my needs. Worse still, don't be like the candidates who have sent me a CV that was clearly used for a previous application. Having expended all of this time and energy in ensuring that you have created the best possible CV for your job search, make sure that the finishing touch, the file name, is just right.

Clare Howard's A – Z of CVs and interviews

A for Achievements

Make sure that you quantify your Achievements in terms of scope, scale, and skills you used to achieve your results

B for Benefits

What were the Benefits of your achievements for the organization, your customers, your clients?

C for Conversion

Convert your achievements and the benefits of your past experience to the current and future needs of the new role or organization

D for Demand

Remember to match what you can offer to what's currently in Demand

E for Enthusiasm

And Energy and Empathy. And e-commerce of course. Make sure you know your bits from your bytes

F for Feedback

Not sure of how to sell yourself? Ask your friends, colleagues, coach, manager for Feedback. Also for Focus, Flexibility

G for Guts

Be proud of the time when you have had the courage of your convictions; where you have taken risks. And if there have been a few failures – can you describe the lessons you have learnt?

H for Hobbies

Leave out! – unless you can sell them as added value

J for Job hunting

Enough said …

K for Key words

Used correctly these are the key to success

L for Limitations

Don't undersell yourself – but don't try to bluff your way out of an awkward question. Limitations leave you room for growth and development

M for Motivation

Be passionate – and clear – about what gets you fired up about the job you do and what you have and can achieve

N for Networking

Because it's still true that 7 out of 10 job opportunities are never formally advertised. Also for Needs – always be sure that you really understand the needs of the employer

O for Organization

The hiring one; do your research. Make sure you know what is important to them

P for People

And Personable, and Performance and Personality

Q for Queue jumping

Use your networking skills to bypass the queues and stand out from the crowd

R for Resume

Are you getting the idea of what makes a perfect CV?

S for Strategy

Keep your job hunting strategy focused yet flexible. Also for Skills, and Selling your capabilities

T for Targeting and Tailoring

Target the right organizations; Tailor your CV to meet the needs of the organization

U for Usefulness

Make sure that you can demonstrate that you will be Useful from day one

V for Value

Always, always ask what Value will you add to their bottom line? And Vision – make sure you have a clear Career Vision

X for eXcellence

Make sure your interviewer doesn't need X-ray vision to clearly see what you eXcel at, and the benefits you will bring

Y for You

You can do it

Z for Zoo

Are you doing enough to make sure that you stand out from the crowd?

CHAPTER 3

GET THE LETTER RIGHT

RESULT: AN INVITATION TO INTERVIEW

Having got your drawer full of different CVs, you now need to work out what you need to write to accompany the particular CV that you have amended to match the needs of the specific vacancy. Usually you will be sending it via the Internet or by post so if it is going by e-mail, make sure you name the documents appropriately. Don't call your CV 'Curriculum Vitae', call it 'yournameCV'. Don't call the letter 'letter' – name it for the person or the company you are sending it to, e.g. 'Cadburyletter 020707'. Be sure that you label everything so it is clear to the reader that this is an application that you have thought through and drafted specifically for them.

What it looks like

Let's take the letter first and how it physically looks. If you are posting it, make sure that it subtly stands out. By that, I don't mean writing in green ink or on pink paper. I certainly don't mean encasing it in those irritating plastic pouches. The message has got to be to make you memorable for all of the right reasons, not the wrong ones. You could invest in a box of high quality A4 paper, such as Conqueror or whatever pleases you aesthetically. You can then send in your applications on a heavy weight, high quality paper with matching envelopes. You could buy cream coloured or off-white paper so that you stand out slightly in the pile of applications and make people want to read it. Whatever you do, please don't tear a piece of paper in half and squeeze your message into that small area or tear a page out of a cheap notepad. Don't use cute paper, pink paper, purple paper or notelets, (yes, I've seen this all done). You are seeking a professional image and a well-presented look so support it with your personal style.

However, if you are applying for a creative role, use this as an opportunity to demonstrate your artistry. If you want to work with an advertising agency, show that you understand branding by applying it to your own CV in your own creative way. If you want to be a graphic artist, then demonstrate your skills in the presentation of your document. You can take risks with typeface and design layout as this is a practical example of your skills.

In general, however, always remember to be appropriate and don't take risks. What can appeal to one person can offend another and you don't know which is which until you have done it.

If you are sending it by e-mail, then check that you do indeed attach the file. How many times have you had to send an e-mail twice as you forgot to attach the file? It doesn't look good. With the correct e-mail address and the appropriately named file, matched with a comprehensive accompanying letter, you are on your way to success.

What it shouldn't look like

This is an easy one to answer. Your accompanying letter should not be a brief one liner that you have hastily scribbled or mistyped. It is better for your application to arrive a day later and for it to be excellent than for it to be submitted promptly and put together badly.

A poor letter:

- Is generic rather than specific
- Is poorly put together
- Is ungrammatical
- Contains spelling errors
- Is not personal, i.e. not addressed to a particular person (unless the advertisement specifically invites this)
- Has inaccuracies of any form
- Does not address the requirements of the role and the applicant's own skills and experience
- Is addressed to the incorrect person or company
- Contains crossings-out or handwritten notes.

This is the time to work hard at your letter rather than throw together something because you are short of time. You risk giving the impression that you are not terribly interested and that this is just one of hundreds of applications that you are making. Your job search strategy will look like one that is focused on volume rather than quality. A poor letter will reflect badly on you and it will show up very badly in comparison with others who have dedicated true thought to the application. If an interviewer has decided to meet ten people and yours is the only one that is curt, off-hand or ill thought through, you won't make the cut.

The letter should not be about why you want a job or what you can offer to the client. The correct emphasis is working out what the client needs and then framing your own experience so that the client will see what they will be gaining from having you as part of their workforce.

Use the following sheet as a check to make sure that you are addressing the points in the advertisement:

The advertisement Specific requirements	Me What specifically have I done to match this?

Applying by post

When you write your letter, be sure to make it crisp, well presented and set out as a business letter should be. This means you should put the date on the letter, preferably on the left-hand side, directly above the name, job title, company and address of the recipient. Your own address will be right at the top and will also have a telephone number and an e-mail address. This is your chance to make it as easy as possible for someone to contact you.

Remember the basic rules that if you begin the letter 'Dear Mr', 'Mrs' or 'Ms', then the letter should be signed off 'Yours sincerely'. If you address it to 'Dear Sir or Madam', then your sign off should be 'Yours faithfully'. I know that you probably know all of this already but we are aiming for perfection here so bear with me.

Should the letter be handwritten or should it be typed? Some job advertisements ask you to send in a handwritten application and this may be because they like to see how you present yourself and it also may be because they use graphology as a way of assessing your personality. Graphology is the science of determining from handwriting the character of the writer. Make sure, therefore, that if you are asked for a handwritten letter that you oblige.

In most circumstances, a typed letter is the best way to apply as it is the easiest and fastest way for someone to read the letter. They won't have to spend time trying to decipher individual style of handwriting. The disadvantage of applying like this is that your letter will look exactly the same as everyone else's. Stand out by your choice of high quality paper or, if you have perfect copper plate handwriting, consider abandoning word processing and handcraft a reply. This is a sure way of letting someone know that you have dedicated time and energy to the application and that it is a letter you are sending out only to them.

Applying by e-mail

If you have the choice of applying by post or by e-mail, the latter option is the fastest way to get into the recruitment system. Because your application is held in electronic format, it will be on someone's laptop or Blackberry and it will easier to access than a document that is only in hard copy. The recruitment consultant or the potential employer can forward e-mails easily whereas a letter will have to be photocopied and might end up forgotten in a pile. As your goal is for people to read your CV and to include you in a recruitment process, it is probably better, on balance, to go for the e-mail option. You could always send it by post as well, making clear in the letter that is a duplicate application.

Your covering letter can be the body of the e-mail itself with one file attachment that is your CV or you can simply attach the letter as a Word file.

Letters you shouldn't send

Have a look at the following letters and see if you have ever been guilty of sending them out:

---

21 September 2007

Mrs Rose Smith
HR Department
Large PLC
Technology Park
Swansea
SK4 2AW

Dear Mrs Smith

Please find enclosed my CV in response to your recent advertisement. I look forward to hearing from you and hopefully meeting you at interview when I will have the opportunity to demonstrate my skills and appropriateness for the role.

Yours faithfully,

Alistair Brown

This is a wasted opportunity. Mr Brown had the opportunity to refer to the requirements of the role and how he thinks he might match it. It is very polite but does not begin to address the issue of 'Why me?' Can I point out again the fundamental rule that if the greeting in the letter is Dear Mr / Mrs / Ms, then the sign off is Yours sincerely and not Yours faithfully.

21 September 2007

Mrs Rose Smith
HR Department
Large PLC
Technology Park
Swansea
SK4 2AW

Dear Mrs Smith

I read with great interest your recent advertisement for a Regional Manager. I believe I have many of the skills and attributes you are seeking and would like to highlight some of the particular areas that might interest you.

I am aged 32 and happily married with two children, Jake aged 4 and Daisy aged 2. Although I have not worked directly as a Regional Manager in the retail sector, I am sure that my experience in property, working in estate agents for the last three years will be beneficial in this role.

I am sending this by mail as unfortunately I do not have access to the Internet at the moment. I would prefer not to disclose my salary at this time but will be happy to talk about it at interview.

I look forward to hearing from you and meeting you shortly.

Yours sincerely,

Jed Jones

Mr Jones seems to be focusing on all the wrong things. Instead of describing his family, he should be looking at the transferable skills he has that he could bring to the role. He needs to expand on what he could bring to the role and how he would address the gaps in his skills and his knowledge.

Lack of access to the Internet is unacceptable in today's job market. There are Internet cafes on every corner of the globe so the excuse that your broadband connection is down simply won't wash.

Why won't he disclose his salary? This is yet another barrier between him and the job.

Received by e-mail:

I reviewed your advertisement in the *Daily Telegraph* for the above position, which I wish to be considered for.

Should you have any difficulties in downloading the information, please contact me and I would be happy to send them in the post to you.

Regards

Mia

Please note: No greeting, no reference to the job, no specifics. This is the assembly line, volume approach to job hunting. It doesn't impress. It is impersonal, offhand and pompous and it gives the impression that it took two minutes to finish. Hasty applications are generally poor ones.

Dear Anne

Please find attached my CV in support of my application for the position of Managing Director as advertised in the Sunday Telegraph.

Regards

Can you hear that one thundering towards the reject pile as well?

Dear Ms Watson

Please find attached my CV in support of my application for the position of Managing Director as advertised in the Sunday Telegraph.

I note from your advert that your client is in the M62 corridor. The M62 is a very long motorway and I would be interested to hear where your client is based.

Yours sincerely

Here we have an attempt at humour that sounds a bit sarcastic, don't you think? Reject pile ...

Dear Madam

I have recently read your advertisement in The Sunday Times for a UK Sales Director. I am an experienced Export Sales manager and I am now looking to move into a UK based role. Please don't let my career path put you off. Export sales are similar to UK sales only in another language.

I live very close to your company head office. The premises and the quality of the company cars parked there indicate that the company is very successful. I would like to contribute to and benefit from this success.

I would be interested in having an initial interview with you.

Best regards

This candidate has started off by planting a seed of doubt and inviting me to be put off. The statement 'Please don't let my career path put you off' instantly puts you off. As for admiring the cars in the car park – I think I would have been more impressed by a statement that he had looked at the products or visited a customer to check the client out.

> Dear Anne,
>
> Kindly review my CV attached.
>
> I am certainly VERY interested in the above noted position and would like to apply.
>
> I have many years of experience in sales and would like to resume my career in this capacity as soon as possible. You will also note that I ran a sales office on at least one occasion.
>
> Please respond with your notes,
>
> Many thanks,
>
> Joseph Bloggs

What Mr Bloggs is doing here is shifting very neatly the responsibility for analysing his CV against the job requirements from him to me. He is expecting the recruitment consultant to make the notes and do all the running. Enthusiasm alone is insufficient.

Dear Anne,

I wish to apply for the above position advertised in the 'Sunday Times' dated 25th May 2007.

I currently operate three franchises with remuneration circa 55k.

The company is changing all sites to direct managed status, which is why I am looking for a new career challenge.

I have attached my CV for your perusal.

Regards,

Fred Smith

This one came by e-mail and I have magnanimously removed all the typos/spelling mistakes. Nonetheless, what remains is a letter that tells me only why this person is job hunting. It does not tell me why I should be interested in him.

What the letter should look like

By looking at letters that are poor and do little to add value, it is easier to work out what you should be doing. Before you start, remember:

- Fresh application – fresh letter. Delete any pro forma letters on your computer
- Date it
- Zero tolerance of typos or spelling mistakes. If you can't spell a word, check it. If you are still unsure, make a friend of a good speller
- When you write 'Dear ...' – get the name right. So many people don't
- If there is a reference number, put it at the top
- When you have finished, check the advertisement and make sure you have included everything that they have asked for
- Be clear, be concise and don't ramble
- Look at the definition of the role and highlight the areas in your career that match it.

There are no shortcuts in this one. The more effort you put into the letter and the application, the more successful you are likely to be. When you have completed it, put it aside overnight and then revisit. Check, check and check again. Put yourself in the mind of the person reading it and see if it stands out. Does it read to you like the letter of someone who should be interviewed? Are you giving yourself the best possible chance in the process?

Nadine Jones, Head of Human Resources, Baugur, says:

Check the gender and name of the person you are applying to – receiving letters addressed to a Mr or indeed Mrs as a Miss doesn't do a lot to ingratiate me to the candidate.

Do watch the length of your application – I'm not precious about two versus three pages but do keep it relevant and concise – most often reviewing CVs is my 'on the train home' job and after seven pages I've either lost the will to live or fallen asleep!

So, let's look at some good examples of strong, applied, intelligent application letter writing and see what they tell us.

Dear Ms Watson

You recently advertised for a managing director in the Capital Equipment sector. Apologies for the delay in responding but I, like your target market, do not often read advertisements. This one did, however, catch my eye and rang some bells.

I have a successful career, predominantly in the turn around of manufacturing businesses or the start up of service organizations. I am used to full P & L responsibility, budgetary management, and cross-functional and cross-cultural operation and I am known as a good manager and a sound 'boss'.

I attach a copy of a CV, which might form the basis of a more in-depth discussion. I am told I have a prodigious work rate and am used to achieving on time and to budget. I do have major project management experience.

My experience covers capital goods to FMCG and encompasses strategy development and implementation.

I hope this has whetted your appetite and I look forward to hearing a little more about your client.

Yours sincerely

This letter sounds natural, personal and specific to this vacancy. It might not be perfect but it felt as if a human being had written it for my eyes only.

Dear Ms Smith

Your ref 32190 – Marketing Week 27ᵗʰ June

I read with interest your advertisement for a Consumer Insights Group Manager in *Marketing Week* and I attach my CV in application.

In order to support my application I would like to highlight the experience I have that is relevant to the role:

- I am a graduate with 8 years' experience in consumer market research
- I have strong international experience, having worked in continental Europe as well as limited Asian exposure
- I have worked in 2 different companies and can demonstrate a flexible and adaptable method of working
- I am accustomed to taking responsibility and managing my own deadlines
- I am a committed team player and know how to motivate myself and others
- I have a proven track record of effective and creative communication
- Campaigns I have run have required new insights and ingenuity

In addition to this I am ambitious, hard working and focused on delivering value to any role I undertake. My combination of large corporate and small private company experience gives me a versatility of approach and adaptability that would allow me to make an instant impact in the Consumer Insights Group Manager role.

I currently live in Nottingham but as I live in rented accommodation, I could easily relocate for this role.

I am currently earning a basic salary of £50,000, plus a bonus of up to 10%, a car allowance of £750 per month, mobile telephone, private health for myself and my family and a contributory pension scheme. My notice period is three months.

I would welcome the opportunity to discuss this further with you. If you require any further information, please contact me either by e-mail or via the telephone.

I look forward to hearing from you.

Yours sincerely

J. Seeker

This is a carefully composed letter that has been put together specifically for this advertisement. It is intelligent and well thought through. It answers some of the questions that might be in the mind of the reader and it gives every reason why he should be interviewed rather than the reverse.

16 Rose Walk
Blackburn
C10 4RL.
jbrooks@email.com
07788 9757654

Sarah Fulham
Human Resources Manager
The Bright Company
The Green
Derham
TS81 9FT

Dear Ms Fulham

Your ref: Grocer 7201 – Sales Executive

I read with great interest your advertisement for a Sales Executive in this week's 'Grocer'. I am actively seeking a challenging career opportunity that will allow me to develop my skills in business-to-business sales. I have been working in a similar industry to your own for the last six months, principally in new business development. This work has been a short term contract so I am eager to secure a position with an organization such as yours where I will be a committed and dedicated part of the team. It seems to me that you have a dynamic and fast paced culture with the market presence and the brand that will allow the sales organization to capitalize on existing success.

You will see from the attached CV that I graduated last year from Lancaster University with an upper second class honours degree in Finance. I worked throughout my university career in a variety of part time customer focused roles and I believe that this has taught me the value of hard work and commitment.

I have always had a strong work ethic and I am very ambitious. I believe that this sales position will provide me with the challenge I need and I would be able to offer you my energy, loyalty and my will to succeed. Although I am currently based in the north-west area, I will happily relocate to anywhere in the UK.

I look forward to hearing from you in the near future and hope that you will decide to offer me an interview.

Yours sincerely,

John Brooks

This is a personal and strong letter that makes a direct link between the job that was advertised and the the experience that John has. His use of vocabulary is interesting as it seems to radiate energy and enthusiasm. This is what a relatively new graduate needs to exude.

Sent by e-mail:

Dear Ms Watson

I am currently an Account Manager for a sales and marketing company in Nottingham and have worked in the business-to-business industry for over 4 years now. I have great experience in working on new and existing accounts and have a demonstrable track record of success in generating contracts, and revenue for them. I believe that your recruitment company could be handling vacancies where my experience could be of interest. I therefore attach my CV for you to review against any possible opportunities.

The main part of my role has been researching, sourcing and nurturing opportunities, making appointments and managing the diaries of the sales teams that I work for. I send out letters/e-mails on behalf of my clients on a daily basis. We work confidentially on behalf of our clients providing them with reports and making sure all of their information is dealt with in the correct manner. Everything is recorded in our bespoke database and managed, good organization skills are essential to facilitate the sales representatives we work with and utilize their time to best effect. Good geographical knowledge has been essential.

In my time at Research Company Ltd I have been responsible for office duties such as staff holidays, stationery, dealing with enquiries, answering the phones and providing refreshments and dealing with new starters. I also take care of the computer systems, liaising with our IT specialist and make sure all our work is backed up.

Although I am very happy with my current company, I believe that the time is right for me to seek a more demanding role where I would be able to develop my skills and make a greater contribution with more responsibilities and personal accountabilities.

I would like to move into a more customer-focused sales role where I could use all of my experience to date to work in a targeted sales environment.

I would be very grateful if you could let me know if you might be able to introduce me to clients where my experience might be a good fit.

Thank you for taking the time to consider this application.

Kind regards

Anne,

Please find attached my CV in application for the vacancy of Managing Director, which was advertised in today's Daily Telegraph.

I have recently returned to the UK from a position in the Netherlands and I am keen to secure a new, fresh, exciting challenge utilizing my business management experience.

Having reviewed your advertisement, I have identified specific areas of my experience that I believe would have an immediate impact on the role of Managing Director as you describe it. I have had full P & L responsibility in my previous two roles and have proven success at driving businesses forward in terms of sales, customer service, distribution and people management. I also have a wealth of change management experience in developing new processes, systems and culture changes in tunnel vision environments to drive through efficiency changes and cost savings in difficult market trading conditions.

My remuneration package in my last position was £75k basic plus benefits. My current salary expectations are to match this at the very least and preferably to improve on them.

I would be grateful if you could give my application due consideration and would welcome the opportunity to discuss the vacancy and my experience with you at your convenience.

Yours sincerely,

Jim Brown

These e-mails are written for the specific vacancies and go a long way towards addressing what the roles demand and what the candidates offer.

Dear Ms. Watson,

Please find attached my CV for your consideration. I would like to be considered for the post of Graduate Trainee as advertised in *The Evening Echo*.

Picking up on some of the key points in the post description, I would like to comment on where I hope I could bring some key skills to your company.

- *Preferably having at least one year's work experience* – although I have only recently graduated, I have worked in a range of roles during my university years. These include office-based positions where I have worked as a temporary PA as well as the normal student jobs, including waitressing, bar work and reception jobs.
- *The successful candidate will have a keen interest in business* – My degree was in business studies and my sole reason for studying this topic is that I have always been determined to pursue a career in business. I read the financial pages of the daily papers and I have applied for membership of the junior Chamber of Commerce.
- *An investigative nature* – research drives me. I have seen the huge changes in research methodologies with the growth of the Internet.
- *Excellent telephone skills* – I am well spoken and confident to carry out telephone interviews and ensure that all telephone contacts are well prepared in advance as well as being able to react to situations that move away from the anticipated paths.
- *Complete command of Microsoft Office and able to manage multiple projects* – I am highly IT literate and fully familiar with Microsoft products as well as web design and other skills.
- *It is essential to have the confidence to speak to people at all management levels and across a number of cultures* – I am confident yet have the diplomacy and tact to speak to people at all management levels. I speak fluent French and have travelled widely so I believe I can handle myself well in diverse social situations.

- *Problem solving, flexible thinking and fast pace are vital within this results focused environment* – I love facing new challenges and I am accustomed to balancing a number of projects. I am quick to react to directives but also have high levels of initiative to suggest, implement and complete my own ideas.

I would welcome the opportunity to talk to you regarding the post and would be delighted if you were to offer me an interview. If you require any further information, please let me know.

Kind regards

This e-mail has been put together very carefully. It is well thought through and it is specific to the vacancy. It shows that the candidate has reflected on the needs of the job and matched these against their own talents.

Mr George Smith
25 Lobelia Avenue
Chidwell by the Sea
Lancs
LC3 4ZT
Mobile: 078850 6453621

Anne Watson
Executive Focus Ltd
21 September 2007

Dear Ms Watson,

Your advertisement for a Group Finance Director has prompted me to contact you. The following criteria are indicated in your advertisement. I feel I meet these requirements.

Your requirements	My qualifications
Finance Director	Two years as Divisional Finance Director of a business-to-business capital equipment organization that experienced major changes and growth. Quick and successful business sale (£93m).
Strategic	As FD worked closely with the MD to realign a seriously flawed strategy, out of control costs and poor reporting. Drafted multi-million pound investment proposals for executive approval.
Commercial support	Negotiated with major customers and suppliers. Produced significant amount of analysis to improve productivity and revenue capture. My team supported multi-million pound bids and the price book with modelling, etc.
Financial leadership	Led and motivated teams of 30+ and 50+ in two recent roles.
Involved at operational level	Performed numerous operational reviews with regional directors involving financials, cash management, investment proposals, pricing, bids and productivity, etc.

| Qualified accountant with experience | ACA (first time passes) with 12 years PQE. |

There appears to be a very strong match between your requirements and my qualifications. I would like the opportunity to meet with you at your earliest convenience to discuss this opportunity. My CV is attached for your further review.

Yours sincerely

George Smith

This letter tells me what I want to hear; George Smith has read the advertisement intelligently and he has given me all of the reasons why I should interview him – laid out in a clear and methodical way matching his skills to the job criteria.

Andrew Harris, Director, Matthews Harris Consulting, says:

When you hear of a job vacancy and read the job description or the advertisement, start thinking straight away about what they need and what you have that they might want. Pull out of your experience elements that match what they are looking for. You can't just send off your CV and expect them to read it and work out how your experience matches their role. You have to do it for them. You have to remember that it is up to you to draw parallels between your experience and their needs. This means that the CV you have spent hours creating has to be modified so that the reader will be able to see instantly that you have many of the qualities they are looking for.

Mobile telephones

The mobile telephone is a brilliant asset in the job search. You are instantly accessible by voice or by text without the need to leave messages on home answerphones or going via the switchboard at work. The whole process speeds up so let's get it right. When did you last listen to your own answerphone message? Go on, ring it right now and listen to it. What impression do you get? If it is the default message from your service provider, change it right now and make it personal. When I ring you and leave a message, I want to be sure that I have called the right number and that I am leaving a message on the right telephone.

If your current answer phone message is a chatty informal one, aimed at friends and family, consider if it is the right one for future employers. Write your message down and then record it. When you speak, make sure that your voice is warm, friendly and professional. How about:

'Hello. This is the telephone of Anne Watson. I am sorry I am not available at the moment but if you would like to leave your name and your number, I will call you straight back. Thank you.'

There you go – easy. I know it isn't exciting, humorous or witty but it is part of your professional image and your impact.

Response rate

Speed of response is everything. If a potential employer wants to talk to you, they want to talk to you straightaway. This for you is success. You have managed to get on their radar and you are about to get to the next stage. Make sure, therefore, that you get the basics right:

- Check your e-mails frequently. Once a week isn't enough and once a day isn't enough
- Respond promptly, even if it is to say that you are away on business or you will have to check on something and come back to them later
- Do not go 'silent' on someone. If you don't want to progress the job application, tell them
- Top your mobile up with credit
- Keep on top of the administration and be efficient.

Gareth James, Director, People Plus and his views on record keeping:
Always remember what job you are being interviewed for. I once was interviewing someone for a Marketing Director's role but in the course of the meeting started to feel that there was some kind of mismatch. I stopped the interview and asked the candidate what job he thought he was being interviewed for. It then transpired that the candidate had got this interview muddled with another and thought it was for a Sales Director. He had been blanketing the market with job applications and had

simply forgotten what the interview was for. He offered as an excuse that he had been applying for lots of jobs but this did not cut the mustard with me.

Record-keeping rules:
- *Keep meticulous records of your job search*
- *Keep copies of the advertisement*
- *Keep copies of the letters that you sent*
- *Keep a copy of any job brief or company profile that you might have been sent*
- *Make sure that you read them all again just before the interview and remind yourself why you are there and who you are seeing.*

The message about this is a clear one and a firm one. You can have the best CV in the world but if you don't support it with a strong covering letter and submit it appropriately, you won't get anywhere. This is the rule whether it is a response to an advertisement, a letter to a company, an agency, a Human Resources Manager or a head-hunter.

The letter has to be right or the e-mail has to perfect. No-one will make allowances for typos just because it has come by e-mail. This is the first introduction someone has had to you and it cannot afford to look sloppy. Perfection is what you aspire to so make sure that applies to both form and content. Job hunting does not accommodate the off-hand and the casual. Take nothing for granted. Take pride in an application that will stand up to the closest scrutiny. It will give you confidence and stand you in good stead for the interview ahead.

CHAPTER 4

WHERE AND HOW TO APPLY

RESULT: YOU TARGET THE JOB YOU WANT

Whoever you are and no matter what you believe your role to be, from now on, you are in sales. Your product is you and your entire focus, as with any good sales person, is on the customer – your future employer. In order to start calling on the 'customers' to sell them this magnificent 'product', you need to know:

- who they are
- what they want, and
- whether or not you can provide it.

Track the process

Before you launch yourself enthusiastically on the job market and before you start sending out your brilliantly crafted letter and CV, take a step back and decide how much time you can dedicate to the job search. If you are out of work, newly graduated or redundant, you will be treating this as your full-time job so you will have plenty of time to take on an ambitious programme. However, if you are already working full time, you need to think carefully about how many active applications you can handle. You need to be cautious not to arouse suspicions at work so if you are suddenly taking three half-days a week off work to attend interviews, the game will be up. Make sure you take on just as much as you can handle efficiently and don't spread yourself too thin.

If you have a two week holiday planned in the near future, make sure you mention this in your accompanying letter. You might decide to wait until you get back before you start the search.

Timescales and targets

Set yourself a target for telephone calls, letters, contacts, e-mails and applications. Set it out week by week to cover a three-month period. Make it realistic and achievable and make sure you check your actual progress against your plan. Consistency of approach is what will win the day. A sporadic search with the occasional letter or application is unlikely to produce the goods. This is a full-time job search and it is going to require effort, time, research and plenty of meetings. Make the space in your diary for them and allocate them the right priority.

An active, measured campaign that shows initiative, ingenuity and determination will win the day. Half-hearted measures will get half-hearted results. Bring all of your resources, all of your energy and your resolution to the task. Set yourself a deadline for getting the job and stick to it.

Managing the administration

If you intend to apply for just one job, or register with just one recruitment company, then it will be simple to keep track of your application. However, you are probably braced for a broad and far-reaching search so you need to make sure that your filing system and administration will not let you down. Gareth James's cautionary tale of the candidate who could not remember which job he was being interviewed for should ring in your ears. The way to avoid this is to make sure that your records are impeccable. Keep a copy of everything that you send out. Remember who you sent it to and remember what version of your CV they received. If you were recommended to someone, then keep a note of who it was. If it was an advertisement, keep a copy. Put it in a file, label it and be organized. When someone rings you up to invite you for an interview, you don't want to be scrabbling around in a pile of papers, trying to remember who they are. There is nothing quite so off-putting as having a candidate whose response to a telephone call inviting them for interview being, 'Er, sorry? Who did you say you are? Which job are we talking about? Do you mean the job that was advertised in the *Sunday Times* or the one in the *Daily Telegraph*?'

Good filing and record keeping will prevent that happening. Invest in stationery, files, coloured pens and sticky labels and make them work for you.

Industrious research

Given that your goal is to find the best possible job that you can, one that will bring you the most job satisfaction and personal fulfilment as well as satisfying your financial objectives, you need to open up all possible lines of enquiry. You might be focusing on a particular job role within one specific sector or you might be quite open-minded. You might be exploring the possibility of employment while you are still considering setting up your own business, going back to full-time study or working as an interim. All of those options will be broader, deeper and give you more choice if your research is rigorous and exceptional.

You need to become an expert in your chosen field. If you intend to follow a new course or programme, make sure you have examined every single one that is available. If you are looking for a job in an SME, (Small and Medium Enterprise) then know where they are. Become an avid reader so that you know exactly who is doing what in your chosen industry sector so you are aware of all of the possible companies you could join. There are reference texts and books available as well as newspaper articles, league tables of the Fastest Growing Small Business, the 500 Best Employers to Work For, the Best Performing Business in the Sector, etc. award schemes, competitions and comparison league tables exist in abundance. Track them down and find out what you don't know. If you are a recent graduate and you are targeting a blue chip organization where you know you will get the best possible training and introduction to business life, make sure you know which are the hottest organizations to work for and what their products, markets and competitors are; do your homework. Analyse their philosophy and their culture and make sure you know what you have to do to get on the inside.

Your research will include Internet-based research where you can track down practically anything you want to know about any topic or any company. In addition to this, you need to become an aficionado of the business pages of newspapers and magazines. Not only will you be reading this week's papers, you can go to the library and pull out archived copies. This ultimately takes less time than accessing them online and has the advantage of being free of charge. Journalists will highlight the business activities of certain companies and you can decide that you have a particular interest in an organization because of what you have read. You may, for example, read that a company has just won a huge contract or has opened up a new manufacturing unit. You may read that an acquisition has been made or a new patent registered. A new department may be opening up and new investment made. This could lead you to think that the company will need someone with your skills to help them in their new stage of growth. Rather than waiting for them to place the role with an agency or to advertise it in the papers, you may decide to write to the Chief Executive, or the Sales Director, or the Human Resources Director, using your keenly researched knowledge of their business to introduce them to the skills that you believe you could bring them.

Andrew Harris, Director, Matthews Harris Consulting Limited, says:

Employers often look at their teams and may have doubts about the performance of one or more of the members. This does not mean that they are going to leap into action and sack them. However, the seed of doubt is there and they might eagerly interview and employ someone who would improve the company's performance, whether this is in sales, production, quality, distribution marketing, IT – any area that impacts on how a business makes money. All Chief Executives know that high-performing people are hard to get and they are therefore always on the look out for good people. People who perform well in an organization make money for the business and this is what it is all about.

Running your own business

Before you embark on a job search, you may wish to address the issue of whether or not you want to run your own business. This seems to be a dream that many people have so if this could be something you may wish to do, why not take the opportunity now to examine the idea in detail to see if it truly is an option or if it will remain a dream? This book is not a guide to setting up your own business. However, it is a career option that needs to be included or excluded from your life.

To begin exploring the possibilities, you might want to make contact with UKTI and your local development agency. Talk to Business Link; look at the listings of businesses for sale. Talk to your accountants to see if they know of businesses for sale. Approach Venture Capitalists and see if they are looking for someone to run one of their investments where you might be able to have a small stake.

If you know what you want to do and you are seeking the courage, the funding, the location, or the timing to do it, research the marketplace well. It is always easier and cheaper to learn from someone else's experience than your own so find someone who has embarked on a similar path and find out from them what potential obstacles might lie ahead. Get tips from other entrepreneurs and discover what you might not know about business life when you are the boss.

You might want to think about buying a franchise. This is a faster, although possibly more expensive route, to self employment and if you are someone who longs to be independent yet does not have the business idea to follow, it can be a short cut to success. To find out more, look at the website of the British Franchise Association, www.thebfa.org, and see what is involved in buying a franchise. There are exhibitions you can go to where you will be overwhelmed by the choice and the scale of businesses that are on offer as franchises.

Whatever you decide to do, remember that cashflow is the biggest single downfall of the growing business. Work out what finance you have in place and be sure that you have it resolved before you set off. It is often said that banks offer umbrellas when the sun shines and want them back when it starts raining so make sure you are in control of financial resources.

Caution!

Before you do anything, make sure you seek the advice of independent accountants.

Becoming an interim

If you are looking for a job with an interim agency, where you will have a specific contract with a company for a defined period of time, generally in months rather than years, make sure you know who they are. There are specialist agencies that will be able to open up opportunities within the most appropriate companies. An interim role may well give you the breathing space that you need if you are undecided about your long-term career goals. It might provide you with the work that you need to see you safely into retirement. It can also be an excellent way of expanding your experience of different organizations, allowing you to crystallize your views on what kind of organization and role you want to work in. It could even lead to a job offer if you find yourself inside a company where everyone likes each other.

The interim role does not allow for much of a learning curve. If you are applying for an interim role, you will be expected to have all of the experience that the role requires and you will be expected to have an instant impact and produce immediate results. This is not an easy option so be sure that when you apply to be an interim that you have the confidence as well as the ability to fulfil the role.

Adele Kimber gives the following listing of the top 20 interim agencies (from her article entitled 'Choosing an Interim Agency', *Personnel Today*, April 2004):

Market share of the top 20 interim agencies

Rank	Company name	Market share
1	BIE International	6.6%
2	Praxis Executives on Assignment	6%
=3	Albermarle Interim Management	5%
=3	Odgers Interim	5%
5	Ashton Penney	4.2%
6	Project Partners	4.1%
7	Impact Executives (UK)	3.9%
8	Executive Interim Management (UK)	3.3%
9	Boyde	3.2%
10	EC International	3.1%
11	Heidrick & Struggles Interim Executives	2.9%
12	Veredus Executive Resourcing Interim Management	2.7%
13	Penna Interim Executive	2.5%
14	KPMG Interim Management	2.4%
15	Hoggett Bowers Executive Interim Management	2.2%
=16	Interim Performers	2%

=16	Barnes Kavelle Interim Executive Services	2%
=16	Calibre One	2%
=19	Brooklands Executives	1.9%
=19	Archer Mathieson	1.9%

There are many others in the marketplace so select the ones that you believe operate in your speciality and in the sector that you prefer.

The interim route can be an excellent way of buying yourself time while you are considering what you want to do next. However, it is not an easy option. The hours are long, you are often working away from home all week and you will be expected to deliver high quality work for every minute of every day

Andrew Harris, Director, Matthews Harris Consulting Limited, says:

Recruitment is expensive and always risky. Make the decision easier for them by volunteering to work for them for two or three weeks for nothing. If you are sitting at home without a job, then this will allow you to make contacts and prove yourself. You have nothing to lose. They can see what you are like and you may be able to stretch it to a six-month contract. You will have a toe in the door and you can grow from there.

Newspaper, magazine and trade press advertisements

The job of your dreams could come from a number of directions. It is possible that it will come via an advertisement in a newspaper, magazine or trade journal. You need to cover the ground in this respect as you have no way of knowing what will be advertised next. All appointments within the public sector are advertised so if this is what you are after, then it is a simple matter to monitor any newspaper or journal where they will appear. *The Guardian*, the *Sunday Times*, *The Telegraph* on a Thursday; all of these papers will be fertile hunting ground. Remember that they often feature different industry sectors on different days of the week.

In order to uncover all of the possibilities, start reading papers and magazines outside your normal scope. Consider the broadest possible range of reading materials, e.g. daily, weekly and monthly publications, and subscribe to them all. Remember to include regional and local papers. Not only that, get online and check to see if you can register for e-mail alerts to be sent to you when they are advertising a role that fits the pre-set criteria that you establish. The job you want is not going to present itself to you on a plate. You need to be reading everything and have all of your antennae out, hunting for something that could lead you to the right place.

Look at the following list of newspapers and ask yourself if you have ever read them or if you think you could; they all contain strong recruitment sections:

- *The Evening Standard*
- *The Financial Times*
- *The Glasgow Herald*
- *The Guardian*
- *The Independent*
- *The Manchester Guardian*
- *The Scotsman*
- *The Sunday Telegraph*
- *The Sunday Times*
- *The Telegraph*
- *The Times.*

And magazines?

- *Accountancy Age*
- *Ad Week*
- Your local *Business Insider* magazine
- *Computer Weekly*
- *Investor's Chronicle*
- *Marketing Week*
- *Nature*
- *New Scientist*
- *Nursing Times*
- *Personnel Today*
- *The Economist.*

And there are many more ...

Broaden your reading material and you will see just where the vacancies lie and how they are being handled, whilst at the same time keeping up to date with the issues of the day in your sector. You need to know who the players are so you know who to be targeting.

Web based advertisements

The Internet is a huge opportunity for you to find out who is recruiting and what they are recruiting for without leaving the comfort of your own home. You can apply on line to a job board such as www.monster.co.uk, www.totaljobs.co.uk, www.fish4.co.uk or any of the hundreds of general job sites that there are now around. If you are looking in a specific sector, then there will be a job site that will focus on what you do, whether it is scientific, catering, nursing, accounting, retailing, manufacturing, sourcing, financial sector – whatever it is, there is a job board that will work well for you. Disregard them at your peril. You cannot afford to make an assumption that Internet-based recruitment will not work for you. Employers are willing to try any method that will work in order to attract talent and they are turning increasingly to the Internet for fast and innovative solutions. Before you begin, though, remember to be selective in your approach. Don't post your CV anywhere and everywhere as you don't want to saturate the marketplace with your CV. Go for quality rather than quantity.

Tim Elkington, Managing Director of Enhance Media specializes in helping companies to use the Internet efficiently for recruitment purposes. He helps companies tailor their own website and resources to control their own recruitment, using technology to attract the best candidates. If you are staring at the Google page and wondering what it can do to help you get a job, then this is a good place to start.

Tim Elkington Managing Director, Enhance Media Ltd, says:

The Internet is for everyone and the starting point for any job hunter should be the Internet. There are 46 million adults in the UK and 28 million are online every month. 12 million of these will use the Internet to look for a job. A recent piece of research carried out by NORAS (The National Online Recruitment Audience Survey) with a sample size of 37,000 showed that jobs have been filled online in the salary ranges of £18,000 to £78,000 and across most sectors and management levels.

A brilliant source of independent and objective information on the audiences of job boards is www.noras.co.uk. It tells you what is happening in online recruitment and has carried out large-scale research to arrive at its findings. In March 2007 the following statistics were published:

1   NORAS uses questionnaires completed by 37,617 online job seekers across 27 job boards
2   Going online every day is normal, 63% of online job seekers use the Internet every day
3   52% of online job seekers have an Internet-enabled mobile phone. This shows a huge (and mostly untapped) potential market in mobile online job seeking
4   The average number of job boards that online job seekers use when looking for a job has fallen from 7 in 2004 to 5.3 in 2007 – online job seekers are becoming more familiar with which job boards work and don't work for them
5   The number of methods used in addition to the Internet when looking for a job is also falling, from an average of 2.8 alternative methods in 2005 to just 2 in 2007 – job seekers are relying more on the Internet
6   Online recruitment is becoming more successful, 56% of online job seekers (that got interviews after applying for a job they found online) got a job, compared to 44% in 2004.

Check out the website and register so that you can see who is who in Internet recruitment and so that you can stay up to date in the cutting edge of technology based recruitment. There are job boards that are general and there are niche boards. The Internet is used by normal people who come from all walks of life and there is a job out there for you. It is not just for IT technical appointments.

Tim Elkington, Managing Director, Enhance Media Ltd, says:

If you are not using the Internet then you are missing out. The Internet is not just a useful research tool to help you find out more about potential employers. In fact, there are organizations that will only accept applications via the Internet. If you want a job with T Mobile, then you have to go via the Internet or you will not be considered.

Make sure you have your eyes open and notice what they are saying.

Corporate recruitment websites

There are large companies who use their website to attract people into the organization. These career sites vary in their degrees of sophistication but it is safe to say that these organizations will have invested significantly in them to ensure that they are a means of attracting job applications from stunningly talented applicants like you. They will use job boards, offline advertisements, search engines, fliers, whatever it takes to make you notice them and go to their website.

The site itself should provide a lot of information about the company, its products, its people, its culture and what it is like to work there. They often use short videos, virtual tours, interviews with current staff – in short, anything that helps to show you the inside of the organization and make you want to work there.

These sites encourage you to apply online so that your CV and application will go directly to their candidate management system. This is a quicker, cheaper and more efficient way of processing CVs. The candidate management system is replacing the tasks that used to be done by an administrator. The CVs are sorted and filed appropriately and then they are reviewed according to the criteria for the job. These criteria have been established and set by the line manager or the Human Resources Manager who is responsible for recruiting. They are not plucked randomly out of the ether but are carefully selected to match the needs of the role. The software will therefore be looking for someone who, for example, has certain skills, has worked for certain companies and is earning within certain salary bands. Every single application will be sorted and sifted against those criteria so you will be going through the most objective and impartial process. You can't be rejected because of your name or anything else that could possibly be an invisible form of discrimination. All in all, you are more likely to succeed when you are up against a software system than when perhaps you might be facing the likes and dislikes of the human equivalent.

Tim's message is very clear:

- If the employer wants you to apply via the web, then don't be difficult. Play the game the way the employer wants you to play it and go via the web.
- Don't be seduced by the apparent attraction of printing off a CV and rushing off to the post box with it. Printing off your tailor-made CV is the path of least resistance.
- Applying online means you need to think again about who you are and how you communicate this in the way that the employer wants to see it.
- Use the tools that are available.
- Don't try to buck the system.
- Remember that the Internet is for everyone.

Finding your way around

One simple starting point is Google, where you can put in the request 'graduate jobs', 'nursing jobs', 'accountancy jobs' or whatever it is that you are hunting for. Instantly you will see the job boards and hundreds of options to examine. You will also see on the right-hand side Sponsored Links, the pay per click options. I have always avoided them, as I perceived them to be some kind of honey trap rather than a preferred option but Tim Elkington put me straight:

Tim Elkington Managing Director, Enhance Media Ltd, says:

Get rid of your prejudice about sponsored links. If a company is prepared to pay for you to go to their website, then they surely must have something to offer.

Perhaps the company has an urgent need to employ and recruitment and it is at the top of their agenda rather than an ongoing process. The hot tip for today therefore is to go to the sponsored links and check them out for immediate offers.

In addition, pay careful attention to the companies who have obviously paid extra in order to stand out on the job board. They have their logo on the site and have clearly invested more time and effort in advertising their presence. Compare this with companies who have not taken any extras and therefore do not tell you too much about who they are. Some of them would be recruitment companies who are trawling for CVs to maintain their candidate data bank. Your task is to work out who is looking for a specific person for an existing vacancy and following these clues will make it easier.

Another option, instead of going via job boards, would be to go direct to companies or brands that you admire and that you think you might want to work for. Go to their website, have a look round and check out their career page.

Tim Elkington, Managing Director, Enhance Media Ltd, says:

Just because Starbucks is a coffee chain, it does not mean that all they are looking for is baristas. They will need accountancy, operations, marketing, sales, legal, property, and administration people just like anyone else. Check out those opportunities within brands that you know and think you may like.

You could also do a regional search and look for jobs in the geographical area that you want to be in. You could, for example, put 'graduate jobs St Albans' into Google and you will be focusing on what you want. Use the flexibility and diversity of the Internet to access precise and individual information.

You should also use the resources of job boards and corporate websites to help you in your research. The site itself will help you prepare for interview and it is vital to have looked at it, otherwise you will be awarded at least one black mark for failing to do so. As well as this, make sure you use tools available on the website to assist you in making your job search personal and active. You can set up e-mail alerts so that you will automatically be sent an e-mail when a job matching your criteria is posted. You can do this across a broad range of sites including job boards, corporate sites, newspaper recruitment pages and agencies. You can set up RSS feeds and make sure that you are covering all the options. Just in case you are a little hazy about what an RSS feed is, it stands for Really Simple Syndication. It allows you to see jobs, news feeds or information in real time, from sites that provide RSS as an option. It is a standard format used to share content on the Internet and receive updates from websites without having to visit each site.

Technology is moving at a fast pace and by ensuring that you stay up to speed, you will always have the advantage. Tim showed me a US-based job board, www.simplyhired.com that allows you to track down who you might know inside a company you are thinking of applying to. By pressing the 'Who do you know in this organization' you can trace people through the social and business network site, www.linkedin.com. Go on – have a go and see what Tim means. The future will be the integration of social networks into job boards. The strategies of Amazon and eBay will soon follow on job boards so Tim's message was loud and clear – keep up to date and be prepared to change your perceptions of job seeking. If technology moves on then so should you.

Feedback and security online

Once you have sent off your CV to a job board or to the website of a company, what can you expect by way of acknowledgement? The good employers who prefer to attract via the web generally respond well to your application and they should send you an e-mail that sets out clearly what will happen next and what the process will look like. They are investing all of this time and energy and money to attract candidates so it makes sense that they should use technology to ensure that you know what to expect. In terms of process it should be transparent and far from the second-class option that you may think of it as being.

One major concern on the Internet is always about security and the risk of sending all of this personal information into 'the ether'. Tim counsels common sense and using the same safeguards that you would anyway on the web. If you are unsure about the site, then check its privacy policy to see just what will happen to your details. Also, all good career sites should be registered under the Data Protection Act. I told him of a Chief Executive I know who spends bored evenings in hotel rooms checking Monster and other job boards to see if any of his employees are actively job hunting. Tim allowed that this could be a risk, albeit remote, but if you look at the privacy policy you may be able to restrict access to your CV and therefore prevent this from happening.

Tim Elkington, Managing Director, Enhance Media Ltd, says:
When you have found your perfect job, take your CV down from the job board. It will prevent people from contacting you about jobs you are no longer interested in and will ensure that there will be no confusion about your status. Equally, if you decide to keep your CV online, make sure it is up to date.

Make it as easy as possible for the employer to find you, to learn about you and to interview you.

Trade press and professional bodies

If you are a professionally qualified person and you belong to a particular trade or professional body, whether this is legal, accounting, health, engineering, catering, insurance, financial advisers, plumbers or graphic artists, if your particular sector has a weekly newsletter or a regular newspaper or magazine, make sure you are in touch. Keep up to date with what is happening and who is doing what. You will find out the facts, the news, the gossip and the intrigue. You will know when there is a conference or exhibition and you should be able to see who is recruiting. The obvious place to start a job hunt is in the sector that is familiar to you. If you are guilty of throwing the trade journal into a pile of unread periodicals, blow the dust off them and start reading them. Become an expert in your specialist field so that if something crops up, you will be in the running for it.

It may pay to attend regional or national meetings to let people know who you are and that you are looking for the next step.

Job fairs, exhibitions and conferences

Graduates will find in their final year that employers make it easy for them by attending career fairs. This is an opportunity for mutual assessment and sizing up. Multinational organizations, lawyers, publishers, accountants, public sector, retailers, manufacturers, logistics; all manner of people will be there, distributing brochures, corporate DVDs, free pens and stress balls and showing you the strengths of their organization and why you should be interested in them. Now is your chance to ask as many questions as you like within this safe environment. You have not applied for a job, you are not being interviewed and you are directly in front of organizations and the people who work inside them. You might approach something like this with a very clear view of what you are looking for and you are just using the career fair as an opportunity to make contact and to discover how to apply for a job. On the other hand, you might just be looking around and keeping your eyes open for career possibilities. When you are doing this make sure that you:

• Talk to as many people as possible

- Collect all the corporate literature to review later
- Keep notes of everything that strikes you
- Get as many business cards as possible so that you have a person to contact
- Make yourself memorable by your professional approach – attract appropriate attention
- Grab as many free pens as possible as they will help with your finals revision!

Newspapers advertise job fairs for graduates and funding is sometimes available for you to attend. Make sure you know what is going on and make it your priority to be there.

Exhibitions and conferences can also be invaluable for the out-of-work executive or the person who is seeking to move. If you work within a defined sector, scan the exhibitions that are taking place in centres such as the NEC, Birmingham; ExCeL, London; the Scottish Exhibition Centre, Glasgow; Harrogate International Exhibition Centre and Earl's Court Exhibition Centre, both in London. Check them out to see if there are any exhibitions taking place that could be relevant to you. If there are, go there and work the hall. Talk to people on stands, let them know who you are and get yourself in front of people who could become your boss or your colleague. If you work in a very specialized sector, you may have to invest in an international conference or exhibition in Europe or elsewhere. When deciding, make sure you know who will be exhibiting or addressing the conference and form a strategy for getting yourself in front of them.

Pieter Schats, Managing Director of Toys LiFung (Asia) Limited, says:

I get recommendations of good people to hire by walking round toy fairs and meeting people. I don't not like hiring 'off the street' so the toy fairs are useful places to network.

Outplacement companies – are they an option?

When executives are made redundant, companies often offer outplacement support to see them through the initial period of readjustment and the process of job search. An outplacement company specializes in providing practical assistance to people who are actively job seeking and generally outplacement support forms part of the redundancy or severance package. People have different needs and respond differently to situations. If it happens to you, you may find that you move on without casting a backward glance, creating a perfect CV and formulating a winning strategy to get a job. However, you may experience anxiety, a dent in your self-confidence and your self-worth and you may worry about how to tackle the job market. You may feel that you have no experience of applying for jobs and that your interviewing skills are rusty and out of date.

If this is the case and if you are offered the services of a reputable outplacement company as part of your severance package, grasp it with both hands. The outplacement counsellor allocated to you will be someone who is a recruitment professional and who will be able to ask you all of the questions that will cause you to analyse yourself and your career plans. He or she will be independent and objective and will be ready to challenge you about points in your background that may be picked up later at interview. You will be able to rehearse and practise for the real thing. You should get the opportunity to do some psychometric tests and to learn what it is like to get feedback. All of this will take place in an environment where you can feel secure and learn more about yourself and where you want to go next.

Whatever you do, however, do not think that an outplacement company will get you a job. They are there to support you and to give you some of the tools you need. There is only one person who has the responsibility to find a job and that person is you.

A major advantage in working with an outplacement counsellor is that you can meet other people in the same situation as you. If you can find someone you hit it off with, why not meet up with them a couple of times a month and compare notes? You can share techniques, strategies and tactics and give your job search a different kind of impetus. Andrew Harris of Matthews Harris Consulting Ltd, a search and selection recruitment business, set up The Black Cat Club, a networking group for job-seeking executives. Once a month he organized a half-day programme where a speaker would address the group on some pertinent issue and the rest of the session was dedicated to pooling resources and experiences. People gained different things from the group but the unanimous opinion was that they were useful at a number of levels. Family and friends can also be invaluable sources of support in difficult times like this. However, the confidence and trust of a stranger can occasionally be more powerful. Find the Black Cat equivalent near you or form one of your own.

> ## Caution!
>
> Remember to listen to advice and feedback you are given and then be sure to evaluate it. Do not blindly accept outplacement advice as being the absolute truth. Retain what is important to you and whatever you do, do not allow the outplacement company to put your CV into their format. It will stand out like a sore thumb and the message you will be sending is that you do not own your own CV. The house style of outplacement CVs is immediately obvious to the professional recruiter so be sure to imprint your individuality on your CV.

Agencies, recruitment companies and executive search companies

Sometimes companies handle their own recruitment and sometimes they outsource the process to a specialist recruitment company. The recruitment would then be handled by companies who work in very different ways. Their approach should be professional and organized, using their expertise in specific sectors or at particular management levels. Their goal is to find the best candidate in the shortest time possible and then to be paid a fee for doing so. A job search should mean, therefore, that you include at least some of these companies in your search, otherwise you will not be covering all of the ground. However, remember that recruitment is an unregulated industry so don't expect consistency of quality. If possible, get recommendations from friends and colleagues so that you have some measure of their track record and reputation. Be prepared for anything and then you won't be disappointed. A recruitment company may have an excellent reputation with advertisements appearing regularly in the broadsheets or it could be a head-hunter known to all. However, this does not necessarily mean that you are guaranteed a wonderful customer/candidate experience. Equally, small boutiques that you have not heard of may do a brilliant job. There is no sure way to tell in advance.

Agencies

Agencies work on contingent fees so they work hard to place candidates and are eager for success-related fees. The advantage for you is that they are working on your behalf and may, if you ask them, target specific companies and try to get you through the door another way. They will add your CV to their database and they will actively try to place you. They are highly motivated and are generally in a hurry to achieve results as, let's face it, they have to be or else they will lose the fee. Remember, though, that they may not be handling the assignment exclusively so they will be pitching candidates in along with other companies. As the client has not paid them up front, there may not be the same sense of commitment that you will find in recruitment companies that are working on a non-contingent fee where the client is committed to a fee. They may not have a strong working relationship with the client and they may not be able to influence and convince them of the skills that you would bring.

If you ask an agency to work on your behalf, bear in mind the power that you are giving them. They will send your CV where they think appropriate and some of them do not consult you beforehand. The CV is often one that they have condensed into their house style and may not be a document you would feel happy to put your name to. Also, they may delete your contact details so that all contact will go through the agency. This may be something that will produce the right results. It might also be like opening Pandora's box. Be sure when you register with an agency that you know exactly what they will be doing and how they will be doing it. Keep control of your own CV as you do not want to discover too late that it is being e-mailed to every employer in Britain.

Caution!

Remember that when an agency sends out your CV to a prospective employer, you are effectively putting a price on your head. If you send the CV yourself, you stand the chance of getting someone to read it, deal with you directly and cut out the middle man who will charge them a fee.

A recruitment company that advertises and uses the web

You may feel that you already have this covered. I do have one more suggestion that could mean you find yourself being marketed by a selection company. Go through back copies of newspapers, magazines and trade publications where you think the right job for you could have been advertised. You can do this on the web or in your local reference library. Go back six weeks and find jobs that precede the start of your job search. Think of this – what if this advertisement failed and the right candidate was not appointed? It is worth writing in just to see. Then go back up to three months. This time, you are targeting advertisements where the person may have been offered the job but decided to turn it down. Your timing could be perfect. Then go back six months as the person may have been appointed but did not like the company or the job and has left. This could be your chance! Then look at jobs advertised up to 12 months ago as the same could have happened.

The executive search companies

Assuming that an executive search company has not called you, how do you get in touch with them? First of all, let's understand how they work. The term itself is very vague and open to abuse. A true head-hunter will be someone who has been commissioned by the client to find a specific person for a particular job. They will be paid a fee, usually a hefty one, that is non-contingent and so they have to deliver results. You can be absolutely sure, therefore, that when they call you up to discuss a role, they are handling it exclusively and if you are the right person for the role, they will move heaven and earth to get you an interview and give you a chance in front of the client. This is absolutely what you want so a meeting with the retained, exclusive head-hunter has got to be an objective. A head-hunter I know who specializes in the banking sector goes even further. He suggests that what you need to do is forge a close working relationship with one head-hunter. Get close to one and make sure that person knows who you are and values your career. This head-hunter will then watch out for you, open doors and generally be the person who nurtures your career. Be a little careful with this advice – I think that this applies to senior managers and executives who are at the top of the tree in specialized sectors and who know that they are seeking limited, high-level opportunities.

Andrew Harris Director, Matthews Harris Consulting Limited, says:

I had a candidate who had excellent textile experience but after months of searching had got nowhere in his job search. He had recognized that there was little future in textiles manufacturing in the UK and had planned to find a role in produce and food. He had sent off dozens of applications and got nowhere. What he had been doing was sending off his CV that just shouted 'textiles' so he kept ending up on the reject pile. When he decided to focus on his experience in quality, Far East sourcing and ISO 9000 and play down the fact that this experience had been gained in the world of textiles, he started to get interviews and soon found a role as Sourcing Manager for a major high street retailer. The moral of this story is that he did not realize what he had and he therefore was not selling it as he was. As soon as he identified his core skills, he began to think laterally and to broaden his search.

If you are actively job seeking, you have to let head-hunters know that you are around, whilst still recognizing that they are client driven and not candidate driven. Your hope is that your CV will land opportunely on their desk, just as they are seeking someone with your exact skills and experience. Otherwise, you can hope that they decide to interview you just to find out about you in case an assignment crops up. Realistically, this meeting is more likely to take place if you are currently in a position where you may considered to be influential and therefore 'someone worth knowing' or if you have been referred to them by a mutual friend or client. You could get hold of a copy of *The Executive Grapevine*, the executive search bible, and plough your way relentlessly through that, telephoning, e-mailing and writing, deciding that if you send out enough volume, then someone may reply. There is a small chance that this could work so why not keep this as a task for the dull, rainy days when you have no meetings, you don't feel up to doing anything more challenging and you feel you will be satisfied by the sight of a stack of beautifully printed envelopes ready to take to the post.

Nadine Jones, Head of Human Resources, Baugur, says:

Think carefully about why you are using a head-hunter/recruiter for the privilege of sending your CV. A potential employer will be signing up to pay as much as 33% of your first salary and benefits as a fee which doesn't leave you a lot of room to negotiate that interim pay review so why aren't you making that call, or writing that e-mail or letter yourself?

If you are working through a head-hunter/recruitment agency, take the time to find out whether they have a relationship with your targeted company. Have they recruited for them in the past? Most companies have preferred suppliers for their recruitment activity and even if you are the best candidate, they will not see you if you have not either applied direct or through an agency they use!

Have you ever wondered how executive search companies find their candidates? It used to be the 'old boys'' network and for some it still is. Some companies maintain a good database and network their way through it until they find the right person. However, the key to finding good candidates is by using a skilled researcher. Some companies have an in-house team and some use the services of specialist research companies. These researchers are the back office part of the executive search process and are often the unsung heroes. They are the ones who compile target lists, search through information on companies and people and who make that initial call to an unsuspecting potential company. As an active job seeker, you need to make sure that the researchers know who you are and call you. After all, researchers are interested in getting the best possible candidates so how do you make sure it is you?

I enlisted the help of Sarah Lacey on this one. Sarah has been in executive research for over 20 years and runs a team of researchers, supporting executive search companies across the UK and Europe. Sarah considers herself to be someone who processes information and then filters it. How do you make sure that you are one of those pieces of information that she is filtering? Sarah is not enthusiastic about people sending in their CV to her in the hope that she might be able to help. Her work, like all head-hunters, is client driven and about filling a specific job. It would take an enormous stroke of luck for your CV to land on her desk just at the right moment.

The way to get onto Sarah's radar is for you to be either highly visible in your role or to get referred to her by someone else.

Sarah Lacey, Managing Partner, Sarah Lacey and Associates, says:
If you want to move jobs, let people in your industry know that you are looking for the next stage in your career. Referrals are like gold dust to us as they mean you come to us with a warm recommendation.

How to respond to the head-hunter's call

When you get that call that comes out of the blue, make sure that you handle it well. The head-hunter will be forming a judgement about you with every word that you utter. They know that their appraisal of you will usually be the same as that of the manager at interview so you have to impress and your response to this call is critical.

- Sound bright, buzzy and switched on
- Answer the questions and be succinct
- You have to grasp quickly what the job is about and be ready to discuss it
- Be flexible, open-minded and ready to talk

- Be obliging and ready to e-mail, telephone and share information.

Most people ask, 'Where did you get my name from?' Sarah does not mind this as she knows you want to be reassured that it is not your colleagues or your boss; however, it is highly unlikely that you will be told as no researcher would divulge their sources.

Talent spotters

Chris Strachan, Managing Director of Organisational Search believes that his brief is to be a talent spotter for his clients. A business needs talented people in order to grow and develop so when he is briefed for an assignment, Chris always adds into the profile the need to find talent.

However, Chris also thinks that this can sometimes be viewed ambiguously within the organization. Although the Chief Executive and shareholders might be delighted to have high powered, entrepreneurial and first class candidates in the company, some colleagues may view them with suspicion. Therefore, if you are bewildered by a rejection letter after an interview, wondering what you might have done wrong, don't worry. It could very well be that you are simply too good for the company. They may proclaim that they want challenging and controversial new ideas in the business, but secretly individuals may be alarmed about the possible impact on their own roles if you join them. Be pleased, therefore, that you were rejected – this job was not for you!

Working in the public sector

The private and public sectors are radically different in their approach to recruitment. To gain an in-depth understanding of what those differences are, I spoke to Rachel Hannan, director of Gatenby Sanderson, who has a seven-year track record of public sector recruitment and also spent a number of years in private sector head-hunting.

Public sector recruitment is driven by fairness, openness and transparency. When candidates are evaluated against the needs of the job, it must be clear that they meet the established criteria. Candidates who don't make the cut will have been evaluated against those same criteria and will not have qualified. It is very important that diversity and equality are the bedrock of public sector recruitment. Within the public sector the workforce should reflect the populace so there is a constant drive to access a more diverse talent pool. It is also vital that this pool should then be assessed fairly. Good candidates are actively encouraged to come forward and then they are treated fairly, based on the objective criteria for the role. Let's face it, this is what should happen in every business across the land, but often the process falls short of these high standards. You hope that objective assessment happens everywhere and yet you know that often the private sector, including companies listed on the Stock Exchange in this category, are driven more by the need to find the best person for the job in the shortest possible timescale rather than ensuring that their workforce is diverse and equal. Share value and profits are driven by high performing people so the selection process can be ruthless.

This does not mean that within the public sector there is positive discrimination in order to meet government targets. The Disability Symbol (sometimes referred to as the two ticks scheme) means that if you meet the minimum criteria for a job, then you are guaranteed an interview.

The good news for candidates in public sector recruitment is that there is accountability in the process and a level playing field. The challenge, therefore, lies with you to make sure that you present yourself in an appropriate way that meets the specified criteria and that you are aware of those vital differences in order to be successful.

Rachel's rules:

Rule no. 1: Dedicate the time

Remember that job hunting in the public sector is very time intensive. You have got to be ready to dedicate sufficient time to the application. If you don't have the time to do it properly, then be selective in the number of jobs that you apply for. The timetable for the process will be set out in the advertisement, so you will know exactly when you are likely to be called for an interview. Calculate the time that you are likely to need in order to be thorough and then decide if you are able to do it. Never enter anything half-heartedly.

Rule no. 2: Always follow the instructions

Read the instructions in the advertisement and follow them to the letter. The recruitment process is a journey. Many set off but ultimately only one person will be appointed so in order to stay in the game, make sure you do not give anyone an excuse to knock you out. The best way to stay in the game is to make sure you read the directions in the advertisement and in the candidate information, then make sure you implement them.

Rule no. 3: Tailor your CV

Make your application a specific one that is tailored to the advertisement and not a generic one that you have got stashed away on your laptop. Read the advertisement, look at the person specification and work out how your experience meets the criteria. Update your CV. Address the key issues that stand out for this particular role and show what you have in your background and experience that match them. Make the person who is sifting the advertisement response believe that you match the criteria. Demonstrate that you match the criteria and you will get an interview. Simply posting off your CV and hoping for the best just won't work. Rachel and other public sector recruiters will be matching your experience against the criteria that are set out clearly for this particular post. If you can't demonstrate that you have what it takes, then you won't get anywhere.

Rule no. 4: Prepare for the interview

Make sure you have done a lot of homework to prepare for the interview. Use the websites that are available, explore the sector, the region, the locality, the individuals and the stakeholders. Get under the skin of the particular sector you are targeting and make sure you understand what all of the issues are. This way you will be prepared for the rigorous interview that awaits you.

Rule no. 5: Talk about the new job – not your current one

When you are being interviewed, don't give a stunning performance that will leave people convinced that you are doing a great job where you are. This isn't an interview for your current job; it is for a different one. Show that you have the capacity for this new role and demonstrate that you are already thinking of yourself in relation to these new challenges, not your existing role. Step up to the challenge of a new role.

Rule no. 6: Second-guess the questions

When you are applying for a public sector role, you will have been given sufficient information about the role for you to be able to work out what the questions are likely to be. It isn't rocket science – you will probably be looking at questions about:

- Leadership
- Managing budgets
- Change management
- Interactions with elected members, stakeholders, board members and trustees
- Technical and professional expertise.

Consider what the questions are likely to be and then take the time to run through them in your head a few times. Do this so that you lose all the waffle, all the padding and all the chaff, leaving you with clear, structured and well thought through responses. Make sure you have a number of examples ready that illustrate your successes in these areas to date.

Rule no. 7: Showcase your talents

Think logically about the process. Put yourself in the shoes of the interviewer and ask yourself, 'What skills and experience would I want this person to have?'

Some of the differences between the public and private sectors

Public sector	Private sector
Vacancies are advertised – open competition.	Vacancies not always advertised – networks and head-hunters provide an unadvertised solution.
Harder to move to the private sector.	Public sector is often eager to recruit from private sector companies.
Recruitment processes are open, inclusive and accountable with a commitment to review every application against set criteria.	Achieving diversity in the workforce is not often a key driver. The commitment is to find someone who will add value to the organization and deliver shareholder value.

Salaries tend to be fixed to a grading system.	Salaries are more flexible with scope for negotiation. Often you are expected to negotiate to show your strength of character.
Shortlists are as long as they need to be – if you match the needs of the post you are on the shortlist.	Shortlists tend to be much smaller and there is no guarantee that you will be shortlisted, even if you are as good as the chosen shortlist. Generally they are looking for 3 to 5 people, no more than that.
Pay levels are slightly lower.	Equivalent posts are generally 3% higher.
Public sector pension benefits are often better than private sector.	Pension benefits vary in quality and size and are generally not as good as public sector.
If you don't get the job you can ask formally for feedback and to have your application reviewed.	If you fail to get the job you can ask for feedback and will often get it. There is no appeal system and no need for someone to justify why you did not get the job or get an interview, unless there was clear discrimination on the grounds of race, sex or age.

Building your network and raising your profile

If you are busy sending out your CV to every head-hunter listed in *Executive Grapevine*, the industry bible, imagining that your CV will be fallen on with cries of ecstasy, you are likely to be disappointed. You could also buy a lottery ticket while you are at it, as you might just win this week's rollover too! This just isn't how the system works. The Data Protection Act makes it difficult for your CV to be kept electronically without your specific permission so this approach could just be sending CVs winging out into the void. The best way to succeed is to have the head-hunter call you.

Philip Eisenbeiss of Executive Access Ltd advises:

Choose a head-hunter and stick to him. Don't work with every head-hunter in town but go for depth rather than breadth. Cold calling is the hardest way to do any kind of business and this is true in the job search. A warm, personal relationship will work well for you in a whole variety of ways.

The vital element, therefore, is to manage your own PR and ensure that you are visible. It is not enough to do a good job. If you want to progress you need to be seen to do a good job.

The radar test

Go on the Internet, go to www.google.co.uk and type in your name. Or go to www.zoominfo.co.uk and type in your name. What happens? If there are no hits, try putting in your name, your company and location. If you still have no hits, then you have found the reason why no-one calls you. No-one knows who you are or where you are so you can be sure that your telephone won't ring.

On the other hand, if you discover that you are there and there are ten hits, all describing your wild social habits or indiscretions that you would prefer a potential employer not to know about, then take action fast. Believe me, just as you will be doing your research on the company and the interviewer, they will be doing their research on you. Google has a long memory so do what you can to remove references from websites. If you have a crazy wall on Facebook, get rid of it. Don't be known for the silly photograph in the newspaper, the Rag week wildness, the stag night excesses or the holiday hilarities. A university student thought it would be very amusing to have a photograph taken of him pretending to sleep soundly in a high profile lecture. It was posted on the Internet and picked up by the national press. Before he knew what had happened, he was the centre of a debate about idle students and he was alarmed to realize that it was not being seen as a joke. He is now on the back foot whenever he is out job hunting.

Although we associate impulsive behaviour more with younger people, the same problem can occur to more senior people if they allow an ill-advised comment or inappropriate blog entry to appear on the Internet. Just be sure that today's good idea will stand the test of time.

Getting on the radar

1. Volunteer

You need suddenly to become the obliging person who volunteers to go to exhibitions, conferences, head office meetings, think tanks or training days. To be noticed by others, you need to be out there, expanding the boundaries of your world. Haven't you wondered why some of your colleagues are always eager to put themselves forward for external events? I bet you have always wondered why they want to give up precious free time for something that has no direct impact on business. It is because they will be noticed and people who get noticed get head-hunted.

2. Join

Now is the time to join institutions, associations, trade associations, alumnae organizations, chambers of commerce, rotary clubs, breakfast clubs, networking organizations and any other business-minded forum that you can track down. There may be groups that are directly linked to your industry or your qualification. Join them and play an active role. This is your chance to appear in directories, associations, handbooks, yearbooks and members' listings. If a researcher for a head-hunter is looking for a Human Resources Manager or Director, don't you think that a logical place to start would be *The Personnel Manager's Year Book*? This is a directory of listings of companies, addresses, telephone numbers and names of people in human resources. Make sure that you have your name in your association listing. You probably thought that you were avoiding nuisance calls by staying out. This is true but you are also missing the head-hunter's call.

3. Write

Now is the time to pick up your pen and start writing. You don't have to publish a bestseller but you can surely manage a letter to the editor of a trade journal, a newspaper or a website. You could write an article for the company newsletter. You could start a blog (with caution!). You can write to *The Times*, you can e-mail a radio programme. You can engage with the world in written format so that people see your name and associate it with particular skills.

4. Take a call

Be accessible. Take telephone calls even when you don't know who is calling you. The dread of any researcher or head-hunter is coming up against the 'Dragon PA', the person who will not let you through to the boss. This person probably suspects that you are selling insurance or coffee machines or water coolers and make it their life's mission to prevent you from getting through.

There are senior executives to this day who remain blissfully unaware that they missed out on a potentially brilliant job because of the consummate skills of their gatekeeper. Be open, be available and be alert.

5. Use business cards

Never leave home without one. Get those business cards out there so people know who you are and can get in touch with you later. If you are not currently working, get a personal business card made up with your e-mail address and your telephone number. You might want to think about making your business card a little bit different so that people pay attention to it and remember it. You could do this by printing something on the back – instead of the company mission statement, maybe you could put the four things that matter to you? Whatever you do, don't put a photo on it and don't be flippant – that wouldn't be the best of starts.

6. Network

Decide on a strategy to increase your engagement with the outside world. Work out how much more you need to do to increase your social interactions and formulate a strategy. Decide how much time per week you are going to engage in new social events and work out how many lunches, dinners, coffees, events, conferences, reunions, wine tastings, football matches, tennis games, gym classes, golf days, etc., you are going to attend. Set yourself a target and measure yourself against it.

Get in touch with people from the past and make sure that you meet up, as you keep promising to do. Make the time for it and value it as a necessary part of business life.

7. Manage the media

Business people in senior and high profile roles need to be aware of both the power and the danger of the press.

I asked Zaria Pinchbeck, Managing Director of ZPR, for any advice she could offer to people who need to stay in the media spotlight and make sure they are noticed.

Zaria Pinchbeck, Managing Director, ZPR Ltd, says:

Managing your profile in the media and with external stakeholders is a key part of managing your career. Whether you choose to have a high profile or a low profile it needs to be managed. Some leaders choose the cult of personality to front their business externally whilst others prefer to let the performance and reputation of the business speak for itself. Either way, the media and key opinion makers cannot be ignored. Work with them and they will work with you. You can choose to be the voice of your sector or you can choose to be famous for what you deliver rather than what you say, but never ignore the media; it is always better to be on the front foot than the back foot. Relationships that you personally build or develop through your PR team will pay back in both the good times and the bad times. Call it a bank of trust – if most of what the media know of you and your business is good, when things get tough, you have some previous equity for journalists to work with. If you are secretive and defensive with the media, they will simply speculate in the absence of anything else to go on. At the most senior levels the media can help make or break careers so it is imperative that your relationship with the media is part of your career management strategy.

The result of all of this is that when the head-hunter is pondering how to find the perfect candidate, one of the research paths will lead to you. The head-hunting world is not for unsung heroes. Take all of these steps so that people know where you are and can find you!

Jeremy Hobbins, Group Managing Director of Li & Fung Retailing, says:

I like to recruit senior people from within my network. I like to listen to recommendations from people I know and trust in the industry, where there is an understanding of who the candidates are, where they have come from, I regard this as a way of reducing the risk involved in bringing a senior person into my company. The suppliers, manufacturers within the apparel and toy industry, all tend to know each other.

In order, therefore, to be considered by one of the global industry leaders, you need to manage your profile and make sure that people know who you are, where you are and what you have done.

> ## *Caution!*
> Networking is not a way to squeeze people of their knowledge and their contacts. It is a way of nurturing relationships, building on them, developing more and ensuring that the benefits are mutual. The simple rule is that if you take, then you must give. You might not be in a position to do it now but you will be able to repay the kindness of others at a later stage. Networking functions best when it is mutual and where there is as much give as there is take. Don't gain the reputation of being a 'taker' or your network will melt.

Building your network – connections

Of the many routes you can take to find a job, one of the most effective and most interesting is networking. What networking actually means is getting out and about to talk to people. There has to be a purpose to your networking so make sure that, when you are meeting people, you stay focused on your objectives. Maintain the required level of sophistication and do not behave like a job hunter I met in Paris. We were at a reception for International Women's Day in the magnificent surroundings of the British Embassy and I was approached by a French lady who thrust her CV and her business card into my hand. She asked me what I was going to do to help her find a new job. She demanded my card and told me she would telephone me at 9 am the next morning for my list of opportunities. She then scoped out her ideal role, although by now I was listening more out of morbid fascination than any interest in her career, and then she briskly marched off saying she was too busy networking with other people to hang around. She did call the next day and I politely brushed her off.

Social and career progression in China relies to a large extent on the strength of your guanxi – your connections. This is who you know, who can open doors for you, who can oil the wheels, exert influence and allow you access to people, places and jobs that otherwise would be closed off to you. Although in an ideal world it would be wonderful to progress purely on merit and your personal strengths, the truth is that the better your guanxi, the greater your opportunities. You need to be developing and growing these people throughout your career, not just when you happen to be job hunting. And remember that the connections run both ways; so, just as you would like to be able to turn to the people you know for help and advice, you need to be someone who is willing to help out when others need your input.

Find a buddy

If you are actively job hunting and your full time employment is finding a new job, then you will be launching a whole campaign to make sure you get the right job. You will be setting yourself goals and milestones. You will be sending out letters, making telephone calls, arranging meetings and attending networking events. Many people are in the same position as you so Andrew Harris suggests that you find someone and buddy with them. You can be each other's conscience and you can compare, contrast, review and help each other to retain the confidence, the energy and the motivation that is needed for a committed job search. You will support each other and be the 'pacesetter' in what can be at times a lonely task.

Widening the net

The job search will be a much better one if you have the active participation and interest of a broad range of people. The broader the range of people and the greater the number, the better your contacts will be and the better the job. It is highly likely that your next role will come from this route, either because you meet someone directly who invites you to come to their office for a formal interview and then gives you a job, or because you will be referred to someone else. Make an impression on someone and they will keep you in their minds and remember you at the right time. I believe that most people are eager to do someone a good turn, keen to help out and to see people succeed. Tap into that resource and you will have an army of assistants working for you free of charge.

Start by making a list. Write down the name and contact details of everyone you know. Friends, relatives, colleagues, suppliers, customers, people you met on the train or the plane, or the bar by the pool. Check old diaries, your computerized address book, old address books, Christmas cards, etc., and work out who you know. Hunt out all of those business cards that you have been given over the years and have a look for the people you have forgotten or have lost touch with. Remember the bank manager, accountant, friends from church, from the gym, from the golf club, the nail bar and the book club as well as all the professional associations. The list is getting longer so let's now divide it into categories.

The A-list

This consists of people who you know well and who are easy targets and easy marks. They will take your call without a moment's hesitation. They are people you are in touch with and they are up to date with where you are in life. They already have a warm feeling for you and they are likely to want to help. They may be sitting on the sidelines, wondering if they should get in touch or they may be completely unaware that you are job hunting. Make it your job to let them know.

The B-list

This is where you may have to work a little harder to warm them up. You may have been out of touch for a while and you may have to put some effort in to get onto their agenda. It could be people you used to work with or people you lived next door to. Perhaps you have been to university with them or spent time with them on a gap year. They are people you once enjoyed a good relationship with but it has been some time since you have been in touch. You will need a strategy for reintroducing yourself and breathing new life into what once was a pleasant relationship.

The C-list

These are people you know only vaguely and you worry that they may not remember who you are. You may only have met them once or met them as part of a group. This is going to take a more carefully thought through approach.

The D-list

This is a list of people that you don't know. You have been given their names by your A-, B- and C-list people so they are warm contacts. You can get in touch using the name of the mutual friend or colleague so they will listen to you. This is the list that is going to grow and grow and you will have the satisfaction of knowing that you are doing a good job. Set yourself a challenge of growing this list by a certain number every week.

The E-list

These are people that you have never met, that no-one else knows and who you are going to find for yourself. It could be the person you sit opposite to on the train, the person you share a table with at a café, someone you meet at the school gates, the scrum line of your son's rugby team or someone you sit next to at the school concert. As soon as you become aware of the vast number of people there are around you, you will be able to start talking to them and enlarging your social circle.

Introducing yourself

Once you decide who you want to talk to, find a way to get yourself introduced. It is always easier to work from a warm introduction rather than a cold start. If you can say 'XYZ told me that you might be interested in talking to me', it is much more powerful than saying 'I am writing to you because I got your name from the Yellow Pages'. How do you get that warm introduction? You may want to search www.linkedin.com to see if there is a contact that could help you. Perhaps your accountant, solicitor or bank manager might know them? Or what about your breakfast club, university alumni association, local branch of Institute of Directors, Round Table, local church, art club – there are hundreds of opportunities to track down the person you want. All you need is the will and the determination so it is back to how much you want the job. Referrals are the route to networking success and this lies in your hands. Some people are natural and easy communicators. They love meeting new people and talk to anyone. Many others find it hard and have to make a conscious effort. The more you do it, the easier it is, so make your focus the art of communication.

Andrew Harris, Director, Matthews Harris Consulting Limited, says:
You are unique and the skills and experience you have cannot be found anywhere else. Get the employer wanting you and a role will be created for you. Show them that you have something that they want so they will invite you in. How do you do this? You do this by researching the marketplace that you want to enter. Can you name five competitors? What do you do when you go to a trade fair? Do you sit on your own stand for three days or do you wander off and see what other people are doing and offering? Find out about other companies' products, marketing, distribution, manufacturing – anything that will give you an idea about what you can do for them because this is the essence of the successful job search. This is not about what they can do for you but what you can do for them. Broaden your knowledge about what else is going on in your business sector and then work out what you have to offer that could interest people. Do not get engrossed and wrapped up in your world. Adopt a different perspective and think about their world.

When you meet them make the focus of the meeting their needs and their business rather than describing your needs. An intelligent conversation about a specific business topic that is dear to the heart of the Managing Director will get you a lot further than a discussion about your career crossroads. Introduce yourself with their language and home in on their problems, not yours. Remember the first rule of any customer-focused business – when you meet, make sure that you make eye contact and that you smile.

Be sure to maintain the focus on others and be interested in them and their lives. This way you will be interesting yourself, and who knows what information you will uncover about them that could potentially be of value to you? Make sure that before the meeting ends they are very clear about what you want from the meeting. It is no good having a fascinating meeting if you miss the opportunity to put forward what you are about. Always go into the meeting with a goal and make sure you achieve it.

Graduates and networking

Networking for graduates is no different from the networking that people do who are at very different stages of their career. You may do it less formally and you have to work harder to apply a potential work or career context to a social contact, operating at a much more conscious level of thought and processing. The way in which you do it and the outcome will be the same. Perhaps one way of looking at it is that all of the socializing you have perfected during your undergraduate years will give you the social confidence to make the connections you need to open up the right door to a career.

> **Jeremy Hobbin, Group Managing Director of Li & Fung Retailing, says:**
> *We prefer not to use head-hunters. We recruit between 30 and 60 management trainees per annum so that we grow our own talent, people who are passionate about our business. We want people who have an affinity with us from the start and who can get linked in quickly.*

You may not have a drawer full of business cards and you may not have golf club membership. However, you know more people than you think you do and it is time for you to think about them in a different way. This is not cold-blooded networking where you are out to grab what you can from people, squeezing all of their usefulness out of them and then discarding them. This is sophisticated, friendly and direct contact to seek the assistance of others. People love to help and will generally put themselves out to assist you.

Who might these people be?

- People you have worked with during vacation jobs
- Someone you babysit for
- Parents of your friends
- Family friends
- University lecturers
- People who graduated before you at university
- Contacts from gap years
- People at the gym
- Neighbours
- Friends from sports clubs
- Friends from book clubs
- Friends from chess clubs.

In short, networking opportunities exist in any situation where you find yourself in the company of others. Be prepared to be the one to break the ice first and say the first words. For some people this is effortless and as easy as breathing. For others it is a skill to be developed. Make a conscious decision to expand your social network and start now. Work out how you can utilize the social networking sites to help you in your job search. If you do not already use MySpace, YouTube, Facebook and LiveJournal, start doing so now and use the Internet to expand your social range.

The Golden rule of networking – say thank you

The golden rule of networking is remembering to thank people who have helped you. A text message may suffice with friends of your own age but I doubt it. Telephone and say thank you; e-mail and say thank you. Send a handwritten letter or card and say thank you. Drop off a small present – a magazine that might be of interest; a bunch of daffodils; a small token that has little intrinsic value but demonstrates your appreciation. The most valuable commodity you can give anyone is the fact that you have thought about them so taking the time to show that you have thought carefully about an appropriate way to demonstrate gratitude will always be accepted gratefully and you will be remembered. The best thing is that you will be remembered as someone who has manners and knows how to articulate it. Making yourself memorable is part of your objective so this is one of the simplest ways to do it.

Internet networking

While you are sitting wondering who else you know and who else you can contact, switch on your computer and find an online networking group that could work for you. This may be www.friendsreunited.co.uk where you can be sure that someone you know will be listed in the 16 million memberships. It could be www.linkedin.com that is a stepping-stone to developing a broader network. It currently has more than ten million members and actively promotes the theory that enhancing your presence online will increase your ability to track down the right kind of job. Another route could be via www.zoominfo.com. This will allow you to start connecting with people in another way. People will be able to find your career summary when they search using the major search engines. Another useful Internet tool is a Skype account. Register on www.skype.com and you will be able to communicate over the Internet. Not only does this save you money on telephone costs, it also allows you to access people in a different way. As you build up your Skype network of contacts, you will be able to see when they are online and you will be able to send them an instant message.

Use the Internet and any new technologies that could give you an advantage. Become an early adopter and squeeze every possible piece of help from the computer sitting on your desk.

How to get in touch

The objective of this targeting is to get people to meet you and to have a chance to discuss your career challenge. You know that these people are not necessarily going to have a job for you but they will be able to help you to get the job you want. If you subscribe to the theory of six degrees of separation, then you will believe that we are only six steps away from anyone we want to talk to. The first step, therefore, is to speak to people you know.

Andrew Harris, Director, Matthews Harris Consulting Limited, says:
The starting point in any job search is to ask yourself, 'Who has got the problem that I am the solution to? Who is looking for me? Who is looking for the knowledge, experience and qualifications that I have got?' As people's careers progress, the job they want is not necessarily an empty chair. There might not be a vacancy in a business. Life is not black and white; we live in a world of grey. That colour grey is your opportunity to go and get a job that doesn't exist. Boldness and active steps are what will get you the results.

The best approach is a telephone call, so if you have the telephone number and you know you can get through, go this route first of all. E-mailing has become the default method of communicating and it just doesn't work in all circumstances. It is fine for transmitting facts and figures but subtleties can be more difficult to get across. It is also much easier to say no to someone in an e-mail than it is face-to-face or on the telephone. You will therefore be increasing your chances of getting a meeting by making a call. This should be simple with the A-list people so just use it. Don't do what one now notoriously frequent job hunter does to me. Every time he is job seeking he sends me an e-mail with an attachment that is his updated CV. The e-mail itself is completely blank. The message he is sending me is very clear, that he is sending his CV to everyone he knows and he can't be bothered to write even a few words to try to make it personal. My response is to treat this as junk mail and to delete it.

With the B-, C-, D- and E-list people, you may find that you can't get through on the telephone. This is your chance to write a personal letter or e-mail to them, explaining what you want, which is the opportunity to meet up for a brief chat to discuss how possibly they may be able to help you in your job search.

This letter or e-mail must be personal and it is essential to ensure that it looks specific and not like a standard e-mail you are churning out to everyone. If I feel I have been sent the same e-mail as 100 others, then I could take the view that I will leave the other 99 to get back to you as you won't miss my reply. However, if I know that this is a single, special letter, then I will reply.

Here is a 'marvellous' example of an e-mail sent to Gareth James from a job hunter, with names changed to protect the guilty:

> From: Mary Smith [mailto:marysmithr@email.net]
> Sent: 27 March 2007 11:05
> To: Gareth James
> Subject: Mary Jones
>
> The other Mary gave me your name and said that you might be able to hlep with my job search. I am looking for a HR Director/Head of HR role with a South West/east base. My strengths lie in the IT/Technology/sectors. I have significiant experience working with TU/TUPE/transformation projects and general change management activities.

There was no greeting, no sign off and two typos and it just gives the impression that it was an e-mail dashed off in a moment. There is no carefully crafted sentence to engage Gareth's interest and to ask him to help a complete stranger, free of charge.

The ironic end to this story is that exactly one week later Gareth received the following e-mail from someone else:

-- Original Message --

From: Louise [mailto:louise@emailhrjobs.com]
Sent: 04 March 2007 17:13
To: Gareth James
Subject: Head of HR Business Partners

Hi Gareth

Hope you are well, do you know of anyone looking for work at the moment? A recruitment consultant friend of mine is looking for a Generalist to fill Head of HR Business Partners on a 9–12 month contract with a major company in the South East – c80k package, not sure if you know of anyone who is looking that would be interested? Please feel free to forward on and use my name as initial contact point.

Thanks

Louise

Mary Smith could have been at the top of the list for this interim assignment. She had done all of the hard work and been referred to Gareth who could possibly help her but she ruined it by sending out a rude and sloppy e-mail. Regard every contact as a golden nugget of opportunity. Cherish it and make sure you extract every ounce of value from it.

Let's look at how Mary might have phrased this e-mail and made a much better first impression:

> Dear Gareth
>
> Mary Jones is a friend of mine and she has suggested that I contact you to see if you can help me with my current job search.
>
> You will see from the attached CV that I have an eight-year track record of working at a senior level in HR within the technology/IT sectors. Until the end of last month I was HR Director of Major Company Ltd but my role was made redundant because of the downturn in trading conditions and the inevitable cost cutting that ensued.
>
> I am actively job hunting now and I am considering interim or permanent positions, preferably in the south of England. I appreciate that you are not a recruitment consultant but I believe you have a strong network and opportunities could occasionally cross your desk. If that were the case, I would be very grateful if you would perhaps consider me.
>
> If you had time to meet up for a brief chat, I would be delighted. Failing that, I am always available on the telephone or via e-mail.
>
> Thank you very much indeed for taking the time to consider the needs of a relative stranger! Mary asked me to pass on her regards to you and to say that she is looking forward to seeing you again at the next Forum meeting
>
> Best wishes
>
> Mary

The message, therefore, is a clear one: for effective communication:

- Telephone if possible. If not, e-mail or letter
- Be personal
- Be concise, say clearly what you want
- Abandon any standard letter or e-mail format
- Be polite, say thank you
- Avoid all spelling mistakes, particularly names
- Be careful about informality
- Call at a civilized time.

When you are the person asking the favour, there is no room for off-handed, hurried communication of any kind. Remember to check your answer-phones at home and on your mobile to be sure that you have a professional and personal greeting. If someone calls you back they don't want to get the default answerphone message as they won't be sure they have got the right person and they don't want to hear your children lisping sweetly on the message. This may be enchanting when Granny rings up but it is hugely irritating in a professional environment.

When you do make the call, don't upset people before you start by calling late at night or at weekends. Just because this is at the top of your agenda, it doesn't mean that this is the case for them. I can't think of too many people who want to discuss business on a Sunday morning so stick to the safe option, Monday to Friday, 9 until 5 pm. Even if you know them, where possible, stick to normal working hours for your telephone call. You want to send a clear message that this is a business call, not a private one. It is not an invitation to a barbeque or to organize a squash match, it is about work and business so deal with it as such.

The meeting – more golden rules of networking

1 Remember you are the one asking the favour so be polite
2 Research the company and the person beforehand. Google is the job hunter's best friend
3 Be on time for the meeting. In this case, on time means being five minutes early
4 Go into the meeting with a purpose
5 Clarify how much time is available before you start and adapt your conversation accordingly
6 Be prepared. Bring along a copy of your CV
7 Dress appropriately. Wear business attire. It is better to be overdressed than underdressed
8 Stick to the agreed timescale for the meeting. If you arranged to meet for an hour, don't settle in for the day. Respect other people's diaries. If your contact suggests extending, that's fine but don't take that initiative yourself
9 Follow up with a thank you
10 Thank the person who introduced you in the first place.

Create high volume and high quality job applications

The greatest problem for both recruiters and applicants is the ease with which letters and e-mails can be churned out. A few keystrokes on your computer and you can create a dozen letters that have just been 'topped and tailed'. When you are eagerly job seeking, you can be sucked into a vortex of activity that occasionally loses track of its objectives. Although it is important to generate a lot of applications and a lot of letters and e-mails to make sure that people know who you are, do not slip into lazy ways so that you send out a letter that has not been personalized or one that contains irrelevant information. The only way to make an impact is to make sure that every letter you send looks as though it has been carefully crafted for that particular job or that particular person. Never send out a letter to 'Dear Sir or Madam' as this shows that you have not bothered to find out the names of the Chief Executive or the HR Director or the Sales Director. It is a waste of a stamp so pick up the telephone and ask who you should be writing to.

Details are important. Never misspell the name of the person you are writing to. Time and time again I receive letters with the wrong name on. These are avoidable errors and ones that alienate people before they have read your letter. Make sure also that you get their job title right and that you send it to the right address.

It may seem obvious, but when you post your letter, stick the stamp firmly on and make sure it is the right value. On a number of occasions we have had to collect mail from the Post Office and pay a supplement, as it did not have sufficient stamps on, only to find that it is a job application. That is not too bright a start.

Be very careful of 'cut and paste' when writing letters. If you are not careful, it could make the letter disjointed and without a natural flow. Although it is quicker to take the production line approach to mass mailing, it is potentially flawed. A letter that is going out to 100 other people will always look like that. Maybe you could have a core paragraph that you include in your letter but then you can include something that is very specific to the person or the company you are writing to. Avoid the 'mailshot' approach to job hunting as it will end up in the final resting place of most mailshots – the bin.

Get past the 'Dragon PA'

Fortunately for researchers and job hunters, PAs are not the force that they used to be as executives become more self-reliant and use technology themselves. However, there is still likely to be a shared secretarial resource, an Administration Manager, a department secretary – someone who may consider themselves to be the protector of the inner sanctum, the one who will defend the boss against any unseemly and unknown incursions.

You may have sent out a letter that states you are likely to call the recipient within a week. If this is the case, then you must do so. However, you may find that someone in the office is going to make it their life's mission to stop you. You may also come up against people who refuse to put you through unless you state exactly who you are and what you want.

Do not, at this stage, be tempted to say what you want. This person will not transmit the message as well as you can and your cover is blown. There are a number of tactics to try to get through. Resist the temptation to say that it is a personal call as you risk incurring the wrath of the target when he or she realises that it is a ruse. Do not tell lies about who you are or use anything other than the truth to get through. If you can mention the name of a mutual acquaintance, then that should oil the wheels. If you don't have that, resort to cunning wiles. It is likely that if you are targeting a senior executive they will work longer hours so try calling the office before 9 am or after 6 pm and you may find that they answer the telephone themselves.

You could speak to reception and ask for the mobile telephone number of the person you want to speak to. Ask for it with a voice of authority as if you are entitled to it and it could just work.

If you are beginning to get desperate and nothing is working for you, work out what the e-mail convention of the business is and send them an e-mail. For example, if you know that e-mail addresses are always initial, followed by surname followed by @ and the domain name, then you are free to get in touch with anyone in the organization.

Coping with rejection

The toughest part of the job search programme is dealing with rejection. You are investing huge amounts of energy, enterprise and initiative and what are you getting back? Inevitably you will get letters of rejection, you will be sent the hated pro forma letter to say that you are being kept on file and worst of all, you may be ignored. Remember that the sheer volume of your high quality output means that you are not looking for a successful outcome from every single letter, e-mail or telephone call.

Although you may not have success with the letter that you sent you can be satisfied that on another level you have achieved your objectives. Someone has read your letter and therefore one more person knows about you. It may not have led to a successful outcome now, but who knows where it may lead in the future?

Particularly hard to take may be the disappointment that certain people have not helped you in the way that you hoped. This is bound to be matched in parts by the surprising helpfulness and constructive support that you receive from relative strangers. You cannot expect the same level of success from every letter. Focus, therefore, on who is helpful, the person who invites you to meet for a coffee and the interviews that you do gain, rather than the ones that you don't.

The best salespeople learn very early on in their careers how to cope with rejection. It is quite simple how they do it. They focus on what they win rather on what they lose. Put the rejections quickly behind you and move on. Learn what you can from the encounter, take the best out of it and get ready for the next meeting.

You may also wish to open a new file and keep in it all of the names of the people and organizations who have disregarded you or dealt with you in anything less than a professional way. Keep this list very safely because you will want to be absolutely sure who they are when you are in your new role or when they come to you looking for help. This will be an opportunity for you to show them how important it is to treat people courteously and professionally at every opportunity. Regard it as your chance to change the world in a small way.

Reading between the lines of the reject letter

Letters of rejection come in all forms and very often are standard letters. This can mean that your letter was not read properly by the person you sent it to. It could mean that the sheer volume of a response to an advertisement means that it is not practical to send out well thought through letters detailing the reasons for rejection. It might mean that your letter or your CV, or even both, might not be good enough and were not sufficiently detailed or eye-catching to make the grade. Good companies and good recruiters should always be willing to take your call to tell you why you did not make it to the finishing line. In the public sector this personal feedback is a right – Rachel Hannan told me that she may spend as much as 45 minutes discussing with someone why they have been rejected for a role, depending on how far through the process they had gone. If you think that you only stood an outside chance anyway, you might not want to bother chasing up the real reasons for your rejection. However, if you have had an interview and you considered that you were in with a strong chance, it is only right that you should know why. Chase it up and get feedback.

When you do so, make sure that you do it in a measured manner. Don't hound people, leaving messages on every answerphone available. I recently had a candidate who bombarded me with texts, e-mails and telephone calls. My explanation of why he did not get the job was just not enough. He kept on going until I reached the point where I vowed I would never put him forward to a client again. He overplayed his hand so be careful not to overstep that invisible line.

CHAPTER 5

HIGH PERFORMANCE INTERVIEWING

RESULT: YOU ARE SEEN AT YOUR BEST

You've got an interview, now what?

An invitation to attend an interview is a major success – first objective achieved! Something about your CV, your accompanying letter and possibly your telephone interview has impressed someone enough to decide that they want to know more. Their purpose in getting you to their offices is not to catch you out but to find out more about your strengths and to be given enough reasons to want you inside their organization. Your objective is to give them as many reasons as you possibly can to make sure they include you on the final shortlist and offer you the job. Their task is to give you the chance to excel and your challenge is to make sure you present yourself in the best possible light.

Martine Robins, European Human Resources Director, Cookson Electronics, says:
You actually want a tough interview so you can shine.

Get ready to dance

Every interview is different and every interviewer has a different way of tackling the process. Some people will have been trained in particular techniques and will have a set formula that they are following. The questions they put to you will be the same that they put to everyone else. They will have planned what they are going to ask and they will have a purpose for every question. It might be a panel of interviewers; it might be a series of one-to-one interviews. It might even be a Virgin-style interview where you have to perform a dance to show how warm and interactive you are. Picture doing that at 8.30 am in a room full of strangers!

The only certainty in an interview is that you may be faced with a more challenging interview than you may have expected. Preparation, therefore, is vital so that you are ready for every eventuality.

Preparation

You cannot do too much to be ready for an interview. One candidate told me that he had gone along to the client's premises and had parked outside for a day, watching the comings and goings and seeing what people looked like. He knew what kind of cars people drove, the hours that they worked and had a bit of an insight into the kind of people who worked there. This may be a step too far for you or may be too impractical but you can do lots more research to get detailed information on a company, its products, its markets and its values.

Graduates and preparation for work

Graduates are likely to face the toughest interviewing, especially if you are fighting for a prized place on one of the blue chip graduate trainee schemes. In addition to all of the hurdles you need to get over, you will be tested in a different way to the exams you have faced during your academic career. Now you need to be prepared to be interviewed about untried potential and you will be facing some tests that you don't seem to be able to prepare for. However, there are many things that you can do to make sure that when you turn up for the interview, you are prepared, energized and ready to make an impact.

The first thing you can do is to use the research skills that you have been honing at university for all of these years. Bring all of your intellect to this process to find out everything about the company to which you have applied. This interview is going to be about them, their world, their products and their markets. You will have to show what you have to offer, what value you can add and how you will fit in. You can only do this if you know what they are about and if you have thought deeply about why they would want to have you. Do more than just scan their web pages. If you are applying to train as an actuary, get the technical vocabulary and understand what it means. If you want to work in the City, be prepared for questions about the difference between the back office and the front office. Know the difference between a PEP and an ISA, a share and a bond. Get on one of your social networking sites and find a friend to give you an insight into that world so that you are not going to be floored by a question you might not think you could know the answer to. Although you can't be expected to have the experience and successful track record of more mature candidates, you still need to make the effort to find out as much as possible. Employers will want to set challenges to find out how you work with others, how you respond to pressure and how emotionally resilient you are.

The appointment

You may receive a telephone call asking you to make a meeting at a particular time. They may be kind and offer you a number of options or they may spring a meeting on you at short notice. Do your best to be accommodating and to fit in with their schedule. After all, you are looking for a job and they have a vacancy that they need to fill. Do your best to attend, change your diary to fit in if necessary. If you can't, be sure to explain exactly why you can't do it. This is the first interaction a prospective employer has with you so you don't want them to think that you are anything other than keen and eager to meet them.

Nadine Jones, Head of Human Resources, Baugur, says:
Be flexible, the people/person interviewing you has a day job and is short of resource – the business needs may require that your meeting has to be rearranged – sometimes at short notice, so make yourself available, be positive and be cheerful. If you weren't the ideal candidate from a skills and background point of view, you'll earn yourself 'points' for attitude, fit and flexibility. I've often been in the situation where I've needed to fill a role quickly and the person who has been the most flexible to arrange and rearrange meetings has been offered the position.

Once you have agreed the time and the place for the meeting, make sure you get written confirmation in order to avoid any possible confusion. Once you get the letter or the e-mail, read it carefully. Make sure you get the date right, the time right and that you pay attention to the details. Don't let the excitement make you blind to simple instructions, such as to confirm that you will be attending. You will be amazed how many people fail to confirm or who turn up at the wrong time or on the wrong day. Check, check and triple check. If the letter does not tell you how long the meeting will be or the format it will take, why not telephone them and ask? This will demonstrate initiative and is another way of showing your approach and your efficiency. Check out the venue on the map and calculate how long it will take you to get there. Build in contingency time and, if you have to, book your train or your bus or your plane. Make all the necessary arrangements around the interview and then focus on everything else.

Research

Now you need to find out everything you possibly can about the job and the company. Start with the job description, the job advertisement or with whatever information you have been provided by the organization or the recruitment consultant. Analyse it carefully, working out what they are seeking and what you have in your portfolio of experience, talent and skill that you can bring to them. Open a file and collate all of this information carefully. Not only are you going to become an expert on the business, you are going to be able to demonstrate this knowledge subtly at interview. This way you will have a head start on any other candidate as you have gone into the subject in more depth than anyone else. Get to know the language of the business and what it means.

Jan Shaw, Associate Director, Barracuda Search, says:
Do your research about the company beforehand. Go out and talk to the people in the business. This might not always be possible, but is very achievable in retail and customer-focused environments. By doing this you will impress the interviewer that you can get up and get out there and that you are prepared to talk to people at all levels in the organization; and you will also learn something about the business. You will demonstrate that you believe that results come through people because you have talked to them.

The Internet

This is such an obvious place to start. Look at the company's website and study it carefully. Form a view on its quality and style and be ready to have an opinion. Now have a look at other information about the business that is in the public domain. There will be financial information available, listings on other websites and all manner of newspaper articles and public comment. Read it all. Remember that it might be written from a number of perspectives and it should not all be taken as fact and etched in stone. Just because you found it in Google does not necessarily make it factually accurate.

Now look at competitors. Who are they? How good are they? What do their products look like? Know who they are and rate your prospective employer against them.

Get out there and look

Your research should not just be restricted to desk research. If you are considering working for a retailer, visit their stores. Don't just visit the one that you pass on the way to the bus stop, visit a few a little further away, showing your commitment and your interest. If it is a product, find stockists or distributors and ask them questions about how it sells and what advantages it has. If it is a publisher, get hold of their key publications and look at them. If it is a university, get hold of its prospectus and visit the campus. If there are brochures, find them. If there is an exhibition or a trade fair, get there and see what it is about. A candidate we had approached on behalf of a client managed to find out where they were exhibiting and he approached them on the stand. He engaged their interest and was accelerated through the interviewing process. Whatever the role is, do more than just look at a website and surf the Internet. Any employer will be impressed by someone who has taken the trouble to investigate and explore.

Again accepting the theory of six degrees of separation, you will know that you are only five people away from the person you want to talk to. Think about who you can ring to get an inside track on the job and the company. You are not looking for clumsy and unsubtle attempts to get a recommendation. What you want is someone who can let you know the unspoken elements of a company's ethos and values, the information that will allow you to make the most appropriate pitch.

Use your initiative and take an active approach. Don't wait for people to provide you with information – go out and get it.

Nadine Jones, Head of Human Resources, Baugur, says about the interview:

Know the company: Who are they? When were they set up? What are the company origins? What is the core business? Who are the competitors? Why will you fit into this business? Find out, ring up, ask friends, ask the HR team, ask your head-hunter about the recruitment format. Ask for a copy of the job description. Be prepared to give feedback on the areas you'll excel at and your development needs. What's the dress code? You can probably predict some of the questions you will be asked so have some answers rehearsed. Why do you want the job? What do you offer above other candidates? Why has your career developed in the way it has? What are your career aspirations? Why should this business employ you?

Take a copy of your research and questions to the interview. Try to ask at least one sensible question about the role, the structure of the department you'll be working in, how the bonus scheme works, how the performance review process works – there is nothing worse than meeting a candidate who says meekly at the end of the interview, 'No, you've covered everything', without referring to notes or research.

Ask the questions – 'How do I match up to what you're looking for? When will I hear?' (if you haven't been told) and 'Will I get feedback on how I performed today?'

Telephone interviewing

Before you get face to face and have your big chance to impress, you may have to face a preliminary screening via a telephone interview. Many companies, particularly at graduate level and the next level up, rely on a 15- to 30-minute assessment via the telephone. This call will be made either by someone in the Human Resources department, a team member in the department you are hoping to join or the functional head, that is to say, the person who heads up the department where you will be working. The format will be designed to test certain aspects of your technical knowledge and personal style. Your challenge is to work out exactly what they will be testing and make sure you make all of the pertinent points in the course of the telephone call. If you are in an industry where there are certain buzzwords and acronyms, make sure you use them. If you are a linguist, expect to use the language. There may be a list of vocabulary that you are expected to use so decide what those words are and work them into the conversation. Make no mistake, this is not an informal chat – it is an assessment process with very clear goals. The disadvantage you have is that all you can use to convince the interviewer of your worth is your voice and your words.

Above all, listen and tune in to what is being said to you. Make sure you respond with what is required. Answer the questions and adapt the tone, pitch, volume and inflection of your voice to match the voice you are hearing on the telephone. Avoid the temptation to have a script in front of you and don't read out prepared answers. Stay alert and let the adrenalin take care of the rest. Pass it with flying colours and be ready for the next stage – the face-to-face interview.

Turning up

It sounds quite simple, doesn't it? Turn up on time and look smart. Let me tell you, it isn't. People arrive late without giving advance notice, they turn up at the wrong time, they go to the wrong office, they forget the name of the person they are supposed to be meeting, they do everything except the simple, uncomplicated task of arriving on time.

Often, this stems from lack of thorough preparation, although it also happens through nerves. A candidate once rang me from Pall Mall to say that she was already ten minutes late for her interview, couldn't find the building and could I help her. Too late – the damage was done. An assumption was made that if she could not find a building in the heart of London, then she would not be much use in an organization that relied on people to be resourceful and enterprising.

Know where you are going, who you are going to see and what time you are going to get there. Have the telephone number of the company keyed into your fully-charged mobile telephone so that if there is a derailment at Grantham or if the wrong kind of leaves are preventing the smooth running of the rail network, then you can call ahead and explain these unexpected events. Sometimes you cannot help being late. It is, therefore, how you handle the situation that will be critical.

In these exceptional events, do not just turn up late. Advance notice will allow your interviewer to reallocate the time and hopefully prevent any possible irritation occurring. Apologize and make it clear that it is a major road, train or plane incident, or family crisis that is preventing you from being there on time. Recognize also that a small minority of people are unrelenting and will discount you from the process, no matter how watertight your excuse. Most people, however, will appreciate that problems do happen that are not of your making and beyond your control.

Expect the unexpected

Be aware that however much you prepare, you are likely to be faced with something that you are not expecting. Hopefully you will have been advised if this is an interview for you alone or if it is a group interview. Graduate roles and the first tier of management, sales roles, team roles and customer-focused roles may plunge you straight into a song and dance act or a group discussion. They are testing how you respond when you are put on the spot. They want to know about the speed of your reactions, how you act when you are under pressure and how you behave with others. You may have claimed all manner of wonderful qualities in your CV but this is the acid test. Do you behave in the way that you say you do? Rather than asking you to articulate your responses in carefully rehearsed words and phrases, they spring something on you that is experiential – this is your chance to show what you are like while trained observers are taking careful note. Advance notice won't change the way that you are but it will give you the opportunity to rehearse your techniques for making maximum impact and building rapport. A winning smile will get you over a lot of obstacles. You can also brace yourself for the unexpected so that you are not beset by a sudden attack of nerves. Be ready to be natural and you will perform well. Be aware of others as well as yourself and remember that team playing is a vital part of any career.

What kind of things might they do? One company I know asks all of the participants to pretend that they are at a cocktail party and to go round introducing themselves to others. In this artificially created environment, you have to abandon any self-consciousness or wish that you had stayed at home in bed. Throw yourself into it, act away with the best of them and be sure that the observers can see that you are at ease.

They might ask you to play a game, such as the Radio 4 game 'Just a minute' when you have to talk on a topic for a whole minute without repetition, deviation or hesitation. The other group members will be there to pounce if you go wrong. You might be given a puzzle to solve as team and the challenge is to make sure you get into the spirit of it straightaway. Immediate energy and impact is what they are looking for, so don't disappoint them.

The unexpected is there so that you can be seen at your best and most natural so be courageous and plunge in without reservation.

Emotional intelligence and the interview

A vital element in personal success in all areas of life, including career management and development is emotional intelligence, a concept made popular by the book *Emotional Intelligence* by Daniel Goleman.

What exactly is emotional intelligence? The term encompasses the following five characteristics and abilities:

1 **Self-awareness** – knowing your emotions, recognizing feelings as they occur, and discriminating between them
2 **Mood management** – handling feelings so they are relevant to the current situation and you react appropriately
3 **Self-motivation** – 'gathering up' your feelings and directing yourself towards a goal, despite self-doubt, inertia, and impulsiveness
4 **Empathy** – recognizing feelings in others and tuning into their verbal and nonverbal cues
5 **Managing relationships** – handling interpersonal interaction, conflict resolution, and negotiations.

Researchers have concluded that people who manage their own feelings well and deal effectively with others are more likely to live contented lives. High intelligence and first class academic qualifications are not enough to get on in life. Emotional intelligence and developing the skills needed to manage your own emotions as well as your relationships with others are the foundation stone of career success.

In an interview situation, if you are tuned into the reactions of the interviewers then you will be adapt your own behaviour and responses accordingly.

Jan Shaw, Associate Director, Barracuda Search, says:
The requirements of the workplace used to be all about labour intensive environments. Look at the textile mills, the car manufacturing plants – the whole host of manufacturing businesses – or the mining industry, where sheer volume was the critical element. Now most jobs require a level of emotional intelligence to fulfil the needs of the role. Service industries where attitudes to customers will win or lose business require people who can cope with stress, handle people and sustain the same level of calm response throughout. This shift from the technical to the social aspects of roles means that employees need to be self-reliant and emotionally reliant, able to interact with people and to motivate and coach their colleagues.

Creating the right impression – impact

We all know that you only get one chance to make a first impression. Many of my clients over the years have boasted to me of their incisive interviewing skills and their ability to assess people quickly. They often say that they can sum someone up in two minutes. Some people take a little longer and say that it takes them three minutes. What they are actually saying is that they go by first impressions. If you think about this carefully, it means that you can be the most stunning person who has ever walked into that office, with skills beyond anyone's wildest imaginings, but that won't matter a jot if you fail to make the right impression. I am not defending this position and saying that it is the right way to assess someone, I am merely describing the reality. Your task when you walk through the door is to make people want to learn more about you, to be curious about who you are and to want to know more. When you are busy making this impact, remember that this is not just about who you are and what you do. This is also about the person's prejudices, likes, dislikes and views of the world. There are, however, always exceptions to any rule and one of those is Peter Dove.

Peter Dove, Managing Director of Watson's the Chemist, says:

I place a huge emphasis on 'fit'. I want to see more than just a technical ability to deliver the results. My company has a clear culture and I need people to fit into it. I believe it would be unfair to bring someone into a company where they might not be able to fit in.

I prefer to give people the time and the opportunity to prove themselves in an interview. By the time I meet up with candidates I believe that their specific technical skills and experiences have been qualified and checked by others earlier in the process. All that I am interested in is 'fit'. I won't judge you in two or three minutes of that initial impact. If you want to impress me and anyone else who takes this approach, come up with case studies, examples and relevant anecdotes. Make sure that:

- *You have done your research and visited stores*
- *You have thought about the customer*
- *You are thinking about the role and not about how to get the job*
- *You have prepared those mini case studies and show how quick you are on your feet*
- *Get inside the mind of the business*
- *You remember you are being interviewed for a reason so stay focused.*

The very first thing that someone will know about you is how you responded to the advertisement. They will also know how you have put together your CV or responded in the application form, how you construct a letter and possibly how you responded to the invitation to interview or within a telephone interview. They will have experienced already your confident and professional telephone call and the e-mail confirming the meeting so you have already begun to make an impact. Now you have to build upon it through your physical presence. Focus entirely on this interview and think of nothing else. No distractions about anything else in your life – just give the best of yourself and be in the moment. Remember to:

- Be there
- Focus on your interviewer
- Maintain steady eye contact
- Maintain a good posture
- Remain calm – breathe
- Listen to the questions, don't interrupt.

Be careful and calm when in an interview situation. Before you enter the room, do whatever you need to reinforce a calm and controlled state of mind. Breathe in. Act as if you are relaxed and you will be relaxed. A friend of mine was going for an interview for a Managing Director's role so she kept an image in her head of a successful Managing Director that she knew. She walked like her, she talked like her and she adopted the posture and mannerisms of this successful Managing Director.

Clare Howard, Director of e-coaches.co.uk, says:
Have a go at creating a PowerPoint presentation of yourself as a 'product'.
NEVER be tempted to show it … But it gives you a way of looking at yourself in a different light.

Measure your personal impact

Here is a practical task that will give you the opportunity to take a step back and see if it helps reveal things about yourself that you might not be aware of. You may find out encouraging points about yourself that you had not recognized or valued before.

If you truly want to put yourself to the test, why not ask someone who knows you well (i.e. your best friend, your mother, your partner, a trusted work colleague) to answer the questions on your behalf? That way you will see if the results are very similar. If they are widely divergent, then that will give you food for thought.

Score yourself 1 to 5 against the following qualities of personal impact where 1 is low and 5 is high:

Quality	1	2	3	4	5
Confident					
Socially skilled					
Poised					
Brings authority					
Has 'know how'					
Energizing					
Credible					
Leader					
Tenacity					
Enthusiasm					
Positive attitude					
Involves others					
Convincing					
Inspiring					
TOTAL					

Add up your scores and see where you stand in terms of personal impact:

- 14 to 20 – You don't believe in yourself so why should others? Now is the time to identify and to value the talents that you do have and to take pride in them. Focus on your skills and your achievements and work out what you have to offer.
- 21 to 35 – You seem a little tentative about life and about your contribution. Work out why you do not seem to believe that you are as good as other people and then identify ways to grow in personal confidence.
- 36 to 50 – You think you are as good as most people rather than thinking you are better. Be more courageous in taking credit for what you are good at and make sure people get to know it.
- 51 to 60 – You have more confidence than most people and it is likely that you will make an impact when you go into a room. People will take notice of you and be impressed. Make sure it is justified and stay alert.
- 61 to 70 – You believe you are the best around and that you bring energy with you into a room. Be careful that this high level of confidence does not come over as arrogance. Make sure you demonstrate humility and self-awareness as well as all these other fine qualities.

Your physical appearance – dress code

As you walk through the door of the offices the first thing they will see about you is how you look. There is evidence to suggest that initial impact contributes 65% to the decision making. You can't change the fact that you are tall, short, fat, thin, blonde or dark. However, there are certain things that you can do to ensure a positive impact. Prejudice comes in all shapes and forms. I have clients who have expressed a sharp dislike for white socks, men without ties, strong aftershave, brown shoes, short skirts, long skirts and so the list goes on. You can't please all people but you can please most people.

Jane Chapman, Development Consultant, Financial Services, says:

First impressions count and it is so important to make the right kind of impact in that first engagement. You have a choice about how to create the right impression so use it well.

When we meet other people we are deciding very quickly.

- *Are you safe?*

- *Do I like the look of you?*
- *Do I want to spend time with you?*

The first information that we will receive is the physical impression, how we look, how we are dressed and how we make an impact. At an interview, you want the people you are meeting to trust and to like you. You are going to meet instinctive reactions and so you need to work hard to reassure people that you are likeable and trustworthy. Start by putting yourself in the other person's shoes and realize that you can do significantly more than you may have thought to influence those first impressions. If you know you have an interview coming up, why not stand outside the building and watch people coming in and out. How do they look? What are they wearing? This is a perfect chance to gauge the formality or informality of a business and see what it takes to fit in.

Before an interview, decide on the impact that you want to make. Do you want to fit in and look like one of them or do you want to make a statement and stand out? Whatever your decision, do it knowingly and deliberately.

You may have been given guidance on what the dress code is for the interview but if you haven't, take the safe bet and go for the formal interview look. If you are applying for a fashion retailer, then wear their clothes. If you want to work for Marks & Spencer's, wear Marks and Spencer's clothes. If you want to show you are an original designer, then wear your original designs. For most people, however, the formal look for the first interview will always be the safe option. However, think hard about what the dress code might be in a newer, younger style of organization where you could look out of place in a formal suit. If in doubt, ring up and ask. I attended a meeting recently with a client I was meeting for the first time. I turned up in a suit, high heels and crisp, ironed shirt. He was wearing jeans, super cool tee shirt and the trendiest glasses I have ever seen. The mismatch in attire was not the end of the world but I could have managed better if I had checked out the style of the company.

Jane Chapman, Development Consultant, Financial Services, says:

Younger people need to take into account that they need to look grown up in order to be taken seriously. It is important to give the impression that you have been thoughtful about how you present yourself rather than having thrown on the first thing that came to hand in a random and uncoordinated way!

Make sure, therefore, that you are well groomed, professional and well dressed. Do the checklist before the interview and get it straight so you are neat, tidy and smart:

- Dark suit, dry-cleaned and perfect.
- Shoes, highly polished with no scuffs.

Ladies:

- Wear a jacket. It might not be a fashion statement or a reflection of your unique style but you are competing with men in suits so wear one too.
- Careful with heels. If you are going for the three-inch ones, don't totter.
- Tights – no ladders, no catches and avoid the bare leg look. We are not on the Promenade in Nice.
- Make-up – wear it as it gives presence. If you are a graduate, it gives greater gravitas and makes you more sophisticated. If you are older, then it makes you polished and professional.
- Lipstick – never leave home without it.
- Perfume – go easy with it as it can offend.
- Hair – make sure you are well-groomed and tie your hair back or wear it up if it is long.
- If you bite your nails, glue on false ones.

Gentlemen:

- Leave the crazy tie at home. Show your humorous personality in the interview, not through your Snoopy tie.
- Abandon the pink socks, as they don't show you have a zany character.
- Be careful about being too fashionable.
- If in doubt, dress up rather than down. You can be overdressed and get away with it but not the other way round.
- Be careful with the aftershave.
- Hide those bitten nails – I might deduce that you have an anxious personality if I see them bitten to the quick.

And finally – resist the temptation to have a few puffs on a cigarette before you go in to the interview. A non-smoker will smell you before they see you and you will be off to a terrible start. Smokers like smokers because they feel a sense of allegiance, as you are becoming an oppressed minority. Non-smokers, however, will get their hackles up straight away. They will already be imagining you smoking in the toilets, lighting up in the car or wasting time hanging round in the office doorway for cigarette breaks and you will find it hard to come back from that. Leave your cigarettes at home for the day so that they can't be spotted in your shirt pocket or in your handbag. For interviewing purposes, behave like a non-smoker and don't create a problem before you begin.

Martine Robins, European Human Resources Director, Cookson Electronics, says:

Interviews can be a big ordeal. Some people can struggle and the interviewer will want to put you at your ease. They are looking for a frank and open exchange on both sides. There is nothing worse than being grilled. This is an artificial situation and you have to have an adrenalin rush and a tinge of apprehension in order to perform well, but beware of appearing to have a complacent attitude and don't swagger through the door. You need a heightened sense of 'this is down to me'. It is never good to arrive ill-prepared or to tell the interviewer that they are just one of a number of companies you are looking at. You need to be able to answer the question, 'If you were offered the job, would you take it?' The interviewer is looking for someone who is eager to come on board and be part of their organization. They want to build a rapport with you as a person.

Walking into the room

This is something else you can practise at home. Walk through the door with your head held high, your shoulders back and a friendly look on your face. Don't walk in nervously or sloppily, as this is no way to make new friends. You need to exude energy and a sense of purpose. You need to make eye contact with the people you are meeting and you need to introduce yourself with a smile and a firm handshake. Then, make sure you remember the name of the person or the people you have just been introduced to. In the high adrenalin environment of an interview, this is the hardest thing to do. Recognize this and form a strategy for remembering their names. You can do this in a number of ways, some of which Heather Summers and I described in detail in *The Book of Luck: Brilliant Ideas for Creating Your Own Success and Making Life Go Your Way*; see especially Chapter 5, 'Sociability'. Some of these techniques include:

1   Repeat the name immediately after someone has told you what his or her name is. Use it again at the first opportunity.

2   Imagine a label over their head with the name written on it.
3   Form a mental link between them and someone you know.
4   Picture names – such as Dawn, Heather, Daisy.

Whatever technique you use, make that conscious effort to remember the name and then to use it so that they know you have remembered them as an individual.

The pitfalls in interviews are potentially endless. Generally, in my experience, they are created by candidates and not by interviewers. For example, it is easy to avoid problems by turning your telephone off before you go into the building. I have had numerous interviews where the candidate has answered the telephone that has rung while we have been talking. What a good impression THAT was!

Arrive in plenty of time so you are not out of breath, agitated and sweating. Remember all of the rules that your mother impressed on you when you were five years of age and embarking on your first day at school. Clean hanky, go to the loo before you leave and don't be late. What could be simpler than that?

Jan Shaw, Associate Director, Barracuda Search, says:

With the increased emphasis on a service culture and developing the strong customer focus, interviews are aimed at bringing out personalities. The Asda way [outlined on p.201] was the trailblazer for new and dynamic ways of identifying the right kind of person for the business. Asda wants to bring into the organization people that they like and will get on with. They need to reflect the brand of the whole organization and be people that you would enjoy spending time with. The brand has got to be translated into people.

The interview process, therefore, is not to find people who intellectually grasp the Asda model but people who do it naturally. The interview is structured to bring out personality, to find candidates who are helpful and who enjoy dealing with people. Background, the right school or the right university won't cut any ice with companies like Asda. Status does not exist, as everyone is a colleague, so the test is, 'Will this person bring added value to the job?'

Avoiding bias

It would be good if all we had to worry about was age, gender and racial discrimination as our protection against them is enshrined in UK law. It is the insidious and unspoken discrimination that is truly worrying and is something that you need to be on the alert for in interviews. I have known clients over the years that have been spectacular in the breadth of their prejudices and in their ability to bring them to bear in their assessment of people. One client always went down to the car park to peer in the windows of applicants' cars to check that the interiors were tidy. What this had to do with someone's ability to fulfil a role in an organization always baffled me. However, be sure that if you turned up with your car full of sweet wrappers, petrol receipts and empty drinks bottles, you wouldn't be getting that job. Another client mistrusted people with beards and would discount them instantly. This prejudice is one that is quite common so if you do have a beard and a moustache go and look in the mirror and decide if that beard is vital. Could you shave it off until you get the job and then grow a long, luxuriant one later? Although you might be prevented from winning a job because of a beard, they can't sack you because you have grown one.

Five o' clock shadow, stubble, earrings (for men) and hair gelled with an oil slick are ways of raising suspicions of interviewers and are to be avoided at all costs. What about brightly coloured socks and ties with pictures of Fred Flintstone? For every person who admires this jaunty expression of your slightly quixotic personality, there will be someone else who simply sees it as an inappropriate way of dressing for an interview.

Nadine Jones, Head of Human Resources, Baugur, says about the interview:
An obvious one – but clean your hands and nails. A slovenly approach will allow the interviewer to draw conclusions you may not want them to! And polish your shoes! Avoid fizzy drinks before and during your interview. Sitting opposite a candidate who is burping is not a pleasant experience!

Other prejudices are around, particularly about weight and height so if you are overweight, think what you can do to dress in a way that is more flattering to the fuller figure. If you are not as tall as you might be, build up your heels, put your shoulders back and gel your hair to a slight quiff – see, you have just become of average height rather than small.

Regional accents are another fertile hunting ground for prejudices. Be prepared to face people who don't like Scottish, Welsh, Yorkshire or Liverpool accents and be quick to head it off. Don't flaunt your allegiance to your region, unless that is where the job is, and find ways to show instead that you see yourself as a UK or European citizen. Whatever you do, don't let anyone know which football team you support as this could be the route to instant rejection. A senior manager I know is an ardent supporter of Arsenal. His office is draped with flags, banners and Arsenal memorabilia, One day, following an evening fixture when Barcelona defeated Arsenal; he interviewed someone in his office who told him cheerfully that he was feeling particularly good as he was celebrating Barcelona's success. The interviewer thus had instant doubts about the candidate's powers of observation, his intuition and his taste in football teams. I can think of better ways to impress a prospective boss!

When you have got the job, there is plenty of time to allow the real you to show through. Give it a couple of weeks and then you can feel free to put your ear stud back in, replenish your stocks of chewing gum and rediscover your tie from the joke shop. At the moment you can't afford anything like this. You are on a serious mission to get the right job and you need to win every step of the way. I am not suggesting that you become bland and indistinguishable from the crowd but I am showing how it is possible to avoid possible elephant traps.

We all bring our prejudices with us into the room and maybe now is the time to acknowledge this and realize that it is not just the people who are interviewing you who have their prejudices but you too will be leaping to conclusions about them. Be prepared to make allowances for people, just as you would want them to make them for you. If someone instantly reminds you of the vile maths teacher you had when you were at school and this brings up all those emotions you had when you were 13, stop and remember that this person is not that maths teacher but is a distortion of your memories. Acknowledge that this is your prejudice and give them a chance to show you that they are a different person. If you have any of those thoughts about smokers, chewing gum, fat or thin people, snazzy socks or Londoners, forget them right now. Be prepared to see the best in people and be ready to let them see the best in you. Legislation is there to protect us from race, sex and age discrimination. In truth, all of these exist in one form or another and to one degree or another so be aware that it is there and be ready to circumvent or challenge it.

If you know a particular organization is one that is likely to display any or all of these discriminatory practices, then you have to ask yourself if you want to be part of it. Would you enjoy working with such an organization? However, some people are good at challenging the system and ensuring that they change.

Building rapport with your interviewer

When you arrive for your interview, you may find that you are being interviewed by a sophisticated and experienced interviewer who has done this thousands of times before and who can put you effortlessly at your ease, making you lose your nervousness and be ready to open up. Equally, you might be interviewed by someone who is not sure how to do it and who may be as nervous as you are.

Sheila Burgess, Director, SBI International, says:
I am not there to find you a job. I am here to find the most appropriate person for my client.

Whatever the situation is, take responsibility for breaking the ice and getting a rapport established that allows people to perform at their best. Sometimes the environment might help you; for example, if you are sitting at a round table in an informal office. It might be harder if you are at one side of the table and you are facing a panel of three or more, when the atmosphere is undoubtedly more formal and more intimidating. Remember it is down to you as much as it is to them to put everyone at their ease so be ready to talk.

Before you have even gone into the room you will have researched the people who are interviewing you. You will know their names and something of their track record. You may know what they look like, allowing you to address them by their name when you are introduced. You might have the chance to comment on how you have heard a lot about their particular successes in a certain field, showing that you know who they are and you are interested in them.

Martine Robins, European Human Resources Director, Cookson Electronics says:

When you come in the room you need to demonstrate some knowledge about the company. You need to Google the interviewer beforehand and show that you have looked at the products. We want to see a spark. My starting question is likely to be 'What do you know about our company?' It starts the engagement. It shows you are keen and interested. You need to highlight your potential during the interview but don't oversell and do it with modesty. We are looking for a considered response.

The interview is a two way street in terms of information flow and impact. You are not a passive participant, waiting for people to drive the meeting. You can subtly make sure that you drive the agenda as well.

When you are offered a coffee or a tea, accept it even if you don't want it. It shows that you intend to stay longer than ten minutes and the social conventions of pouring coffee, offering milk and tea biscuits are a good way of interacting and allowing people to get settled.

Now is the time to establish rapport in a different way. You will be using your knowledge of people to show that you value them as individuals. Listen harder and identify their particular linguistic traits. Softly-spoken people may wince if faced with loud people. Once you have identified people's traits, use them and see what happens. You will find that you find yourself at ease quicker and you establish better, deeper and more meaningful communication. Used in an interview situation, this will give you an instant advantage.

What you must also do now is to be alert to the kind of vocabulary that they use and make sure you incorporate it into your own. For example if they use words like passionate, energetic, high yield, dramatic, exponential, multicultural, global and dynamic, then adopt them too. You need to become part of their world so steal their words and replace your own.

Then look at how people are sitting. Examine their physical posture and the opposition of their bodies and their legs. If they are sitting at an angle, then you do it too. If they are sitting forward or if they are sitting backwards, then you must do it too. Look at the angle of their spine and the tilt of their head and match it too. Maintain strong eye contact. I once interviewed an Engineering Director in a hotel in Glasgow and he stared out of the window the whole time. He never looked at me once so I felt disengaged and unsympathetic. Look people in the eye and maintain that contact. Now is not the time to be staring into space in a reflective kind of way.

Notice also the tones of people's voices. Everyone talks at a certain pace and a particular pitch. Have you ever listened in to someone else's conversation where one person is speaking rapidly and the other person is slow and measured? It just doesn't work, does it? I am not suggesting that you go so far that it sounds as though you are mimicking people and causing offence. We are not looking for Rory Bremner impersonations. I am just asking you to have a more flexible and versatile way of speaking. Make yourself liked by:

- Using their vocabulary and linguistic style
- Slow down or speed up appropriately
- Watch the volume and pitch – get it right.

Narrow the gap between you and the interviewer. It is down to you and to no-one else. Whatever the pitch and the tone of the voice are, make them your own.

Clare Howard, Director of e-coaches.co.uk, says:
Tune into and then match the energy levels of the interviewers. If they are quick and lively, be animated, lean forward; show you are engaged. If they are quiet and reserved, stay calm, be measured, nod wisely. If there is more than one interviewer – make sure you give each of them in turn your attention, matching their different styles if appropriate.

All of this matching requires a light touch. If you over do it in any way, you will look obvious, unnatural and will arouse the suspicion that you are making fun of people. Do it with subtlety and you will establish a good level of rapport that will cause them to listen to you carefully.

Interviewing with a professional recruiter

Every recruiter brings their own individuality and style to an interview. Although Sheila Burgess specializes in recruiting bilingual PAs, her interviewing methodology is applicable to all situations. You may find it useful to go through it and see how you would fare if you were being measured against an equivalent seven point plan.

Sheila Burgess's seven point Parisian plan for interviewing

The seven points:

1 Impact, presentation and overall impression
2 Personal circumstances
3 Ambition and motivation
4 Intelligence
5 Technical skills
6 Education and experience
7 Personality.

1. Impact, presentation and overall impression

What are you like in the first stages of a process? How are you on the telephone? What do you look like and how are you dressed? How do you walk into the room? Do you walk in confidently or do you slope in? What about the handshake? Are you someone who inspires confidence and who can be seen to represent the organization?

These are things you have probably never given any kind of deep thought to before yet they are part of the initial impact you will make. When you shake hands make sure that it is a firm grasp. Although it is something that takes ten seconds, great assumptions are made about your personality from it. Have you ever shaken hands with the clammy-handed? Remember what that felt like and avoid it like the plague. What about the person who grasps your hand with both of his (sadly it is usually men who do this)? This seems false, over the top and obsequious so if you were ever tempted, forget it.

Remember too that the firm handshake on its own is not enough. It is imperative that you must smile simultaneously and make direct eye contact.

2. Personal circumstances

- Family background
- Commitment
- Working hours
- Transport
- Accommodation.

Sheila likes to know about people's home circumstances so that she can be sure that she is introducing people to the right kind of job. The reason she needs to know about home life is that there is not a lot of point in being interviewed for a job that is likely to have regular late nights if you need to be home for 6 pm when the childminder leaves. Sheila tends to work a lot with young graduates so she likes to check that they have organized their accommodation and that they have a clear view of where they can travel to and where they can't. Openness about your home situation will not lead to discrimination against you but will help prospective employers put you in the right slot. The wrong job where pressure is put on you to work in a way that conflicts with your home life will bring unimaginable stress and will be short lived. Get the interviewer on your side by being straight with them.

3. Ambition and motivation

This is the point when Sheila is going to grill you about what it is that you like to do, what kind of people you get on with, what kind of boss you like and what it is that you don't enjoy in a job.

She will also be asking you about your last job, why you left it and what you did and didn't enjoy about it. She will ask searching questions about your long-term ambitions and where you want life to take you.

These are standard questions in any interview so be sure to have reflected on this beforehand. Think about the content of a job, the culture of the company and the kind of people you like working with. Make sure you have formulated in your mind some kind of answer so that you can make an articulate and sensible reply.

4. Intelligence

Are you bright? Sheila never makes assumptions about people's academic ability so she always includes some form of written exercise that will show her your capacities. For example, if she is interviewing a prospective secretary/PA, she will ask them to write a simple letter to a supplier who has sent an order with missing items. Be prepared for deceptively simple tasks that will show how you pick up on things and how practical you really are.

5. Technical skills

Sheila, like all consultants who represent a client, will be making a recommendation for the client to see you. Her priority is therefore to ask questions of you while she is asking herself the question, 'Will my client want to see you?' Her sift, therefore, will be thorough and rigorous with searching questions. She will need to test you on your technical competence to do the job. This is the easy bit for you. The job specification is clearly laid out and you know what they need. Make sure you highlight all of those skills and experiences in your career that demonstrate that you have the technical competence to get you the job.

6. Education and experience

Your education is very important. You need to include all of your qualifications and your diplomas in order to demonstrate your capabilities. Be thorough, detailed and meticulous in your record of academic achievement. Do not assume that someone will know that you have a particular skill or qualification. List it, record it and make sure it counts. Where possible, use your education to show that you already have some of the experience needed in the role you are applying for, or at least be able to demonstrate similarities. Make sure that you have carefully thought through how your experience matches up.

7. Personality

Sheila is constantly being asked, 'Why didn't I get the job?' Sometimes she can't be definitive and give one clear answer, as it is just a jumble of impressions and conversation that leave her feeling uncomfortable. Let's be clear here: if a consultant is feeling uncomfortable you will never get to the client. What leads to this feeling? Sheila mentions the person who does not ring to say they are going to be late but apologizes when they get there. Other times it is that intangible element called 'fit'. It may be what you wear, your manner, your attitude and your demeanour. She talked about the person who walked oh-so-slowly into her office. This may have been fear (perfectly understandable given the circumstances) but it gave the impression of lack of pace or, in Sheila's words, that they were 'slothful'.

Be the best person for the job

The only way to win is to make yourself the best person for the job. Disregard who else may be on the shortlist or who may be waiting for the next interview slot, remember that you are the best person for this role. Even if you are now attending your 20th interview, having failed to get the other 19 jobs, make sure that you are just as fresh and motivated for this one.

Clare Howard, Director of e-coaches.co.uk, says:

You may have been interviewed 30 times already but this is the first interview with these people so make sure you maintain the adrenalin and that you make this interview as animated and powerful as your first. If you have to, wear something other than your 'interview suit'. Put on a different shirt or blouse. Do something that is different and don't come out with stock replies that you have churned out before. It hasn't worked before so change it now.

How to listen

It is said that in an interview, the candidate should talk for 70% of the time and the interviewer should have the other 30%. Having said that, the true talent is to know that what you are saying is what people want to hear so you can only be a good talker if you listen properly.

There are people in conversations who are dying for you to finish saying what you have to say so that they can pitch in with what they have thought of. Now is not the time for that. Listen carefully to what is being asked of you so that you answer appropriately. Have you ever listened to the *Today* programme on Radio 4 when John Humphries is grilling a politician and asking very specific and tough questions? Have you listened to the experienced politician neatly sidestep the question asked and then go on to say what they want to say, straight from the rehearsed script and what has been agreed with the PR gurus? Do not use these people as role models. When you are asked a question, you can only answer it with a straight response.

Gareth James, Director, People Plus Ltd, says:
Never rubbish your former company or your former boss. Be positive about your achievements, your responsibilities and what you have learnt. The firm rule is 'No whingers!'

Never interrupt and always allow someone to finish their sentence. I hate it when people finish my sentences for me. How do you know what I was going to say? The courtesy of a dialogue is that each person listens to the other and uses the content of that contribution to form a response. This is the meaning of intelligent debate. Make sure that you allow the interviewer the opportunity to set out what they want you to talk about and then respond. Make no assumptions about what they want to hear – listen to them.

The important thing is also to listen actively. You may know that you can gaze out of the window, write notes, drink coffee and simultaneously listen to a conversation and hear every word; however, the person opposite will still think you are not listening. Therefore, engage eye contact, look interested and focus actively on what they are saying.

When to talk

Consider every word that you utter to be a jewel. Do not waffle, do not ramble and do not get sidetracked. People are listening to you in the same way that you listened to them so make sure you make your point. Don't be monosyllabic and don't talk forever. A question will have been put to you so you can show your strengths and show how good you are. It is not the time for a monologue and it isn't time for a six word answer. Don't take over and eat up whatever limited time there is for your interview with a focus on this single issue. If you are struggling to keep going, ask a question of them and open up the debate. This will buy you more thinking time and will deepen the rapport in the meeting. The balance of talking and listening is a delicate one and it is something you must be careful to maintain. Beware the hobby horse – don't get onto to a theme that is a favourite of yours and hammer it to death. Maintain crisp, professional and focused responses throughout. However friendly the interviewer may be, they are not your friend. They are there to assess you so don't lower your guard.

Jan Shaw, Associate Director, Barracuda Search, says:

- *Forget the positioning statements about who you are and what you have done. Back up whatever you say with facts.*
- *Just because you have or you have had a big job title and a big job, do not make the mistake of thinking that no one will challenge you about what you have achieved. Be ready to be challenged.*
- *Do not 'overtalk'. It will be seen that you are not listening, trying to dominate or that you are 'over flowering' your experience.*
- *Listen for cues from the interviewer. Respond to them in a factual manner. Do not waffle. Be very clear and back up your statements with evidence.*
- *Get your punch lines in quickly. Do not think that the interviewer will wait for you to blossom in the course of the interview. Don't go in with the attitude that 'I am wonderful and they will find this out.' No they won't. It is up to you to shine. Don't come out of the meeting saying, 'I should have said this' – get it in during the interview and take control.*

It is to be expected that interviewers will be taking notes during the interview. It is also likely that you will be there too with a notebook, a file or a filofax. You may want to jot something down or to refer to notes you made earlier.

Taking notes is important. It is much more important for the interviewer to take notes because, let's face it, they meet a lot of people and they need to make sure they get down every thrilling detail about you so that they can remember who you are and then write their interview comments about you later when you may, surprising though this can sound, have disappeared into a fog of faces. You, on the other hand, do not have a report to write. You are concentrating on making a good impression. You are actively listening and you are using all of your wit and intellect to ensure you give of your best. A notepad is always a good prop and occasionally you may care to write down a pearl of wisdom but don't over do it. A candidate of mine went for a final interview for a senior role but was rejected as he was not considered to be sufficiently serious about the job. A contributory factor was that he did not take a notebook and pen into the final meeting. A fascinating psychological insight is that, for some people, the person wielding the pen and the notepad, taking copious notes during the interview is the one who is in charge of the interviewing process. Some candidates match me word for word as I write away, thus demonstrating that they consider themselves to be as much in control of the interview as I am. However, as you are the one being interviewed, I think it would be magnanimous to allow the interviewer a position of control!

Caution!
How not to do it

I had arranged to interview a candidate at the Institute of Directors at 9 am and got there early. By 8 am I was sitting at a desk in their coffee lounge, waiting for my candidate. At 9 am prompt I had a call from the candidate asking where I was. It transpired that he was a member of the IoD as well so he had not checked in at reception but had decided to position himself at a desk in the same room. He insisted that I join him so my well-ordered and well-planned meeting was now going awry. I scrambled my papers together and found Mr Nuisance totally in control. He ordered the coffee, took notes continually and took complete control of the meeting. He was in charge and he showed it. Unfortunately, having hijacked the meeting he showed me more about himself than he imagined. He had shown me his insecurities and his arrogance. He had shown that he had to be in charge and he was discounted from the short list. On the plus side, at least he paid for the coffee!

Mastering the art of answering difficult questions

Interviews come in many shapes and sizes and interviewers have different ways of approaching the interview; therefore, you are going to have to be at your most flexible and adaptable to cope with the questions thrown at you. You may find yourself in a long interview that does not seem to follow any particular format or you may find yourself in a short sharp scenario with a few set questions.

The goal of the interviewer is to get a firm grasp of the kind of person you are, your set of values and the particular style that you have. They will already know about your experience and they may have a few particular points they want to raise about achievements or reasons for moving on. The main thrust of the interview is to ask questions that will get under your skin and reveal the true you. You need to show that there is a strong link between their needs and your attributes. As candidates are getting more and more sophisticated in their ability to manage interview situations, interviewers are having to be more cunning and adept in how they interview. I often feel that there is a glass screen between the candidate and me. I get carefully prepared answers and beautifully rehearsed speeches. This is not what I want, I want the real you.

I am not aiming to provide you with a portfolio of pat answers that you can learn by heart in your forthcoming interview. My objective is to start you thinking about how you might begin to answer them in your own way, drawing on your own experience and relating it to the demands of the job. All of the recruitment insiders I have spoken with are unanimous in their view that they want you to be honest and direct.

These interview questions will allow you to practise your answers, think about who you are and bring to the front of your mind the important aspects of your career and personality. There is no substitute for honesty.

Preparing for the obvious

Before you go into the interview you stand a very good chance of knowing what kind of questions you are likely to be asked. You can find this out by studying the job brief and the advertisement very carefully and deducing what it is that they are likely to be looking for. If they are seeking experience in managing and motivating cross-cultural teams, you would be well advised to have delved into your experience and come up with examples of occasions when you have done this and achieved success. If the job requires experience in managing service contract performance, then have a couple of examples of how you have done this at the front of your mind. Go into the interview with a clear picture of what they are looking for and what you have to offer that is relevant. If there are gaps in your skills and experience, acknowledge them and formulate a plan of how you can address them. You can talk about how you have signed up for a specialist course, a language course or an IT programme. If the job requires an MBA and you haven't got one, don't be tempted to fake it but apply for an MBA programme. Demonstrate that you are ambitious and that you can fill the gaps through your own efforts and it will be considered to be as relevant as the skill or qualification itself.

Rachel Hannan's rules to make the interview go your way:

1   *Ask beforehand what kind of interview it is going to be so you are pre-pared.*
2   *Take every opportunity to get ahead of the game.*

3   *Remember the interviewers are probably more nervous than you. They may well be inexperienced in interviewing and nervous of questioning you in front of their colleagues.*

4   *Put them at their ease. Engage with them. Introduce warmth and personal engagement in this formal setting.*

5   *Take control in a subtle way. Maintain respect and don't take over.*

6   *Never put any interviewer on the spot. Don't ask a question that they may not know the answer to.*

7   *Let them see you are serious about this job, that you are well prepared and that you have researched it well.*

8   *Do not give them any excuse to discount you from the process.*

Don't be tempted to lie about experience that you don't have. You will be found out sooner or later and that will be the end of the road. It is much better to raise the issue of the gap or the 'learning curve' yourself and show that you have thought about how you would address it.

Gareth James, Director, People Plus Ltd, says:

Never be tempted to lie in the course of an interview. This demonstrates the assumption that you think you are cleverer than the interviewer. As this may well not be the case, settle for the truth, as it is much simpler.

At face value, questions such as 'Where do you see yourself in five years?' or 'What are your life goals?' seem pretty silly if they're merely requests for information. But you can view them as opportunities to demonstrate the serious thought you've given to your values, priorities and driving motivational forces. Your responses should reflect optimism and the ability to reality-test forces that shape your career development. 'I'd like to have your job' probably isn't the most insightful answer.

When an interviewer asks, 'What are your greatest strengths?' they may, in fact, be asking several distinct questions:

- In what ways could you add most value to us?
- Can you organize your capabilities into distinct functional categories?
- What evidence or proof can you provide to substantiate your claims?
- Can you prioritize?
- If a lot of things are true of you, what things are most true of you?

Providing a laundry list or a mixed bag of self-laudatory adjectives – 'I'm kind, trustworthy, brave, clean, reverent, wholesome, goal-orientated, innovative, collaborative and strategic' hardly addresses or suggests that you are aware of the interviewer's concerns.

Internet answers

A quick search on Google for possible answers to tough interview questions produced a possible 16 million hits. I suppose that this means that you are not the only one who worries about the right response to the hazardous questions. It means that we are awash with information and answers but how do we evaluate the accuracy and relevance of what they are saying? Just because it is on the Internet does not mean to say that it is right. If you consult Wikipedia, how do you know that what is there is accurate? Stock answers will not ring true so you have to make sure that you add authenticity by making sure that your answers are grounded in your own experience and reflect your own values.

There is no simple solution to this. There are no ready-made answers sitting on a shelf, waiting for you to collect them and have a winning ticket on the shortlist. If you know accurately what an employer is seeking in terms of skills, education, experience, personal style, ambition and 'fit', then you might have a sporting chance. Nothing can match the firm foundations of rigorous research and then the determination to run the process and to showcase your talents. Assembly line answers that you have learnt by rote won't work. The simple, direct, honest and specific answers will win the day. The truth, therefore, is that it is not the smart answer that will win the day but the clear thinking, highly-focused and well-prepared candidate who knows what the job is, knows how his or her experience applies and then can articulate it – having also ensured a timely arrival in a well-dressed and friendly manner.

It sounds complicated but it can be done. What might these questions be, therefore, that you should be rehearsing? The real question that is being asked here is: do you have the experience to do this job, will you fit in and will you deliver results? So long as you use the time and the other questions to answer this satisfactorily, then the job will be yours.

30 common questions and how to answer them

In addition to technical questions relevant to the role, most interviews include some general questions, intended to reveal more about you, the person. Some of the most commonly asked questions you may face along the way could be:

1. If I were to talk to your boss, what do you think he or she would tell me about you?

Think carefully about this one. Before you go into the interview, work out what skills they are looking for and what kind of personal attitude is likely to fit. For example, if you are being interviewed for a role with a charity, you might find yourself in an organization that is caring and sharing so let's avoid words like 'ruthless' and 'hard-nosed'.

A good exercise to do before the interview would be to write about yourself in the third person. Write an appraisal of you and your achievements as well as your personal style.

What would you *want* your boss to say about you?

2. If I were in a bar and found myself sitting next to your boss, how would he or she describe you?

This is a variation on question 1 and is tackling the same issues. One difference is that it is perhaps is tapping into a more informal use of language.

3. What would you consider to be your single greatest personal success?

You probably have dozens of examples you can come up with here. This applies to anyone from the age of 16 to 90. Before you go into the interview, review your career successes and use the example that is most likely to gel with the role and the company you are talking to. Be careful not to bring in too much about your personal life. This interview is about your career and not about a hobby that is dear to your heart. Use every opportunity to demonstrate how important a part work plays in your life.

4. What would you consider to be your single greatest business success?

Again, select very carefully a career success that will have some relevance for this particular role. This is your chance to show that you will be bringing pertinent experience and added value.

5. Describe an occasion when you have wrenched success from the jaws of defeat.

Now is the opportunity to show that when the going gets tough, you are resourceful, enterprising and able to drive through results. The relevance of this example is key. Make sure that you link it with the business you are considering joining.

6. Why are you interested in this role?

Please don't say that you are looking for a challenge. This must be one of the most hackneyed expressions of all times and has become completely meaningless. You may sincerely believe it but find other ways of putting it. You might want to say:

'I have reached a stage in my current job where I rarely encounter difficult situations. I am comfortable and confident in my role. I feel that I am at my best when the adrenalin is rushing and I find myself in uncharted waters. I am ambitious and ready to learn from new situations so that is why I am very interested in this new role. I recognize that it is a different sector and that I will initially have a sharp learning curve. However, I am confident that I will be up to the challenge.' Isn't that better than the alternative, 'I am looking for a new challenge'?

7. Describe an occasion when you have been faced with the impossible and yet you have succeeded.

This is a great chance to show that you slay dragons, you don't feed them. Awaken the warrior that is inside you and remember when you rose to a seemingly impossible challenge and achieved results. Everyone has done this at some time in their lives. If you can't think of good examples, ask your friends, your partner, your mother, your colleagues and find that time when your input made that crucial difference. This is what people are seeking so give them what they want – and make it relevant.

8. What is your greatest disappointment in life?

You are not sitting on your therapist's couch now. Be careful what you display here. It is alright to confess that you are disappointed that you did not make it as a professional footballer or that you never became fluent in a foreign language. It is not all right to make the true confessions about wishing you had managed to create a more cohesive management team in your last job. Focus on what is self-evident from your CV, not deep confessionals from your subconscious.

9. If you could rewrite your career history, what changes would you make and what would you do differently?

Again, you can now talk about how, for example, you wish you had gone to university at 18 rather than doing it the hard way by working and studying simultaneously. This is a brilliant way of showing yourself to be hard working and highly motivated.

10. Who would you consider to be the three people who have had the most influence in your life?

If you haven't thought about a question like this beforehand, you might flounder. There is no right answer to this one. Just show that you can put forward a well constructed argument about why you have chosen Captain Cook, John Lennon, Fidel Castro or whoever it is you think has influenced you, and you will be fine. Most people include a family member, showing that in order to have a true impact, that person has to be known and physically present.

11. What do you think are your greatest strengths?

This is not an opportunity to reel off a list of fabulous adjectives. You will have carefully evaluated the role beforehand and you will have thought through what type of person will succeed in the role. You will know what strengths they will need and you will play them back. You will also use the opportunity to link them directly to the job. So, when you claim to be an excellent leader and team player, you will point out that this is required in the role. If you have experience of implementing a particular type of software, point out how this could add value in the role. Use this as an opportunity to demonstrate your appropriateness for the role.

12. We all have weaknesses – what are yours?

This is the question that you have to sidestep. Don't confess to your poor timekeeping, your inability to finish off projects or your pathological fear of flying. You could say that you have always carefully targeted career opportunities where you will only be playing to your strengths. If you are applying for a job training to be an accountant, admit that your artistic side is sadly lacking. If you are applying for a highly creative side that has no budget responsibilities, it is all right to own up that you prefer not to deal with statistics and VAT. All in all, reflect long and hard before the interview about the kind of weakness it would be alright to have and use for this application.

For there to be a real fit for the job, the answer should be true. The common approach of turning a strength into a weakness can often ring false. It sounds manipulated and it probably is, and few astute interviewers will be fooled.

13. If I employ you, what value will you add to the organization?

This is an easy one. This is where all your hard work and preparation will pay off. You will know what they are looking for and you will rattle off the skills that you will bring. Rehearsal beforehand will mean that you will be thoughtful, articulate and fluent.

14. If I ask your current boss what your weaknesses are, what would he or she tell me?

This is just another way of pushing for a more direct answer to question 12. Keep plugging away at weaknesses that would not have a direct impact on the success of the role. Avoid the temptation to induce nausea in the listener by claiming that he or she might say that you work too hard. You could focus on their disappointment that you are not fluent in ten different languages or that that you would not relocate to a remote village. You can justify this as a lifestyle and family matter. We don't want to hear that you miss budget every year.

15. If I were to ask someone who disliked you to tell me about you, what do you think they would say about you?

Don't get drawn into this one. This is a potentially hazardous path. First of all challenge the assumption that you have enemies. It is better to recognize that we all have different styles and approaches and that what works for some people simply jars on others. Therefore, your direct and forceful approach might be difficult for some people to accommodate. Or your collaborative and understated way of ensuring everyone gets on board can frustrate those who champ at the bit for action and don't mind a bit of blood spilt along the way. Practise this one and be ready to work round it.

16. How would you describe yourself?

Keep reminding yourself that the interviewer is only interested in you in so far as it affects your candidacy for the job. Whatever you reply, make sure it continues to describe a person who could make an impact on the role you are applying for. However interesting it might be to hear about your cooking skills, your cycling interests or your family, it is not relevant and it will not add value to your application.

17. If you could wave a magic wand and change the way that you are, how would you like to be?

A fantasy question like this is one that can be answered in a light hearted way so it depends on its context and how it has been put. If you are applying for something artistic, creative and inventive, give full rein to your creative talents. If it is for a role as a senior manager in an organization, treat it as seriously as any other question. Use the opportunity to reinforce what you do have, not what you don't. You could, for example, suggest that you would like to be a fluent Mandarin Chinese speaker, as this would give you a true edge in a global economy.

18. How many other jobs have you applied for?

Be honest and tell them what you are looking at. However, if you have a vast number of applications on the go, it might be better to reduce it dramatically. You need to let them know you are serious about this role, so whatever you say, make sure you finish it with an expression of absolute interest in this one job.

19. Tell me about yourself.

This is a killer question as it could potentially open the floodgates to a long and rambling monologue about life from the age of five. I remember sitting in the France Ameriques Club in Paris interviewing a candidate who responded energetically to this question. One hour and 20 minutes later he had still not stopped to draw breath. I was slumped at the desk and had practically lost the will to live. Having too much information to put into your answer is as potentially lethal as not having enough. Begin your discourse by saying 'I will give a brief three minute overview of what I consider to be the highlights of my career to date. You can then focus on any areas that are of particular relevance and interest'.

20. What newspaper, books or magazines do you read?

Whatever answer you give, make sure it is true as it is very easy to be caught out. If you claim to read *The Times*, the *Financial Times*, the *Independent* or the *Guardian*, make sure you have read it for at least a full week before the interview. Be ready to talk about your favourite columnist. If in truth you read the *Sun*, keep it to yourself and if you can't, then please do not try to justify it by saying you read it for the sport. There are some things that you ought to be doing as a serious business person, and one of those is reading a quality paper.

If you are actively job seeking, you should be reading widely anyway so it should be easy to answer this one. If the job you are applying for has a trade paper, then you could mention that you have had a glance at that.

21. What was the last book that you read?

This is the point when the most well-read person sometimes goes blank. Have something suitable at the front of your mind and be ready to discuss it. I know a few people who have embarrassed themselves by claiming to have read a book but when they are questioned on it, show a lamentable lack of knowledge about it. If you are caught out in one lie or exaggeration, it will put your whole interview in doubt so stick to the truth, even if you have had to manufacture that truth in the weeks leading up to interview.

22. Describe someone who has acted as a mentor to you in your career.

This one should be simple too. Think of a person in a senior position who has urged you on and made you realize that you have more potential than you may originally have thought.

23. Describe to me your 'shoes-off self'. What do you like to do in your spare time?

OK, don't bore me now. Don't talk about football, don't talk about socializing and don't get into the intricacies of war games. Now you can talk about leisure pursuits that indicate you lead a healthy lifestyle, have an active mind, a broad range of interests, an interest in the community and the world at large and nothing that we might flag up as potentially quirky. Don't get into religion as this will not fit with everyone. Keep it brief and keep it relevant.

24. Where do you plan to be in five years' time?

Do not say, 'I will have your job'. That is just too pushy and insulting. You may want to paint a picture of career progression and personal growth. If you do have a very specific career plan in mind, particularly within a profession where this could be expected, for example, in engineering, nursing, medical or army environments, then that is fine. For anything else, just ensure that you point out your energy and enthusiasm for growth.

25. How will we know that you will be committed to the company and the role?

This is the time to point to your track record of loyalty, achievement and success. However, one candidate offered as testimony of his dedication the fact that he got divorced as a consequence of his utter single-minded dedication to the job. Avoid this at all costs.

26. Why do you want to work for us?

All of your research will pay off now. Everything you know about the company, their competitors, their products, their markets and their values will come into play. Do not say, as someone said to me once, that he had looked at the cars in the car park and he wanted to be part of an organization that was so clearly car-minded.

27. When I am describing you later this evening to colleagues, how would you like me to talk about you?

As you will already have written your third person description of yourself in answer to question 1, you will know exactly what to say. It will be linked to the needs of the role and it will highlight the skills that you have to match it.

28. What changes have you made in your life that you are most proud of?

This is the interviewer's opportunity to find out if you are capable of switching gear and embracing change. Look into your past for an occasion when you have moved location, changed departments or taken on a new role against the odds.

29. What are your expectations of this role?

Do not, at any price, mention money. This is not about what you expect to earn. This is about career opportunities, the chance to develop and learn new skills, the opportunity to make an impact on the organization and create successes that you are proud to write your name against.

30. Do you have any questions for us?

If the interview has been conducted properly, there is every chance that all of your questions will have been answered. If this is so, don't be embarrassed to say that for the moment you have nothing further to say. Alternatively, you may have some burning issues you want to bring up so you may now safely introduce them. However, there are some danger zones in this deceptively simple question:

- Please do not get into layers of detail that are just too deep and irrelevant. Do not bore the listener.
- Do not ask a very 'clever' question that confounds the interviewer. No-one wants to be made to look stupid so don't get too complex.
- Do not produce sheaves of paper with vast lists of questions.
- Do not spend five minutes carefully viewing your notes to make sure you have covered every point, leaving the interviewer silently contemplating you.

Gareth James, Director, People Plus Ltd, says:
Always ask questions but make sure that they are focused on strategy, the business or where the business is going. Don't ask about BUPA, holiday entitlement or trivial matters. They may be very important to you but now is not the time to get to this level

of detail. Beware the killer final question that is thrown at you. It is often something as simple as 'What was the last book that you read?' Have something ready for this and don't say it was Victoria Beckham's autobiography.

Be ready for the off-the-wall questions. This might not be about facts and figures but could be some little strand that the interviewer is pursuing. Your job is to be prepared for everything but be careful – don't be too polished and prepared, as there is a difference between preparation and rehearsal. Excellent preparation will allow people to see the true you whereas too much preparation will look like a performance.

The animal question

Bear in mind that sometimes, interviewers like to catch you off guard and throw something at you that will leave you speechless and perhaps reveal something of the real you, demonstrating how quick off the mark you can be and how fast thinking you are. An old favourite is 'If you were an animal, what kind of animal would you be?' This is not the time to show your quick sense of humour and claim to be a skunk because sometimes you forget to wash. Neither should you be a giraffe, as the neck would come in handy for peering into other people's affairs.

Now, this is a ridiculous question. There cannot be a right answer, there can only be an answer that you can justify and explain. Let's think how this could be:

A tiger – if you are applying for an aggressive sales position, then you can say that a tiger is out there fearlessly stalking the territory, hunting out new opportunities all of the time and making sure that it survives in the finest style. You will bring all the qualities of a tiger to this job.

A golden retriever – if you want to work in a caring role, then you could assume the qualities of a dedicated, loyal and thoroughly reliable and dependable animal that will be undeterred by anything.

A parrot – a secretary or personal assistant could lay claim to its high intelligence, its astonishing memory and its ability to repeat conversations verbatim. You could have this for an actor or performer as well.

A cat – The highly independent cat who owes little allegiance to anyone, except the person who feeds it and allows it to sit in comfort on a sofa or a knee would be an excellent consultant. This would be someone able to operate on their own, without the input of a team and able to give their unvarnished views.

No such thing as an easy question

The only way, therefore, to be ready for the interview is to be prepared for every eventuality. Every question at interview is potentially tricky. Before you go in, look at your CV and check what you have put. If you have followed my advice and you have a portfolio of CVs, make sure you know which one you have submitted for this application. Get out the job advertisement or the job description that was sent to you. Focus on what they are looking for and then extract examples from your own career history that match those needs. This interview is not about what you want and need. It is about what this potential employer wants and what you can give them. Research and good preparation will pay off.

Some interviewers 'freewheel' their way through and seem not to have a specific format. They may run through your CV in a chronological way, starting with your GCSEs and working their way through to the current day. This may seem like the easiest option but in fact it holds the biggest potential pitfalls. The best aid in an interview is the surge of adrenalin you have when you are facing the unexpected. If you are asked a hard or an unexpected question, then your mind races and the best will come out. If, however, you are asked to run through the familiar facts of your education and experience, the danger is that you ramble on in an unstructured way, giving too much irrelevant detail and reducing the interviewer to a state of boredom. You want the interviewer to be interested, giving you their full attention and not thinking about what they are having for dinner that night. This is your chance to shine so make sure you are prepared. If you have the deceptively easy questions, make sure you are crisp, concise and interesting. No one is particularly interested in the art project you did when you were 15 so please don't give us the detail.

In summary:

- Be prepared – research, review and rehearse
- Arrive on time in a calm and measured manner
- Make an impact – look good, maintain eye contact, good posture and a bright smile
- Listen

- Talk
- Be structured and relevant in your replies
- If in doubt, ask for clarification
- Be honest and straightforward – be who you truly are.

Interview notes – how did you do?

At the end of every interview, I write notes about the person I have just met. I write about their personality, their impact and how they match up against the needs of the job. I describe their personal style and how they came across in the interview. These notes may find themselves in a report I send to a client and will form an important part of the decision making process.

Think about yourself and your performance. Were you happy with it or do you think you could do better? Where precisely did you think you let yourself down? What will you do to make sure that you improve next time? Take the time after every interview to measure your impact at interview and think about how you did.

Second-stage interviews

Having gone through the first interview, hopefully you will be invited back for a second. This might be a formal assessment centre or it could be an interview with a number of people from the potential employer who want to give the interview some structure and a theme. They have already had one meeting with you and they have liked what they have seen. They have questioned you about your career and your experiences to date and now they want to see you again. They are likely to hold the meeting in a different setting and possibly with different people; therefore, be prepared for a different combination of people and a different style of meeting. They already know something about you and you know something about them. This time you must demonstrate your future potential and you need to focus on how you can meet the demands of the new job, not concentrate on your previous performance. Your research needs to be tip top and you need to have invested hours of effort into getting this right. You may be offered a lot of information about the company and you may be offered their accounts. If you haven't, get hold of them. This is easy if it is a public limited company as they are available to all. If it is a private company then you can go online to Companies House, www.companieshouse.gov.uk/, the official register of UK companies, and order the accounts at very low cost.

When you get the accounts, make sure that you take careful note of the data, such as the turnover and the profit. Look at the balance sheet and see what assets the company has. Look at the list of directors and remember their names and their roles in the organization. If you don't know how to interpret company accounts, then find someone who does and ask them to help you read them. There are plenty of books about finance for non-financial managers so now may be the time to start reading them.

You can go into this meeting with your confidence sky high. You know you have got through the first sift and you know that you are the kind of person they are looking for. It is now up to you to rise to the challenge of ensuring that you maintain the strength of that impact.

You may well be asked to make a presentation on a particular theme. It is likely to be related to their business and the objective is for you to show how you use data to inform your thought processes, how you interact and how you can convince people. PowerPoint presentations are an obvious way to go forward. This allows you to show the interviewers the depth of your preparation and for them to see how good you are at grasping information quickly and making appropriate recommendations. If you do this, print off copies and distribute them at the end so that you stay in people's memories. I am not even going to mention the need for grammatical and spelling accuracy. How many times have you been in a presentation or a conference when all you can see in the PowerPoint slide is someone's spelling mistake? Don't let that happen to you.

Make sure, as well, that you are not constrained by this format, as perhaps there is a better way of doing something. Andrew Harris of Matthews Harris Consulting Ltd, tells the tale of a short-listed candidate who wanted to be Marketing Director of a wine company. She was asked to make a presentation about the first 100 days in the company, and instead of coming along armed with a PowerPoint presentation, she arrived with six bottles of wine, a corkscrew and six glasses. Instead of it being an interview, it suddenly looked like a board meeting and that the candidate already was the Marketing Director. She was talking about the product that they all loved and showed that she was not talking about business theory but about their product. She got the job.

Be memorable, be confident and be creative. Show that you are different and that you have something dynamic to bring to the business. Use the presentation to talk as though you are already part of the business. Speak as if you are already in the job and forget that you are an applicant.

Assessment centres

The final hurdle may be when you are invited to an assessment centre. You can be confident that if you have received this invitation, you have already made the right kind of impact and the employer wants to know more about you. This should give you a great boost in self-confidence and the knowledge that what you have shown about yourself so far is a good match and a good fit.

The purpose of the assessment centre is to measure your intellectual capacities and your future potential. No two assessment centres are the same and they are each designed to focus on the qualities required for the particular role. Graduates face more assessment centres than most people as they have less work experience to draw on. The assessment centre will allow you to show your personal style and your way of communicating with others. It will show how you work, how you assess information and how you act upon it.

Whatever format it takes, it is likely to be a full day at the very least. Often it is two days. Remember that it is an artificially created environment and the ones who do best are the people who throw themselves into it and act as though it is real. Let's face it – it doesn't get more real than this as a job depends on your performance.

The instructions you receive in advance should include details of the format that this will take and will often include some or all of the following:

- Psychometric tests, both ability and personality based
- Group exercises/activities
- Role play
- A presentation
- In-tray exercise
- Individual interview
- Trial by sandwich.

It should also indicate to you what the dress code is. If they are going to send you into the countryside to ford a river with the aid of string, two plastic buckets and a stanley knife, they will advise you to bring along casual clothes. If they don't mention what to wear, put on your interview attire.

Gareth James' advice on attending assessment centres:

Be appropriate

Make sure you are dressed appropriately. This does not necessarily mean a suit, but something that fits the style of the business. If it is e-commerce, then smart casual might be better than a suit. For an old world company, a suit, shirt and tie are essential, but please bin the waistcoat. A crumpled linen suit might be a fashion statement in Islington but it might not be right for the role of Production Director. Short skirts and high street fashion may be very up to date but could hit the same discordant note in an assessment centre as they would at an interview.

Get ready

Think hard about what you are going to face there. Psychometric assessment is usually inevitable as many organizations will not make a decision to appoint just on the basis of an interview. A good track record is no predictor of future success so the evidence from assessment centres is essential. You are likely to have a couple of aptitude tests, a personality questionnaire and a competency-based interview to add to the data. You might also be asked to make a presentation. In some circumstances, there may be a work simulation like an in-tray exercise or – if meeting other candidates is acceptable – a group exercise. These are opportunities to convince that you want the job and also that you can do it.

Start off by making sure you ask before the date of the assessment centre itself if there is anything you can do to prepare. It is not a secret or a mystery and any decent assessor will supply you with leaflets and practice tests or links to websites where there is information and practice tests. Do whatever you can to prepare and also let the assessor know that you have prepared by asking up front what you can do.

Doing your best

The best way to approach psychometrics is openly, honestly and candidly. No one will like you if you try to be cleverer than the psychometrics and fake the results. Believing you can be smarter than a carefully developed psychometric test is patronizing beyond belief so be sure to be direct and honest, otherwise it will backfire on you.

Getting feedback

You should always receive feedback about your performance at an assessment centre and there should be an opportunity for an assessor to tell you how you did. Don't start making excuses if you have not done as well as you think you might have in the ability tests. These excuses have all been heard before so settle for expressing your disappointment and saying that you do not think it is a fair reflection of your capabilities.

How to prepare for a psychometric test

It is inevitable that along the job hunting path you will be faced with a psychometric test. Two-thirds of medium to large organizations use such testing alongside traditional methods such as interviewing, references and assessment centres. Moreover, it is estimated that nearly half of UK managers applying for a job sit some form of online test.

These come in many forms and some are more accurate and more acceptable than others. Whatever the test is that you will be facing, it is not an option for you to refuse to do it. It is better, therefore, to see them as an opportunity to learn more about yourself than a fear that you may fail. Psychometric ability tests seem to inspire fear and uncertainty in the most confident of individuals. No-one likes to sit a test where there is a prospect of failing or not performing well. We were all accustomed to this constant testing at school, but somehow, along the way, we have forgotten what it is like.

There are two main categories of psychometric instrument: one is the ability test, questionnaires that tap into your verbal, numerical and spatial skills. These tend to be tests that are timed and therefore you need to be alert, ready for action and keeping an eye on the clock. They can be at a number of levels and for more senior positions are likely to be tougher than most. However, many graduates will vouch for the fact that they have had to go through many psychometric hoops in order to secure their place on a graduate training scheme. This is a way of weeding people out of the process so make sure you are prepared for what is coming.

Most tests will be 30 minutes long and will take place in examination conditions. Everyone doing the test will receive the same instructions, the same exam conditions and the same questions. The process will be scrupulously fair with everyone evaluated against the same measures.

There are many websites where you can do practice tests and a good practitioner will have sent you either practice papers or a weblink to an appropriate site. Use them to practise. Actively seek out more. The whole point of psychometric testing is that it presents a snapshot of your potential and, while you can't rehearse and research for it in the traditional way, having an understanding of how they work can help you to improve your performance on the day. Get yourself into the frame of mind where you work against the clock and your brain is functioning in a different way. If the test is verbal reasoning, word games or crossword puzzles can help tune you into the right way of thinking. If it's numerical, practise your mental arithmetic.

Some good places to start finding practice papers are:

- www.bps.org.uk – This is the British Psychological Society and it offers a service to candidates and test users. Any publisher of a psychological test will be registered with the BPS so it the best starting point of any.
- www.shl.com – Saville and Holdsworth have practice tests and provide instant feedback.
- www.ase-solutions.co.uk – ASE offer practice tests and the opportunity to look at what psychometrics mean.
- www.opp.co.uk – This site does not currently offer practice tests but it is interesting to see the array of tests that they publish.
- www.kent.ac.uk – This website currently offers six practice tests and feedback.

Who are you?

In group sessions in assessment centres, you may be asked to introduce yourself to the others in the room as an informal way of breaking the ice. Imagine now that someone has just asked you to introduce yourself. What would you say? How much would you say? How long would you talk for? It isn't as easy as it seems. At a recent conference, I watched one of the platform speakers, a high profile Chief Executive, read out who she was and what her company did. I believe that she instantly lost credibility as this is not something you need notes for. You are describing who you are so what could be easier to describe than that? Or is it? The best apparently spontaneous speeches are usually those that have been meticulously prepared and rehearsed. Start now and prepare that introduction. Make it interesting and make sure people will want to listen. Make sure it is relevant to the job you are going for and take the opportunity to highlight something about you that is very relevant. You could follow the format of the Spoken Business Card (as described in *The Book of Luck*, Capstone 2004):

Well, you know how … (describe a generic or universal experience)
Well, what I do is …
The result is …

You can choose your own original way of describing yourself. A bit of humour never goes amiss and makes you memorable. Speak up and make sure that your tonality engages interest. Don't drone on in a monotone and above all don't hesitate or waffle. This is not rocket science – it is about you.

When you have finished saying your bit, don't sit back and tune out, mentally reviewing what you said and how it was received. Sit up and make sure you listen attentively to all of the others. Remember their names and a salient fact about each of them. A group session is about how you perform in a group, not just how you are as an individual. Make sure that not only are you listening but that you are being seen to be listening. This is not the time to hide your light under a bushel. Your objective is to be noticed for all of the right reasons. You don't want to be caught staring out of the window, doodling on your pad or fiddling with your mobile. Turn that telephone off and put it away. No secret texting or leaving your phone on silent as someone is bound to notice. You need to be in the room both physically and mentally.

> ## The Asda way
> Asda devised a hiring method design to identify people who could contribute, work as part of a team and, most importantly, provide good customer care. The job application emphasized experience with customers over formal education and included a personality questionnaire that asked a number of forced choice questions. A shortlist of candidates was brought in for a group interview. Candidates were paired off around a large table and they interviewed each other. Each candidate then introduced the person they had interviewed. The process was similar to an audition and was successful in bringing in the type of people who wanted to work in the atmosphere in Asda.

You need to be in the moment, focusing on who you are with, what they are saying, what you are saying and what else is going on in the room, either overtly or covertly. Trained assessors will probably be positioned around the room and will be taking careful notes about everything that is going on. They will be judging you not only on your own abilities but also on how you interact with others. They will be assessing every element of your interaction in this assessment centre and they will be informed of what has led up to the invitation to this final stage. They will know about your telephone manner, your letters, your e-mails and every conversation along the way. Many employers will ask the receptionist, the security man at the gate and the PAs about what you said and how you said it. Do not find out to your cost that it is not good enough to put in a splendid performance on the day. You must make sure that you do not give anyone the slightest reason to doubt you and therefore to exclude you from the process. If you are not already, become detail conscious and detail driven. Everything matters; if it helps, imagine that you are on camera all of the time, with every action and word being recorded, then this could help you stay on your guard and maintain a high level of performance throughout. Remember that however friendly people are, they are not your friends. They are professionals who are assessing your performance.

Group exercises

Every company will have their own way of putting groups together and giving them diverse tasks to see how individuals perform. The exercises you will be given will be tasks that in themselves are unimportant. It is not about the task, it is about the process and how you handle it.

An example of the kind of assessment centre exercise you might face is the Egg Task. A group of six people will be given:

- An egg
- A black plastic bin liner
- Six drinking straws
- A two-metre length of string.

You will then be given verbal instructions on how you have to find a way of dropping the egg from a height of two metres to the ground without breaking it. The instructions are deliberately not written down, as it is a test of how well you listen and take note of what you can and can't do to achieve success.

On the surface this looks like a simple challenge and it will be fun to do. You need to work out what they are looking for. It is not a test of your engineering skills and it isn't a way of giving the assessors a ten minute break.

People will be looking to see:

- How well you understood the instructions
- How well you contribute to the team effort
- Who takes the lead
- How well you communicate with each other
- How well you listen

- How the team celebrates the success or failure of the task.

Asda's assessment centres focus on getting you to participate and seeing how you communicate and interact with others. If they ask you to work in a group to design a new poster campaign for a new style of pizza, it is not to find out how creative you are. Think hard about what the purpose of the exercise might be and make sure you behave accordingly.

The two-way street

Part of the purpose of the assessment centre is to let you know more about the company that you hope to work for. They are likely to bring along colleagues who will make presentations, both formal and informal, about the role. Meal times will probably be another occasion for them to introduce new people to you and it is an opportunity to gain another insight into the organization. Use it. Remember that you are evaluating them just as much as they are evaluating you. You do not want this job at any price – you want it only if it is right for you so make sure you find out as much as you can. At the end of this session you may well be offered the job so be sure you have found out enough about it to know whether or not you want to accept it.

Personality questionnaires

Many employers also like to have further information about a candidate that can be gained via a psychometric personality questionnaire. Again there are many variations of these on the market and you are not likely to know what you are facing until you get there.

The best way to approach a personality questionnaire is openly and honestly. The information that you and the tester get out of it will be as good as the information that you put in. If you try to juggle or manipulate your responses to match what you think the test is probing, you will inevitably get it wrong and it will be obvious. The result of this is that you will look as though you have something to hide and that you are not open. The result of the questionnaire should be like looking in a mirror. It should reflect who you are so there is nothing to fear.

Whatever you do, don't:

- Offer me a print-out of a report that you have from a previous question-naire. It is irrelevant.
- Tell me that I will now find out that you are a 'psycho' – this is neither original nor amusing.
- Offer excuses at the end of the test about your headache, your lack of preparation or your late night.

Best practice states that everyone should be offered feedback after a personality questionnaire. Make sure that you make the most of this as it is an opportunity to explore who you are and what your motivations are.

How and when to follow up – be keen, not a stalker

Now that you have gone all this way through the recruitment process, you are anxiously awaiting a reply. The company may well have let you know when they will be in touch and so you know that you will hear within one week or two. All you have to do, therefore, is to wait.

However, there are some things you can do in the meantime that will make you stand out. You can send a short letter or e-mail thanking them for the interview and letting them know that you enjoyed it and that you are still interested. If you think that you failed to make an important point, then now is the time to do it. You could also send in a quick summary of the issues as you see them, thus helping reiterate the point that you are the right person for the job.

Scarcely anyone gets in touch with me after an interview. The ones I remember are those who telephone or write, letting me know that they are still there. This is a courteous and simple way of edging ahead – make yourself memorable and show your manners.

If you don't hear within the agreed timescales, then it is perfectly fine to telephone and to enquire about progress. Don't call ten times a day but equally, don't sit passively waiting for something to happen. You will impress if you are alert and aware of timescales. The silent candidates can be overlooked so be tenacious whilst striking a balance. Don't persecute and don't harass but be clear that you are keenly waiting the result.

Feedback

This is the point where you are celebrating a job offer or reading your rejection letter and wondering what you did wrong. Any self-respecting HR person or recruitment specialist will talk to you about your performance if you ask them. It is only fair that you should know why you didn't get the job as you have invested so much time and effort.

If you haven't succeeded in nailing this particular role, then regard it as a rehearsal for the real thing. The whole point of rehearsals is that they present you with an opportunity to practice and to improve. People who have seen you will be able to let you know how they have perceived you and this thoughtful consideration about how you appear to others is what will allow you to excel next time. As you have graciously given a lot of your time to the interview and the preparation beforehand, it is right that you should insist on getting real reasons why you didn't get the job. Maybe you did not have sufficient experience in which case you can shrug your shoulders and move on, as there is nothing you can do about that. However, if it was something about your impact, your research or the way that you answered questions, then this is valuable personal coaching so grab what you can.

Nadine Jones, Head of Human Resources, Baugur, says:
If the interviewer is gracious and generous enough to provide feedback – listen!
Even if you disagree, thank them for their time and ask them what they feel you could do to improve your chances of being successful next time.
Most interviewers struggle to give 'bad news' but if you genuinely feel you were a very close second, make it hard for them to forget you. Ask the recruiter to keep your details on file and contact you if the first choice candidate doesn't work out.

Listen carefully. Don't be defensive, don't argue and don't try to rewrite history. No-one is going to change their minds on this occasion so make sure you get the best help you can for the next one.

Giving feedback is a vital part of public sector recruitment and most professional recruiters take candidate feedback very seriously and are willing to talk to candidates face-to-face or on the telephone to discuss their performance and why they did not win the job.

Rachel Hannan, Director, Gatenby Sanderson, advises:

Before you rush to pick up the telephone, be cautious and reflect on what you might hear. The purpose of feedback is to give you the objective appraisal carried out by others. Only ask for it if you are prepared to listen.

Abandon defensiveness and just listen to what people think about you. This will probably be the best form of personal development when you have someone tell you how you are perceived by others. You might get some very simple tips that could help you next time. You might be told that you are too softly spoken and that you need to project yourself. You might not have sufficient eye contact; you might not have ensured that you spoke to everyone in the room. Whatever it is, this feedback will be given on the basis of observed behaviour so it will be valid. Listen to it and learn from it.

And finally ...

Patience

When you have been interviewed for a job and you are waiting to hear what the next step is, whether it is a second interview, an assessment centre or a job offer, please practise patience. I have learnt that decisions are always made in other people's timescales, not yours. One person's speedy is another person's slow. While you may be waiting for what could be the most important decision of your life, this could be just another job on a long list of priorities for someone else. If you get to this stage remember:

- Jog memories – a thank-you note; a brief e-mail reminder.
- Get the secretary, researcher or assistant on side so they will push your case.
- Don't hassle.
- Keep up your job search – do not rely on a promise. Rely on a contract of employment.

CHAPTER 6

NEGOTIATING THE BEST DEAL AND MANAGING THE JOB OFFER PROCESS

RESULT: THE RIGHT JOB WITH THE RIGHT EMPLOYER

Current package

Generally, when you are applying for a job you are asked to include details of your current basic salary, bonus and package. It is important that you should include all of the extra benefits that this could include. Remember to include the mobile telephone, the home telephone bill that is paid, lunch allowances and the laptop as well as the big issues like pension, life assurance and a particular kind of car. If you have been head-hunted, it is likely that the researcher who makes the first approach will want to know what you are earning and you will be asked to clarify this at first interview. It is fair to assume, therefore, that by the time you are at interview stage, the prospective employer knows what your current financial status is and therefore believes that they can afford to pay you.

A strong word of caution – do not be the one to initiate the discussion about the rewards package when you are being interviewed. This is a topic that needs to be driven by the interviewer. It is pointless to get embroiled into a debate about the car scheme that the company operates, or the various merits of its pension scheme if no-one ultimately is going to offer you the job. If you are pursuing a job in sales, it is perhaps to be expected that you might ask about the bonus scheme that the company operates but keep the conversation general. Your challenge at the interview stage is to get the employer to want you, not to worry about whether they can afford to pay you or to plant seeds of doubt in their mind about whether you are avaricious and only interested in the pay rather than the role. Don't look greedy, look keen.

A gentle broaching of the package is sometimes the case in first interview. A common question is 'Tell me what you are hoping to earn in this role? What kind of package would attract you?' Do not be lured into showing your hand at this stage. Don't frighten them off and don't sell yourself too cheap. Think of a general statement that would allow them to see that you are not a pushover but neither are you greedy. What about saying that you are looking to improve your current position and that a good financial basic and bonus would form part of the whole picture.

Caution!

Whatever you do, never lie about your current package. Do not be tempted to add on any amount whatsoever. When you start work the first thing you have to hand in is your P45, your record of what you were paid in the last fiscal year. The game will be up and the first impression your new employer will have you is that you tell lies.

Beware also of the trick question that is sometimes played at the end of an interview. If someone asks you, 'What are you expectations of this role and this company?' it is not about money. This is your chance to talk about other kinds of expectations, the ones that are about personal development, scope of the role, reporting structures and impact. It is not about the particular kind of car you like to drive, the intricacies of your pension scheme or other details of the package. This is not the time to be talking about money.

The job offer arrives

Job offers come in many forms. You may get a letter through the post that is an offer with a contract of employment attached. This is the fait accompli, non-negotiable, take it or leave it kind of offer. This occurs in graduate training schemes and some public sector roles where the package is cast in stone with no room for negotiation. However, generally packages are negotiated either face to face, on the telephone or via the recruitment consultant. This can be the most perilous point in the recruitment process. It can be perfectly simple as you might be so delighted with the job offer that you accept it unhesitatingly. However, if you are being considered for a sales role, you might be expected to negotiate and to improve the offer.

Nadine Jones says:

Consider the offer on the basis of the total package, not just the basic salary.

If you're accepting – be clear about your start date, any commitments to study, time off or holiday you have.

Ask about the induction: where will you be, what will you be doing, is there any reading or research you can do to get ahead?

Weighing up the offer

In order to work out what a job offer needs to be in order to get you to accept the role, you need to carry out a critical appraisal of what the new package looks like. Look at the following table and use it to help you assess the pros and cons of the package on offer. Employers offer different benefits that you may take for granted so make sure you include all of these in your calculations. For example, you may currently enjoy gym membership, a staff restaurant and flexible working hours with the opportunity to work from home. You may wish to review the company's policies on maternity/paternity leave. If you are a parent, job sharing or flexible working in school holidays might be vital. Another important factor is the distance that you have to travel to work, the amount of time you may be expected to be away from home and the possibility that you could relocate, either nationally or internationally. These may be plus or minus points for you. Whatever you consider them to be, make sure you have included them in your decision making.

	Current job	The offer
Basic		
Bonus		
Car/car allowance		
Pension		
Private health		
Holidays		
Permanent health/insurance		

Expenses policy		
Share options		
Notice period		
Any other benefits, e.g. home telephone paid, home office allowance, training, funding MBA, etc.		
Total		
Remember also … (This includes flexible working, gym membership, staff discounts, possible secondments, training possibilities, etc.)		
Career potential and promotion prospects		
Date of next salary review		

Negotiating with prospective employers

Sometimes it is the easiest thing in the world to negotiate your package. Some roles fall within a clearly delineated rewards scheme so you can see at a glance where you will sit on it. You will know all about the pension scheme and the fringe benefits so you will either accept or reject the role.

However, many jobs will bring with them the possibility of negotiating your own terms and in many situations you will be judged on your ability to sort out a good commercial deal for yourself. After all, if you are responsible for any commercial negotiations in your new role, your new employer will want to see the first example of your keen negotiations skills when you are resolving your own package. Your new employer will want to know that you have a sharp commercial edge and that you can implement it in a pleasant way without letting people feel that they have been ground into the dust by you. The best contract negotiation is one where everyone wins.

The starting point of the salary negotiation is that your prospective employer knows exactly what your current salary is or what your last salary was. This may seem that you are setting off with a disadvantage but this is not the case. By the time an employer has got to the point when they are discussing a salary package, they have made up their mind that they want you and not anyone else. The recruitment consultant has a vested interest in ensuring that the negotiations go well and the Human Resources Manager/Director needs to demonstrate their credibility to line managers by getting the deal closed. Your challenge is to work out how far you can go in the negotiations so that you strike a healthy balance between being a strong negotiator without appearing unreasonable. If you have been recruited via a recruitment consultancy or an agency, it is sometimes easier to conduct your negotiations via this third party. Someone else is negotiating on your behalf and you may prefer this position of indirect negotiation. Generally recruitment consultants are on your side; they want you to get the job as their own fee may often improve as a consequence of your higher salary. It is important to know how far you can trust them and when it is better to get involved yourself. Your future employer may not want to negotiate with you so use all your emotional intelligence to work out the way that will ensure you get the best deal you can without damaging any personal relationships.

It is important to look at the whole package and work out how it compares with your current one. Sometimes you may have to take a view on the salary and decide that you are prepared to take one step backwards in salary terms in order to move forward in career and opportunity terms. This can be an important thing to do if you are working for an organization where they reward people very well. If you are currently with a company on a high basic, an excellent bonus scheme and good fringe benefits, it is very hard to leave for something that you perceive is a better career option but with a lower salary. However, sometimes career advancement comes at a price and you may have to pay this price rather than your employer.

Overcoming obstacles

What happens if you love the company, love the job, you want to accept it but the offer is too far away from where you need to be financially to allow you to accept it? Now is the time to get creative and to resolve that you will find a solution and will make it happen. You might find that you are offered the job by someone who is prepared to think up ways to make the offer more acceptable. You may be helped by the agency or recruitment consultant if they are involved. After all, they have a strong commercial incentive to help you get over the finishing line. However, the best person to find the solution is you.

First of all, measure the gap in the salary package. Work out exactly what the offer is and exactly what it is worth to you, taking into account pension scheme, share options, longer notice period and so on, and be sure that you have a precise valuation. The career prospects, personal development and promotion may not necessarily seem to have a monetary value but they will enhance your attractiveness within this organization and any other so it is important to consider them. You may well be paid slightly more in your current role and short term it might be painful to lose income. However, remember that you are building a long-term career and you may need to move in order to get to where you want to be.

Then, think about possible ways to solve this. If the issue is that the basic salary is not enough, think about asking them to guarantee your bonus for the first year or for the rest of the financial year. In my experience this has happened a lot. Realistically it is going to take you a while to settle in your new role and so you will be lucky to hit maximum bonus in year one. An employer might not be able to increase your basic salary because of the organizational pay structure and because of what they have to pay your peers. However, a guaranteed bonus can slip effortlessly through the system.

You could also ask for a pay review to be written into your offer letter so you could have a review three or six months after starting. This would mean that you have a chance to perform brilliantly in the first 100 days and thus make it easy for someone to justify paying you more.

If you are asking for a car that is outside the company car policy, ask for a car allowance so you can negotiate your own deal and get what you want.

If you are worried about the risk of moving from a secure job where you have been for a number of years, ask for a long notice period. This way, if the job does not work out then at least you have the security of a six-month pay cheque to give you the time to find something else.

A step too far

When negotiating your package or when you have that first informal chat about your expectations for your package and your working environment, make sure that you do not plant any seeds of doubt in the employer's mind. You still haven't got the job so make sure you stay on guard. This is not the time to get into trivia and into housekeeping. Some people make the fatal error of getting into the detail of needing every second Friday afternoon off or asking how often they can work from home and what kind of mobile telephone is provided. By talking about housekeeping you are placing doubt in their minds. Do not talk yourself out of a job by getting bogged down in logistics. Keep the negotiations about the big picture and important topics, not the kind of detail that you can sort out once you have started work with them. The best person is the one who says 'yes' and who does not start finding negatives and bringing up issues that do not have any relevance at this stage. If asked whether you would accept the job if it were offered to you, say yes. Why jeopardize your position by expressing any hesitancy? Please don't say that you have to go home to discuss it with your husband, your wife or your partner. We all know that these big decisions are made by consulting people in your life so there is no need to say it. You are in danger of letting people think that you can't make a decision on your own. I am not advocating lying or messing people around. You have not yet been offered this job so keep your options open and say that you want it. Just as they can change their mind and not send out the hoped for offer letter, so you can change your mind about wanting it or not wanting it. Don't make a final decision until you are asked to. The time you will be asked to make a decision is when the offer is put to you, either verbally or in writing.

Relocation

What happens if the job you are offered means relocation? You may be absolutely adamant that you will never move from the South, the North or the Midlands. You may think that nothing could ever make you change your mind. If this is the case, recognize that you will be closing off a lot of career options. Perhaps you need to think about whether relocation is as insuperable an obstacle as you think it is. Perhaps you could maintain your main home base and arrange to stay in a rented flat during the week? Perhaps you might find that other locations have things to offer. A closed mind will restrict your job search and give the impression that you are inflexible.

If you join a company on the proviso that you need to relocate to be near head office, then you have at least six months before this becomes a reality. You need to put your house on the market and find a place to buy or to rent. This won't happen instantly unless you want it to. The first six months in any job are a probation period for you and for your employer, whether this is formally or informally recognized. This six-month period will allow you to decide how to resolve the location issue. You might find that you can work from home for part of the time and you may be able to demonstrate that you can handle the requirements of the job without relocating.

Don't close off options where you don't need to. There is always a solution but not if you refuse point blank to move.

Clare Howard, Director of e-coaches.co.uk, says:

A client of mine lived in Paris and had recently married a French lady. They were expecting a baby and were totally committed to living in Paris. Unfortunately, the telecommunications company he worked for downsized and the perfect job that he found for himself insisted on relocation to London. He agreed to move and initially commuted weekly via Eurostar. Two years later he is still commuting and he has never told his employer that he has not moved. He uses a relative's address for all of his correspondence and no one is any the wiser. He carries out his job to everyone's satisfaction and he pays for his own travel. This is a win/win solution with no fuss.

The bonus scheme

When you are negotiating, pay particular attention to the bonus scheme. I have seen more disputes and discontent arise out of misunderstandings over the bonus scheme than any other element of the package. This is a time for you to demonstrate your ability to get into detail. Be sure that you know exactly how a bonus scheme is structured. Work out exactly how much of it depends on your own personal performance and how much is driven by company results. A good question to ask is, 'How much did the bonus scheme pay out last year?' You could ask what the highest performing salesperson earned. This should give you a good sense of how much of the bonus is achievable. It also needs to be written down. If the bonus scheme is not written down, then you can expect it to change.

Company cars

Company cars are not quite the thorny issue that they used to be as the car allowance is beginning to take over, as it can be more tax effective.

However, there is nothing quite like a car to get emotions stirred up. If you are one of those people who think that a car is just a means of getting from A to B, then skip this paragraph. If, however, you think that a car is an extension of your personality, your values and your social status, then you need to make this known in a subtle way.

For some people, a car is a piece of engineering excellence. They need to have a car that has a V8 engine, 350 brake horse power and style in abundance. Not for them a Ford Mondeo – they want a BMW, an Audi A8 or a Mercedes Benz. Others may see it as a status symbol and an opportunity to show friends, relatives and the neighbours that life is on the up and up. Some people have concerns about environmental impact and may have definite views about unleaded fuel versus diesel and they want something that will minimize their carbon footprint.

Wherever you sit on the car spectrum, you will come up against the company car policy. These can be flexible and they can be rigid. Be very careful when you are discussing the car that you are not asking the impossible. Be sure to use all of your skills to be diplomatic yet assertive. Let your employer know where you stand on the car issue and know when to back off. I remember once I conducted a high level search to find a Managing Director for an engineering company. It was the job of someone's dreams as it was a role that would lead to a management buyout and potentially a huge capital profit. Everything went swimmingly. The job was offered and was accepted. The contract of employment was sent out and – disaster struck. The owner of the business would allow only his staff to drive diesel company cars – not petrol. My candidate was an engineer by background who believed that diesel impaired the performance of cars. Neither person would give way so they went their separate ways.

Reference checking

Any employer worth their salt will check your reference. The timing of this is generally after they have agreed to offer you a job. The formal offer letter to you will frame an offer that is subject to satisfactory references and a medical. In some instances, references will have been checked earlier. For instance, within the public sector, given their open way of recruiting, references will have been checked before the assessment centre.

It is unlikely that someone will send out a form by way of a reference check. This might work if you are registering with a temping agency or looking for temporary vacation employment. For a serious role in an organization, the more likely way of taking up references will be by making a telephone call. Make sure, therefore, that you think carefully about who you offer as a referee. It needs to be someone who can talk with authority and knowledge about you in the workplace. It has to be someone who knows you well and who will offer a fair reflection of your personal style and your successes. Preferably it should be someone you have worked for. It could be a customer or a supplier. It could be someone you have worked alongside. It might be someone who has worked as a consultant in your organization. It could be someone who has funded your organization so it could be a banker, a venture capitalist or even a competitor.

What it can't be is a relative, a neighbour or someone you know socially. A member of the golf club might be able to testify to your ability to manage an adept golf swing but this is not what it is about. This referee will be backing up your account of who you say you are and what you said you have achieved. They will be describing your style and your successes. Make sure, therefore, that they know what the job is that they are supplying a reference for so that they focus on the right areas of your experience and your achievements.

Before you even consider offering someone's name as a referee, make sure you have asked their permission. Even if someone has given open permission to use their name anytime as a referee, afford them the courtesy of a call or an e-mail to check that it is still OK. This can be your opportunity to give them some subtle coaching on what you want them to say. An e-mail would allow you to attach the job description and a synopsis of what you think you will be bringing to the job. That will focus the referee's mind on the areas that are important to you.

Ready for the medical?

If you know you are likely to have a medical for your new job, consider long in advance what you might be facing. A lot can be achieved in a few weeks so you can start a fitness regime, start visiting the gym and cut down on alcohol intake. Then, when you are asked what your weekly consumption of alcohol is, you can look the doctor squarely in the eye and not lie. You can begin a healthy eating programme and you can start to make different choices about how you live your life so that you reduce the risk of flagging up potential health problems at a medical. If you think you have high blood pressure then you can take steps to reduce it. If you are overweight you can start a diet or fitness regime. Remember you are duty bound to disclose medical conditions that may influence job performance or safety at work.

If you have some illness that a potential employer might be worried about, it probably would be better to discuss this during the interview process. If, for example, you have just had a triple heart by-pass operation, then make sure that you mention it, probably fairly late in the process, and emphasize how well you are and how your life has been transformed for the better. It will come out during the medical so it is better to disclose something yourself than have it appear in some medical report. In my experience, employers are likely to take a pragmatic view of any disclosed health issues. The ones they worry about are the ones that pop up unexpectedly in the course of the company medical.

Your new notice period

Your notice period is your security. If your new job doesn't work out and you decide to leave or, worse still, you are asked to leave, the notice period you have agreed to will cushion the impact of the lack of salary. If your role is made redundant, then the longer the notice period, the bigger the cheque.

Whatever you do, focus on this notice period and get it for as long as possible. Some people regard it as shackles but I see it as something that will add financial security at a time when you might be job hunting. If you are offered a month's notice, go for three months. Often, you will be leaving a company where you have spent some years and you will have the financial security that goes with it. Any career move is a risk so reduce the potential impact of that risk with a long notice.

The contract of employment

When the contract of employment arrives, it should very much be in line with what you have already discussed.

Any lawyer will tell you to read it carefully and know what you are signing. Make sure that it contains every element of your discussions and that nothing is left out. Check that the bonus scheme is included, as are the company policy on reclaiming expenses and the details on the pension scheme.

An important area to look at is the restrictive covenant or the clauses with regard to working with a competitor. A German company I know ensures that all employees sign a bar out clause, forbidding them to work for a competitor after leaving the organization until two full years have elapsed. This is possibly unlawful and, if it were challenged in a court of law, would probably be overruled. However, it is unlikely that a prospective employer will be happy to begin their employment with you by embarking on a court case. Equally, you are going to be the one sitting at home with your career on hold while the battle takes place in a courtroom. Avoid this by ensuring that the clauses you sign up to are reasonable and enforceable.

If you have any doubts about your contract, take it to an employment law specialist to have it checked out. A small investment will give you the reassurance that you can sign the document with confidence.

How to resign

You may be working in an environment where your boss or your team knows you are actively job seeking so it will be no great surprise when you announce your resignation and your imminent departure. However, generally, it is going to be a bit of a bolt from the blue so it needs to be handled properly. Don't do what a researcher did to me once: she announced her resignation via mobile telephone when I was driving in the fast lane of the M1 on a Friday night. There is a time and a place for everything. It is better to delay the time of your resignation and to do it properly than to announce it in the wrong circumstances.

If possible do it face to face rather than by letter as this is the most courageous and courteous way to face it. Always have a formal letter written, as this is required under the terms of your contract of employment. If you can't do it in person, do it by telephone and only if you have to, post a letter or e-mail. Texting is just not an option, no matter what the job and what the level of disgust you may have with your current employer. There is a proper form to follow so make sure you do the right thing.

Once you have delivered your bombshell, be prepared for a full range of emotions. It is nice to think that when you resign there may be some overt signs of alarm, upset or concern. You want your current employer to wonder how on earth they are going to manage without you. The last thing you are looking for when you resign is the cheerful and blasé acceptance of your resignation letter with a carefree smile and a cheery wave as you close the door behind you. You don't want the reassurance that you can leave straightaway without working your notice and that it is absolutely not a problem that you are going. Recognition that you have been doing a good job is when your resignation is met with upset, disappointment, frustration or even anger. You can expect to come up against the full range of emotions so be prepared for the lot.

Whatever the reaction of your boss, it is good to walk away and let them think about the implications. The initial reaction that they are going to hold you to every minute of your notice is an extreme position that may change once they have reflected and come up with solutions to cover your departure. An Export Sales Manager I once head-hunted helpfully found a replacement for himself in order to facilitate his own departure and make life easy for his current employer. Helping them out to this extent may be impossible but you may wish to offer solutions to cover the gap that you will leave. You may wish to suggest promoting someone or transferring someone from another department or perhaps a restructure that could take out your job and provide cost savings for the company. Be helpful wherever possible. Be patient and wait to see what happens. Don't walk out and don't renege on your notice period. Leave a company right and join it right. You will not impress your new employer if you walk out on your old one.

Coping with the counter offer

The most dangerous response to your resignation is the counter offer. This will be when, having accepted your resignation, your boss decides to try to buy you back. They will have evaluated the damage that will be done to the company through your departure and they have decided that they don't want you to go. They will have found out why you are leaving, who you are joining, what new role you will have and how much you will be earning. They will be alarmed that another company or a competitor finds you so attractive and they will wonder why they have not promoted you themselves. They may do a cynical calculation of the cost of recruiting a replacement, taking into account the cost of advertising, a recruitment agency fee, the management time needed and the effect of the gap in the organization while they are looking. The answer to that question, as well as their dismay at seeing you leave, may lead them to make a counter offer.

Although it is very flattering to be the centre of this attention, with everyone suddenly interested in your career and your future, maybe you should ask yourself why it has taken something as dramatic as a resignation to bring it all about. If your current employer had been doing their job properly, you would have had regular appraisals, both formal and informal, where you would have had the chance to express any concerns or frustrations that led you to job hunt elsewhere. These concerns were what led you to respond to the advertisement, look around on the Internet, listen to the head-hunter or make a telephone call to a friend. Your vulnerability to another job offer was caused by a gap, whatever it was, in your current role. Maybe you did not articulate your concerns strongly enough or maybe you were ignored. However it came about, you may now be in a situation where you are feeling guilty and disloyal as you have discussed the company's inadequacies with someone else and agreed to leave them.

An astute employer will assess your excellent qualities and, having measured the cost to the business of replacing you, will form a deadly strategy. The pragmatic solution is to buy you back. The counter offer will at least equal your new package and will probably better it.

So, now what are you going to do? You may well have decided to leave because you felt unappreciated, underpaid or insufficiently challenged. Now that the boss has come up with solutions to all of these issues, you face a bit of a problem. At face value, you no longer have a reason to move. But wait a minute – think about what you had to do to wangle this radically new package and these new responsibilities out of them. You had to take them to the brink and threaten to leave. However earnest and reassuring they may appear in their conversations with you now, I bet I can picture what is going on behind closed doors and behind your back – and it won't be complimentary. Your resignation will have caused a nasty shock, causing tremors in the normally serene echelons of senior management. A well-known characteristic of senior management is that they don't like the tranquillity of their lives disturbed by rebellion in the ranks. Remember, therefore, when considering whether or not to accept this counter offer to work out if, once the dust has settled, you will be as valued as you were before. Maybe it will work to your advantage and you will be valued more than you were before. You have demonstrated with a tangible job offer that you have a good market attraction and other people want you. This could lead to you commanding more respect in the future and having a stronger voice in the team.

On the other hand, you have sown a seed of doubt in the mind of your boss. He or she will have been mulling over your activities during the previous weeks, trying to work out when you went for the job interviews. A fundamental element in your working relationship – trust – may have been damaged and have you worked out what you can do to repair it?

Take time to reflect on exactly what it was about your new job that attracted you so much. Focus on why you went so far as to accept the job offer in the first place. There is not necessarily a right or a wrong decision about this agonizing career crossroads. The right answer may only become apparent with the benefit of hindsight. Remember why you were prepared to be so brave and to take a risk in a new sector or new role. The secure, the known, the tried and the tested are very seductive but are you just nestling down again in the fur-lined rut?

Accepting counter offers is a high risk strategy. You run the risk of offending people all around you. You stand to lose face with all of the people you have told about your new and exacting role. You are also sending a clear message that, despite everything you said about seeking new challenges and wanting to test yourself in a different environment, it was actually only about securing a better financial package. Your card will be marked by everyone involved in the process and the doors that opened so welcomingly to you in the recruitment consultancies and in the new company may be firmly closed forever.

Turning down the offer

Just as your future employer has the choice whether or not to offer the job to you, you have the choice to accept it or reject it. During the interviewing process you should have found out enough about the organization to know whether or not it is the right one for you. A word of caution – if in doubt, then don't do it. If you have a number of options and you are waiting for more interviews or the results of more applications, you may want to be brave and to decide to turn the offer down. If you are short of cash and getting seriously worried about the financial survival of you and your family, then you may have to take a pragmatic decision and decide to ignore your misgivings and take the job.

If you do have time on your side, never ignore your intuition. If you have a doubt now, then the danger is that you will prove yourself to be right as time goes by. You don't want to have a CV that gives the impression that you are a job hopper. Having said that, most people at some point in their lives make a career mistake and learn more from that mistake than they ever did from the jobs that went brilliantly. Balancing the willingness to take a risk to advance your career and the need not to throw caution to the wind and end up in a mess is a difficult one to manage. The more information you have, the better the outcome will be.

Nadine Jones, Head of Human Resources, Baugur, says:
If you're declining an offer do it swiftly and graciously – you never know when you will come across the recruiter again or under what circumstances.

If you decide that you don't want to accept the job, be candid and upfront with the recruiter or the employer. Tell them why you are turning it down and be gracious. This will give them an option to resolve the reservations you had or to offer the job to someone else. Resist the temptation to play games and to keep them hanging on. All recruiters have come across this tactic before and they will know immediately that you are either having second thoughts or you are waiting for the results of another application. You could tell them the truth and let them know that you have another offer coming through. People respect the truth and you will not do yourself any favours by trying to play one off against the other.

A candidate I had was once offered a job with a prestigious multinational. The role was based in Hong Kong and during the interview process the candidate and his wife visited Hong Kong twice, once for an interview and the second time for a fact finding and house-hunting trip. He accepted the job and resigned. The client broke all of its normal rules and signed a three-year lease on a house that the candidate's wife had set her heart on. During the notice period, the candidate accepted a counter offer from his current company and just disappeared from sight. He did not return any telephone calls, did not respond to letters or e-mails. The client was left with an expensive house that no-one else wanted and the candidate had achieved a marvellous promotion and huge hike in his salary. However, he must look back with shame at his behaviour and will have trouble ever moving from this company as the tale spread throughout the head-hunting community.

Managing the start date

A key question you will be asked during the interview process is about your current notice period. The more available you are, the more attractive you are. However, this is directly in conflict with the advice that it is usually better to seek a job from a position of employment where inevitably you will be tied to some kind of notice period.

When asked at interview what your notice period will be in practice, the best position to take is a firm one that the maximum time will be whatever it is that you are contractually held to, whether it be a month, three months, six months or longer. However, you can point out that you will do whatever you can to negotiate with your employer to shorten it. Point out that it is important to leave your current employer on the best possible terms and to act properly and professionally. You must be clear that however eager you might be to start your new challenge, you would not dream of leaving your current company in the lurch. Although your new boss will be impatient for you to start, there will be recognition that this is appropriate behaviour. It will reassure people that you are full of integrity and someone to be trusted.

It might be easy to convince your boss to let you leave early. They may decide to let you go immediately. They may insist on a full period of 'gardening leave', holding you to your notice period by stopping you from working but paying you your salary. This means that you will be in some kind of limbo, not working for anyone and waiting for your contractual notice period to elapse. They may also ask you to work up to the very last minute of your notice period. Contractually they are entitled to do so and in theory they probably will. In practice, however, it is possible to influence the leaving date. Psychologically if not physically, you left the business when you resigned and your boss knows it. Allow a few days to go by and then approach your boss again. You could suggest establishing certain goals, targets, projects and milestones that you could achieve and agree that you can leave the business once this has been done. By setting the achievement of tangible results against a revised leaving date, you will be demonstrating your commitment and determination to leave matters in good order. This will strike a positive chord with most reasonable people. Although it is not unheard of for people to be kept to their full notice period, it is unusual. Insistence on contractual rights with regards to notice periods can be a cause of frustration and resentment so employers need to think carefully before they insist upon exercising their rights.

Certain professions have developed their own protocols and standards for behaviour in resignation. Teachers generally accept that anything less than a full term's notice is unreasonable. Public sector has a more open attitude to external recruitment. It is perfectly acceptable in many areas of the public sector to declare your candidacy for other roles. You don't need to worry about your employer finding out in the same way that people in the private sector have to do, taking days' holidays or meeting after work in order to disguise their job-seeking activities. The disadvantage for public sector employees is that this openness is matched often by an insistence and expectation that you will work your full notice period.

Whatever your situation is, make sure that you do not allow short-term expediency to overshadow the long-term need to maintain good business relationships. It is likely that you will meet former employers again so be sure that you can meet them with your head held high.

CHAPTER 7

TECHNIQUES TO HELP YOU MAKE THE BEST OF WHO YOU ARE

RESULT: MORE POWERFUL COMMUNICATION

Work out who you are: logical levels

If you are feeling uneasy about your life or slightly uncomfortable about how you are living, if you feel unsettled and wonder whether life could hold more for you, then you need to consider everything that is happening around you, not just the job that you are doing.

Let's look at one way of structuring your thinking to allow you to examine where you are in life and what is important to you. Robert Dilts, a Californian psychologist, has built a simple model for thinking about personal change. It is known as neurological levels of learning, or logical levels. It is a model that asks you specific questions about six vital elements of your life that all contribute to your sense of purpose. People who have a strong sense of purpose in their life are driven by their passionate beliefs and have certainty about their direction. This is how you tune into your mission, your vision, your connection with the universe and the true meaning of life. Work out what that is and you won't have any problem working out what your most fulfilling job will be.

Use this model of logical levels to work towards defining your own purpose. Decide where you need to make changes to make sure you are pursuing the right career. It will give you the self-confidence that you know who you are and that the changes you are making are the right ones in your life.

The first logical level: environment

This is your physical context where you are living, working, interacting and behaving. It is the country you are in, the climate you are experiencing, the building you work in, the house you live in, the context you operate in and the team you are part of.

Ask yourself some of the following questions:

- Are you working in the right country, region, town or place? Is it where you like to be?
- What kind of work environment suits you best? In a big office surrounded by people? Operating from home and only visiting the office occasionally?
- Does the routine or pattern of your job mean that you are too structured in what you do or not sufficiently structured?
- How well does your home suit your work life and vice versa? Do you have a big commute? Is your commute too short?
- How many hours a week do you work on average? Are they out of balance or are they right?
- What are the external influences that impact on your daily life?

You might be living and working in the perfect place and you may decide that you want to protect this at any price. You may decide that you are in the wrong location and that now is the time to change it. Perhaps you have moved to a job where you are spending time in a home office and you miss the companionship and stimulation from interaction with colleagues. Maybe it is the other way round and you need the thinking time and reflection that a home office brings you. Whatever it is, decide now what is important to you and let it form the starting point of your decisions.

The second logical level: behaviour

This describes the specific actions or reactions that occur in your environment. It is not what you are capable of doing. It is what you actually do. It answers the question, 'What am I doing?'

So what is it that you are doing? Ask yourself some of the following questions:

- Are you enjoying life and doing interesting and enjoyable things?

- Do you leap out of bed, glad to know that you are going to be doing all of the things that lie ahead of you?
- Are you surrounded by people with whom you have a lot in common?
- Do you do the things that are important to you? This could be, for example, sport, music, reading, travel, making new friends, cooking, gardening or voluntary work. In the work context, it can be focusing on matters that are important to you and playing to your strengths. It could be selling the right product, meeting the right kind of customers and working with people you respect.
- Do you spend your time doing things that you would rather not? For example, avoiding issues that you know are important, smoking, leading an unhealthy lifestyle or doing what others want rather than what you want?

Think about how you spend your time, what you do and what you don't do, who you talk to and spend time with and who you don't meet and spend time with. Think about where you put your energy and decide if it is where you want it to be. If you find there are gaps between what you do and what you would like to do, work out what they are and decide on a strategy for change.

The third logical level: capabilities

This is what you are good at. These are the natural talents and skills that you have and the things that you know instinctively how to do. Not everyone has what you have and these talents and skills go towards making you who you are. When you are being interviewed for a job, part of the assessment process will focus on whether or not you have the skills and knowledge for the job. However, far and away the most important part of this will be your attitude. You may not have the specific skills needed, you might not have the technical knowledge, the language skills, the degree or the track record of already knowing something, but if you can show that you are fired up to learn and to develop, giving yourself the technical competence for the job, then you will be looked on favourably. You can learn anything and you can always learn capabilities.

Ask yourself some of the following questions:

- What are you particularly good at? Do you use these skills at the moment in your current role?

- What don't you know that would be particularly helpful in this job or the one you aspire to?
- What talents do you have that you think are lying dormant?
- What would you love to learn about or love to learn to do?
- Could a good friend/colleague tell you what they think you are good at?

This should be the easiest part of change for you. If you are sufficiently motivated and if you want it enough, you can learn to do anything. Many people move to France or Spain to start a new life, following their dream, and never ever get to grips with the language, probably telling themselves that they were useless at languages at school and therefore they just can't do it. Abandon all such limiting beliefs and find the right route to get the skills you need. If you left school and decided not to go to university, and you now find that this lack of a degree is holding you back, get yourself on a degree course through the Open University or your local college. There is no excuse in these days of flexible learning not to get what you need.

If you find that you are competing with people who have MBAs and you don't have one, then work out how you can find the 12 hours a week you will need to do such a course and commit to doing one. If your computer skills are nothing like anyone else's in the office, sign up for an online course, an evening class or a weekend course.

Learning what you need in order to progress will improve your self-confidence and it will enhance your marketability. Don't set off with a disadvantage when you could be doing something to improve it.

Maybe you would be happier in your work life if you were spending your spare time doing something that you were enthusiastic about and you felt was developing another side of you. Bring more balance into the 'work' you and the 'home' you by growing other talents that have no relevance to your work life. If you have ever wanted to become a great tennis player, bridge player, artist, chef, golfer, allotment owner, flower arranger, therapist, counsellor, acupuncturist, Samaritan, gardener, then now is the time to start.

The fourth logical level: beliefs and values

Beliefs and values are what direct and guide your life, often at an unconscious level. Ask yourself some of the following questions:

- Why do you do something?

- What do you believe in or value?
- What do you believe to be true about yourself and the way that you live and behave?
- What are the core values that you hold most dear and are an essential part of the way that you run your life?
- How do these match the organization that you are currently working in?

If you feel a sense of unease in your organization, is it because there is a conflict with your own beliefs and values? In order to be motivated to perform well, you need to be sure that they are in alignment. The beliefs and values of an organization form its corporate culture.

As a high performing individual you may find that your performance dips if you are in an organization where you don't find yourself in alignment with their values. If, for example, you are working in a company where their sole focus is profit at the expense of the customer, you may feel uneasy and this will impact on your performance and your confidence. You may have strong views on the environment, global warming or corporate social responsibility and these may be being ignored. You may find yourself in a company where the staff are not being treated in a way that you think is appropriate. This all creates conflict and will mean that you are at odds with others and with yourself. Use the table overleaf to help you define your values and beliefs and then define those within your company. Work out what you would like them to be and see what you can do to narrow the gap. A few examples follow to get you started on what you might want to be thinking about:

Your value or belief	Your company's value or belief	Your ideal company's value or belief	Ways to narrow the gap
Example 1 Integrity is everything.	Always maximize profit.	Whilst it is vital to be commercially aware and always to maximize profit, make sure that it is not at the price of integrity.	Lead by example. Demonstrate by the way in which you act and the way that you manage that integrity enhances reputations and ultimately long-term rewards.
Example 2 Environmental awareness is an essential part of every company's strategy.	Environmental policies are costly so we will only pay lip service.	Global warming is one of the major issues facing the world and our company will play its part to bring about change.	Start initiatives in the organization that show how to make a difference at no cost. Involve colleagues and make things happen through your own efforts. Be a leader.
Example 3 It is important to make sure the organization plays a part in the local community.	Always maintain focus on core business.	The company is successful partly because of the local communities in which it is based and therefore will play an active role within them.	Begin to forge links with schools, colleges and form relationships with them. Encourage a switch to local suppliers. Get marketing to allocate some of the budget to local charities. Sign up for local charity and sporting events.

Your value or belief	Your company's value or belief	Your ideal company's value or belief	Ways to narrow the gap
Example 4 The customer always comes first.	Profit always comes first.	The focus of our business is our customer and everything follows on from that.	Decide where change could happen with customers and begin to introduce small changes yourself. Train your team to act differently. Take small steps rather than radical change and see what a difference it makes. Show practical examples of success.
Example 5 Flexible working and job sharing is important to me and will be more so in the years to come.	Staff need to operate from the office and to work standard office hours.	So long as employees add value through their contribution, where and how they do it is not the first consideration.	Work with Human Resources to develop a policy of flexible working. Show how this would increase the work output and value of contribution rather than diminish it.

Your value or belief	Your company's value or belief	Your ideal company's value or belief	Ways to narrow the gap
Now over to you!			
1.			
2.			
3.			
4.			
5.			

The fifth logical level: identity

This is about who you think you are. You may express it through your values, beliefs, capabilities, behaviours and your environment but you are always more than this. Your behaviour and your identity are separate as behaviour is a not a reflection of who you are, it is just what you said or did at that particular juncture.

Ask yourself some of the following questions:

- What kind of person do you think you are?
- Who do other people think you are?
- What 'labels' do other people put on you?
- Do you agree with other people's views?
- How would you like to be described?
- What kind of person would you like to be?
- Are you who you want to be or what other people want you to be?

A strong sense of who you are will give you the confidence to make the career change that you need. If, for example, you see yourself as a successful person, then it is very possible that you would hold the belief that you can easily get another job or even create a business of your own. Find out what you truly believe about yourself. If you find that negatives are sneaking in, take steps to change such an unhelpful belief that could be holding you back.

The sixth logical level: purpose

You have now reached the level where you are questioning the meaning of life. You are now entering the realms of vision, mission, spirituality and the whole purpose of your existence.

Ask yourself some of the following questions:

- What are your personal skills that you can add to the universe and the world around you?
- What is your contribution now and what would you like it to be?
- What would you like your epitaph to be?
- What would you like to be remembered for?

Making change the only constant – embrace it!

Once you have thought about these overwhelming questions, you can decide whether your current life plan is taking you on the track where you want to be. Are you going in the right direction or do you need to change something?

The whole model of logical levels works by recognizing that as soon you implement change at one of the levels, it will impact on the next. Albert Einstein said, 'The problems of today can only be solved at a higher level of thinking than that which created them'. This can be achieved through this way of thinking. If, for example, you have a problem at the Environment level, you can only change by moving up to the Behaviour level and taking action to solve the Environment issue.

By asking yourself these types of questions you will challenge how you think about yourself and will be able to bring about change. The only way that you will find a more rewarding role is if you embrace change, facing the risks that this brings with it and accepting that staying the same is simply not an option.

Self-image – silencing the negative voice

How you think about yourself and therefore how you project yourself to others will have a significant impact on your job search.

Clare Howard, Director of e-coaches.co.uk, says:
During our lives, each of us builds up an image of ourselves – a picture based largely on the feedback we received from other people as we grew up. Parents or carers, siblings, teachers and friends have all had some input, giving us some idea of the way others see us and the ways in which we relate to other people in different circumstances.

Once we are grown up we carry on maturing and developing, but we no longer receive the same amount of direct feedback. As a result we can be left with an outdated and inaccurate image of ourselves. The voices of people in our past repeat themselves in our minds, affecting the way we feel and the way we think, as well as dictating fundamental and sometimes unhelpful beliefs.

The following activity is intended as a first step in reappraising your self-image and will help you to begin the process of becoming more aware of your current self and the influences upon you. To gain maximum benefit from this exercise, plan to spend an initial half-hour on it, and then take odd moments over a few weeks reflecting on what you have discovered. If possible, talk to colleagues, friends and relatives to help you tease out and clarify an up-to-date picture of today's you. You are probably aware sometimes of conflicting thoughts and feelings voicing themselves in your head. Often, these are contradictory, a positive and a negative. These internal conversations are often based on messages we received as children and we have stored them in our memories at a very deep level. Normally, we are not aware that they are there, or we may not realize where they come from. Sometimes we speak them aloud, for example, 'Pull yourself together!', 'Why are you so stupid?' or, 'You're a genius'.

These 'voices' express some of your self-image and are largely based on childhood messages. Spend some time thinking about the messages – positive and negative – that you received during your childhood. Who gave you these messages? What words did they use? Do they stand the test of time? Are they still relevant or are they outdated and wide of the mark? What messages could you replace them with to make the picture of yourself more realistic? Now in the space provided make a note of some of the old negative messages that have influenced you and possibly hindered you in developing yourself and your career. Think of examples from work and from your private life. Then, in the positive voices column, list some of the useful messages that have stayed with you, again from work and private life. Also list useful positive messages that you may not yet have heard, but would very much like to hear.

Negative voices	Positive voices

Exercise to develop the positive voice:

Think about any negative statements that you tend to tell yourself. They may be statements like:

- 'I am not confident.'
- 'I am not very good with people.'
- 'I don't seem to win as much business as others.'
- 'I don't know how to deal with the financial aspects of the business.'

For each of these suggestions that you give yourself, invent positive reverse statements:

- 'Confidence comes naturally to me.'
- 'I can build good relationships with people.'
- 'I have won some excellent customer accounts.'
- 'I can develop my financial skills to supplement the other strengths that I have.'

Keep on giving these positive suggestions to yourself in the new, more confident inner voice that you have in place of the old, hesitant one.

Exercise to silence the negative voice

If, at any time in the future, you find that you are talking negatively to yourself, try the following techniques:

- Take a deep breath and stop.
- Repeat all the positive suggestions in your mind three times.
- Keep doing this until it becomes an established habit.

Develop this technique in order to believe in this new positive internal voice and the negative suggestions will no longer affect you. Practise these steps every day until the negative voice is quashed.

Manage your own development

Part of the success in achieving a high-flying and satisfying career is making sure that you keep growing as a person, developing the skills and the knowledge that will keep you from settling into a rut that might be quite comfortable at the moment but will not last forever. It is not possible to sidestep the responsibility for this and put it on the shoulders of an employer or the Human Resources department of your organization. They may be supportive but the person driving this change has to be you. Having accepted that change is a constant part of working life, part of that change must embrace personal change. If you remain the same, you may find that the world will rush past without you. Change happens at every level, whether you work inside an organization, in the public sector, in a small business, or for yourself.

Clare Howard, Director of e-coaches.co.uk, says:

By managing your own development you will be managing your own performance, ensuring that you add value to – and are valued by – your colleagues and your chosen business. It also means you are always ready and in control when you want to change jobs, or when change is forced upon you.

Successful, self-managed development involves:

- Identifying your current strengths and development needs, as well as identifying your focus for development, based on a mix between business priorities and your personal priorities.
- Choosing development activities, e.g. training, on-the-job activities, reading, etc. to meet your specific needs.
- Developing yourself in your current role and preparing yourself for future roles you might undertake.
- Deciding for yourself how much development you want to commit to. This will depend on the direction you want your career to take and how it fits in with other important aspects of your life, such as family and leisure activities.
- Setting challenging but realistic goals and being clear about what you expect to gain from any development activity you embark on.
- Constructing your own personal development plan and setting up the right support to ensure that you achieve your goals.

At the core of a self-managed development approach to your career is a focus on continuously improving yourself and your skills. It is about planning your current development and preparing you for the future. It is about taking decisions about your development at work, whilst also considering these in the context of your life goals, both at work and socially. Underpinning your development, therefore, must be an understanding of yourself as an individual.

You have the greatest vested interest in your own development and therefore have to take responsibility for making it work.

Self-managed development is for you if you want to:

- Meet the challenges of a rapidly changing world by taking control of your own development
- Review your current approach to professional and personal development (whole person, whole life)
- Commit to developing your skills in partnership with the opportunities available through your employer, educational providers, television and Internet, and the community.

An excellent starting point in your personal development plan would be to:

- Undertake a personal audit of your current skills, motivations, values and preferences
- Identify aspects of your present skill portfolio that will need to change to meet the future demands of the working world
- Explore the best ways of negotiating support from your organization, or other network sources of support
- Produce a robust personal development plan to address your ongoing development needs.

Development as a way of life

While you are working through your Personal Development Plan you will continue to analyse your skills, reassess your goals and consider suitable learning activities. You may have more than one plan running at the same time, handling different aspects of your personal and professional life.

Clare Howard, Director of e-coaches.co.uk, says:
It never stops. Development is not something you do once or twice in a lifetime. You do it all the time. It is a way of thinking and a way of life.

Career changing – setting the goals

Sometimes the hardest part of being in a job that you don't like, or being out of work and job-seeking, is the feeling that you lack any control over the situation. You might feel that there is nothing you can do to change the situation and therefore you lack the power to control your own life. It might be that you can't get a promotion or you feel trapped in a job that you have been doing forever. You might have been job hunting for six months and feel that there is nothing more you can do to increase your job opportunities.

As soon as you slip into this frame of mind, you create your own lack of success. How much more powerful would it be if you decided that you are in charge of your own destiny and you control what happens in your own life? In order for this to happen, you need to decide that you are not a victim, that you choose your response to what happens to you. No-one else has control over your life – only you. You might not be able to control what happens to you in life but you can control how you respond to those events.

Instead of dwelling on the problems that you are experiencing with your job or your job search, change your focus so that instead you are thinking about what you positively want. You need to establish your goals and where you want to get to and before you do that, you need to work out what you want from a job. Don't waste your energy reflecting on what you don't want. Spend time concentrating on the critical qualities of your perfect job. Make a conscious effort to shift from a negative to a positive.

Use the following chart to list what is important to you:

Critical qualities	What I have now	What I want
Responsibilities: 1. 2. 3. 4. 5. 6. 7. 8. 9. 10.		

Location		
Colleagues		
Training		
Salary		
Value		
Influence		
Appreciation		
Product		
Technology		
Attitudes		
Working environment		
What else? 1. 2. 3. 4. 5.		

Now that you know what you want from a job, design a goal to make it achievable.

Make sure that the goal is SMART, that is to say:

S = specific
M = measurable
A = achievable
R = realistic
T = timed.

Using the SMART method means that you won't set yourself a goal that is unachievable either in its aspiration, execution or its timescale. There is no point in saying that you will be the managing director of an organization within two years if it is your first job after university. However, you could say that you will achieve at least one promotion a year – that is possible and feasible.

In order to test how robust your goals are, ask yourself the following questions:

1. Is the goal stated in the positive?

Rather than saying 'I don't want to be working in this company in 12 months' time', it is better to say, 'Within 12 months I want to be working in a privately-owned organization that has a high-profile brand and aspirations to increase its turnover exponentially'. You need to be as clear and as precise as possible in order to have the right focus and direction. 'Earning lots of money' won't do – but stating percentage increases will be sufficiently specific.

2. Is it yours and is it within your control?

This goal has to be yours and no-one else's. It cannot depend on someone else for you to achieve it. It must come from within you and not be something that someone else wants for you. It must lie within your sphere of influence and be something that you can do without relying on other people.

3. Is its context defined clearly?

This means that you need to have gone into the kind of detail that challenges your thinking so that you have total clarity about where, how, how much and with whom.

4. Does it identify what you need to do and what you need to have in order to get there?

Now you need to reflect on what extra skills, funds, support, beliefs and attitudes you might need in order to achieve your goal.

5. Does it fit with who you are and with your values and beliefs?

Make sure that what you decide fits with all aspects of your life and who you know you are. There is no point in setting a goal to find a job with international dimensions and lots of travel if you know that it is important for you to spend lots of time with your family.

6. Does it identify the first step that you need to take?

The first step is the most important one so decide on the first things that you are going to do. You might decide to draft a CV, join a club, enrol for a language course or telephone a few friends to ask their advice. Whatever it is, it will ensure that you begin to gather the momentum to arrive at your goal.

Finally, make sure that you maintain your level of self-belief. Change rests in your control and you know you can get there.

Luck and your job

How about making up your mind to have luck in the job search? You would rather be a lucky job hunter than an unlucky one, so what can you do to become lucky? Heather Summers and I have strong views on this topic, as you might expect, so before you begin, visit www.switchtosuccess.co.uk and do the Luck Questionnaire. The results of this questionnaire will flag up the qualities of a lucky person and show how lucky you seem to be at the moment. Accepting the premise that luck lies within your control, now is the time to change your mindset to that of a lucky person. How does this work on a practical basis?

Heather Summers, Director, Work Magic Ltd, says:

Let's say that you have been made redundant and you've already been rejected for a dozen jobs. You've just been rejected again – this time for a post you really wanted and felt you could add value to. The lucky person will be able to look at this event in a positive light. They will see it as an opportunity to learn, a platform for future job applications, the chance to ask for useful feedback and they will view the interview itself as useful practice in honing their interview skills. They are likely to conclude that things worked out for the best, as clearly this job was not meant for them and that there will be something better round the corner.

Result? *More motivation and determination to succeed.*

The unlucky person will see this situation as a personal rejection. They will conclude (again) that it's going to be hard or impossible to get the job they want and that the world is against them.

Result? *A decrease in motivation, feelings of despondency and powerlessness.*

Which would you rather be – lucky or unlucky? The choice is yours. Even if you are one of those who naturally find it hard to see the upside of difficult situations, you can practise this skill by regularly asking yourself the following questions:

- What's good about this situation?
- What could be good about it?
- Looking back on this situation from the future, what might be good about it in retrospect?
- What is/could have been worse about this?
- What are all the good things in my life that I am grateful for? Make a list and refer to it any time the going is tough.

Happiness and your job

Research has shown that the most powerful source of happiness is human contact, whether this is with friends, family, colleagues or closer relationships. If you are not as happy as you might be in your current role, have you considered how you have the power to change that status within your company? You can do this in a number of ways, including forging new alliances with colleagues in your company. If you are dissatisfied with the way the job is going, it is highly probable that others will share your feelings. Sometimes moving jobs seems easier than resolving the issues that you face inside your company. Once you have clearly defined what it is that is causing you to hunt for another job, decide whether it is something that is impossible to fix. If you don't get on with your boss or if your career path is blocked with no possibility of promotion and personal development, then you have to move.

If the issue is something that could be fixed, such as wanting more responsibilities or a higher salary or more personal development, then perhaps this could be achieved if you talk to your boss. If the issue is about working conditions and the environment or a clash of values, consider talking to colleagues and getting someone else's view on the topic. If you are all agreed on the need for change, then you will be more likely to achieve it if you act together.

Work is an important part of what constitutes your happiness. It is also important to have excellent relationships, good health and sufficient money to do what you want. In your pursuit for the perfect role, measure the impact that it will have on your life as a whole.

Visualizing your perfect role

While it is important to form and follow your strategy to achieve the perfect job, writing brilliant CVs, composing stunning letters and performing brilliantly in the interviews you have orchestrated through your own powerful networking, you can always use other methods to assist you. After all, the power of the mind is more powerful than the body so use your imagination, the power of your unconscious mind and your belief in your ability to create your own future to aid your search.

Add into this a simple visualization exercise and your job hunt will be more rounded and complete.

1   Find a quiet place where you won't be disturbed and cause alarm to those who know you. This is not something to do in the middle of the office or the pub.

2   Start by dreaming about that perfect job that you are looking for. Think about where it is, which company it is in and what role you will have. You have already defined what it is that you want so use your imagination to build up a clear picture of where it is. Imagine the building, the office, the desk, the business card in the company branding with your name on it and see your colleagues in the office.

3   Now, having created this clear picture of the role, imagine floating out of your body and into the future to a time when you have achieved this role and secured the job.

4   Notice the pictures, the sounds and the colours that you can see. Bring them into sharper focus and make them even clearer. Having done that, make them even sharper and brighter.

5   From that place in the future, turn and look back to now and let your unconscious mind notice what it needs to know so as to help you to achieve that goal. Notice what the steps are that you need to take in order to get there.

6   Spend time focusing on that dream and remember what you have to do to get there.

How to get help from others

The job hunting process can be a lonely process and you can't do everything on your own. I have already suggested finding a 'buddy' if you are unemployed, teaming up with someone who is in the same situation as yourself.

However, everyone needs someone to talk things over with, to get a second opinion and feedback on your ideas and to offer suggestions of their own. Everyone will have something different to offer so the broader your support network, the better your job search will be. Make sure that the people you have in your network are aware of the need for confidentiality. Don't include the office gossip or the people who don't know the meaning of discretion.

We all need people to help us in this critical hunt, to:

- Encourage us
- Give us feedback
- Challenge us
- Set us an example.

How strong is your support network? Do you have people to support you or for you to learn from?

Draw your support network in the box overleaf, placing yourself in the middle:

Ten good excuses for doing nothing

Procrastination and the pace of everyday life often can step in the way of taking action to sort out something, even something as vital as where you work and how you are building your career. Let's get rid of all those excuses now by setting out what they are so you can never use them to cover up the fact that, in truth, they are no more than brilliant avoidance strategies. I have filled in the first two excuses to give you a starting point for reflection:

Your good excuse	How to overcome it
1. I can't think about changing jobs until the children have finished their education	Decide that you can still get the best job for you without disrupting your family life. You can work from home, stay away a couple of nights a week or find some solution that will give your family the security that they need as well as giving yourself exciting career options.
2. I haven't got a degree so my career path is blocked	Decide to gain the qualifications that might be stopping you from achieving your potential. You can sign up for distance learning and give yourself the tools you need for more career success.
3.	

4.	
5.	
6.	
7.	
8.	
9.	
10.	

Making friends and influencing people

It is irrefutable that your job search will work better for you if you can establish better communications with people and get them to listen to you. If you have real rapport with people they will want to go the extra mile to help you, they will put you in touch with others and you will have a stronger network. Good rapport will help you make a stronger and more powerful impact at your interview. You will be more likely to get people on your side and want to work with you. Not only that, you will enjoy your meeting more and give a better and more accurate impression of who you are.

How can you do this without sounding artificial or being someone that you aren't? You can start now to practise these techniques that will help you in your relationships with others, both with people that you know and people you are meeting for the first time.

Before you decide who you want to establish rapport with, work out why you want it. In networking, remember to focus as much on what is important to them as what is important to you. Consider what they might want to get out of the relationship as much as what you might want to get. Just as you are under pressure, the person you are talking to may also be under pressure. Think about what that pressure might be.

Techniques to build rapport

When you turn up for your meeting or your interview, remember that your impact depends on three factors:

- How you look
- How you sound
- What you say.

This impact can be measured as being partly the tone of your voice, it includes your facial expressions and, of course, it matters that what you say is relevant, appropriate and engaging. It is important to remember that every single aspect of your presentation matters so bring all of this to a conscious level.

I have focused on what you need to say and I have also touched upon how you need to look and sound. Let's now explore that in further detail.

Pacing and leading

In your conversation, you will establish better rapport if you are making 'pacing' statements. These set up a response pattern of 'that's true' in the other person's mind. You are stating what is familiar and getting agreement. You will achieve this by listening to them, understanding their point of view and being ready to take your time to get there.

Only when you have achieved this can you move on to lead them. This will be when you want to influence them and to get them to agree with your point of view.

When pacing and leading is done naturally and effectively, it is possible to move from saying mostly things which are 'verifiably true' to saying things that you want the listener to believe. For example, your pacing statements may be around the role and the vision for the future, something that you have already established as being fact. The leading statements will be about your ability to do the job and your achievements that match those needs.

The overall structure of your conversation would be as follows:

Pace – pace – pace – lead
Pace – pace – lead – lead
Pace – lead – lead – lead
Lead – lead – lead – lead … with an occasional pace thrown in now and again.

Be very careful when using this technique. There is nothing worse than witnessing an eager, newly qualified NLP practitioner trying out their new-found skills and using them clumsily and obviously. If your interviewer gets a whiff of any attempt at linguistic manipulation then you will be out on your ear. Practise this with friends and see how it works out.

Matching and mirroring

Rapport is the ability to enter someone else's world, to make them feel you understand them and that there is a strong connection between you. A technique to enhance the communication between you is known as matching and mirroring.

Mirroring is as if you were looking into a mirror. To mirror a person who has raised his right hand, you would raise your left hand, that is to say, a mirror image. To match this same person, you would raise your right hand, doing exactly the same as the other person.

When matching, you should first focus on body language, then voice and finally words. Body language includes body posture, facial expressions, hand gestures, breathing and eye contact. As a beginner, start by matching one specific type of behaviour and once you are comfortable doing that, then match another and so on.

For voice, you can match tonality, speed, volume, rhythm and clarity of speech. We can all vary the way that we speak and we have a range in which we feel comfortable. If someone speaks very fast, much faster than you do and at a rate at which you would not feel comfortable, match this person by speaking faster, while staying within the range that is comfortable for you. Make a conscious effort to use the same vocabulary as the person you are talking to.

The next time you are talking to a friend or someone you get on very well with, take the time to notice how you behave when you are together. You will probably find that you are already using all of these techniques. The only thing is, in this very natural and warm communication, it is not a technique; it is your natural and easy way of behaving and talking. In order to be more effective in your relationships with strangers in a recruitment process, you need to bring to a conscious level all of the things you already know unconsciously.

If you think of it like this, then you will be able to overcome any uneasiness you may feel about something that may appear at first glance to be manipulative and artificial.

Keep practising these techniques and soon they will come naturally to you.

APPENDIX A:
ANNE'S TEN TOP TIPS TO STAY ONE STEP AHEAD OF THE CROWD AND MAKE THE RECRUITER LOVE YOU ...

1 **Be accurate**: When you respond to an advertisement or write a letter, get the basics right. Spell the person's name properly – I hate being called Ann or Mr Watson or Mr Bryant. If you are e-mailing, make sure that the CV attachment is properly labelled and is not the same one that you sent off last month for that NHS vacancy or the sales job with Raytheon. Please don't call the attachment 'CV' either as it is a fairly safe bet that the recipient might just have received more than one of those already. Make sure that the person reading the letter knows that this is a one-off singular letter, not a mailshot. Make it specific, make it relevant to that particular job and make it personal.

2 **Follow-up**: To check your application has been received and to say thank you after interview. But do not hound people by telephone. By all means ring people and do whatever is reasonable to stand out. Ten messages a day on their voicemail is making yourself notable for all of the wrong reasons.

3 **Be on time**: Punctuality is the courtesy of kings so be on time. Get there early and find out the lay of the land. You might think you know where the offices are, but are you certain? Have yourself announced ten minutes early, not half an hour early or five minutes late. Arrive composed, calm, focused and ready to sparkle.

4 Abandon all clichés: Avoid at all costs 'I'm looking for a challenge'. By all means say that you want to expand your horizons; that you want to develop skills you never knew you had, that you want to introduce a bit of risk into your life and do things differently but please do not say you are looking for a challenge and expect to impress. Most people hate challenges because what that really means is being faced with a horrendous problem that is difficult to handle.

5 Do your research: Research the company properly. If you are being interviewed by a head-hunter, find out about them as well. Make use of Google and be sure that you have the facts at your fingertips. However, do not immodestly trumpet that knowledge. You could have the printouts peeping out of your file so the interviewer can be secretly impressed by both your diligence and by your modesty. Everyone wants to employ a bright and ambitious person but no one wants a Smart Alec. Subtlety is the name of the game.

6 Be open-minded: Keep an open mind about the resources that could help you get a new job. Be willing to explore all avenues and be ready to go down paths that you normally would avoid. A comprehensive job search is the one that will open up all kinds of options to you. The choice is then yours.

7 Build rapport: Change the focus from 'me' to 'you'. This interview is not just about letting the interviewer know about your experience, your skills and your talents. This is about getting the interviewer to like you. Learn the skills of building rapport. Get a book on NLP and find out the techniques you need to make sure that someone likes you. Learn to match their tone of voice, their pitch, the speed of their speech and the volume. Watch how they sit and how they position themselves. Be like them and listen hard. Talking hard means you are in your own world. Listening hard and picking up the signals will mean that you are in their world and that you will become their friend. Someone who is disliked will never get onto a shortlist so get practising!

8 Don't lie: On your CV, or at your interview. Do not tell me you were 'head-hunted' to each of your previous roles because all cynical head-hunters know that this means a mate in the golf club tipped you the wink about a job and you got it through the network.

9 Network like mad: You will get that elusive, critical next career move through who you know. The strength of your job search is wholly contingent on the strength of your social circle. Take a pen and write down the name of everyone you know, dig out all those business cards you have been given over the years. Ring people you used to work with and meet them to ask their advice. People love to help so get out and talk to them, let them know you are job hunting. Now is the time to become the keenest member of the PTA, the IoD and any other organizations you are part of. Talk, network, meet, engage, chat. Social interaction is the name of the game. One day someone is going to say to their HR Director, 'You know that vacancy for a senior whatever manager – I think I know someone because I met him/her at lunch last month ...'

10 And finally: The final interview question is usually, 'And have you any questions for me?' This means, 'I have heard all I need to and I have made my mind up. I now want to go to the bar and have a large glass of cold white wine. Do not paralyse me any more with this topic.' It does not mean that I want you to pull out two A4 sheets of clever questions. This is not the time to ask about the car policy, the bonus scheme or the European patents on their gismos. Now is the time to come up with the odd easy little question that I stand a chance of being able to answer quickly, like, 'What is the next stage in this process?' Show me to be an intelligent and competent person and I will like you. Ask me hard questions that expose my ignorance and you won't impress.

11 Always remember that if someone offers you ten top tips to help you get on, they usually have a lot more up their sleeve!

APPENDIX B:
RESOURCES YOU MAY FIND HELPFUL

RESULT: A WELL-INFORMED AND EFFECTIVE JOB HUNT

1. Bibliography

The general advice when you are actively job hunting is to keep reading. If it is in print, if it is relevant, if it is thought-provoking, then read it. Keep up to date with business news and read magazines, trade press and journals. Interviewers are generally impressed by people who are up to speed with their knowledge and who show that they are interested in what is happening in the world of business. Scan the bookshelves at any airport or railway station and you will see what is in vogue and what is in the top ten. Skim the book and see if it is likely to have something to offer. Check out the business pages of the daily and the weekly papers.

What appeals to one person might not appeal to another so try them all. You may pick up something that could help you in your search. Equally, an informed opinion on a business bestseller can only help you at interview. Visit www.amazon.co.uk and use their facility to read pages from their full range of business books. See what is in vogue is the USA by looking at www. amazon.com and be one step ahead of others.

Look at the reading list I suggested in Chapter 1 and choose one book you might like to start with. You might also want to add the following to your list of possibilities:

1   Collins, Jim, *Good to Great* (£20, Random House, October 2001)

2　Lencioni, Patrick, *The Three Signs of a Miserable Job: A fable for managers (and their employees)*, (£15.99 Jossey-Bass, August 2007)

3　McGee, Paul, *S.U.M.O Shut up Move On: The straight-talking guide to creating and enjoying a brilliant life* (£7.99 Capstone Publishing Ltd, May 2006)

4　Millman, Dan; von Welanetz Wentworth, Diana; Canfield, Jack and Victor Hansen, Mark, *Chicken Soup to Inspire the Body & Soul* (£6.39 Health Communications, December 2003)

5　Kline, Nancy, *Time to Think: Listening to ignite the human mind* (£9.99 Cassell Illustrated, December 1998)

6　McKenna, Paul, *Instant Confidence* (£10.99 Bantam Press, January 2006)

7　Parks, Steve, *Start your Business: Week by week* (£14.99 Prentice Hall, November 2004)

8　Jones, Peter, *How to be REALLY Rich* (£16.99 Hodder & Stoughton Ltd, December 2006)

2. Websites

Given the sheer scale and size of the worldwide web, the best job search will be one that is supported by Internet research. Make sure you don't get stuck in a rut, visiting the same sites all the time. Experiment and be prepared to take a chance. Listen to other people's recommendations and then make sure you bookmark the site properly so you can revisit it later. Have a look at http://del.icio.us/ and use it as a way to store and to share website information with your network. Become someone who is an early adopter of new technologies so you are the first in the queue when something new comes along.

The Internet can be inspiring as well as informative so use it as a way to inject creativity into your job search. Why not set up a separate e-mail account for subscriptions to newsletters from websites so when you are looking for inspiration you will have a ready-made supply of e-zines to read on the broadest range of topics?

Here are a few websites you can look at and that you can use to get you started on your exploration of knowledge in the stratosphere.

1　www.switchtosuccess.co.uk
　This is the website linked to the *Book of Luck* and the *Book of Happiness*. You can do the luck and the happiness questionnaires online and test how truly lucky and happy you are, as well as getting ideas of how to change.

2   www.noras.co.uk

This site leads you to all the job boards so will open up the world of online applications. There are job sites galore on the Internet and some will be more appropriate for you than others. There will be some that appeal more to graduates, some to specialized sectors and some for general levels. Use these as a starting point to find out where you should be looking and keep a watchful eye open for new ones that crop up. Whatever you find, there will be more.

- www.jobcentreplus.gov.uk
- www.totaljobs.com
- www.jobs.nhs.uk
- www.monster.co.uk
- www.reed.co.uk
- www.jobsite.co.uk
- www.jobs.tes.co.uk
- jobs.guardian.co.uk
- www.jobs.ac.uk
- www.jobsgopublic.com
- www.fish4.co.uk
- www.broadbean.co.uk
- www.gaapweb.com

3   www.timesonline.co.uk

If you go to their job pages, you will find an excellent source of up-to-date advice, lists of employers who are currently looking for people and generally up-to-the-minute stuff you need to know to help expand your horizons

4   www.Top100GraduateEmployers.com

If you are a graduate and wondering how to identify a blue chip employer, then start with this to work out what the standards are that you should be looking for.

5   www.fsbonline.co.uk

Federation of Small Business have a directory listing their members. Sometimes they have a listing for a small business that cannot be found anywhere else, for example, a small start-up business working from home. This will help you if you are looking for a creative job search that includes companies that are outside of the mainstream.

6 www.yell.com
Yell.com contains business names, addresses and telephone numbers. This free service lets you search by name, business category or keyword in the super search.

7 http://reference.com/
This is a compendium of information that is a dictionary, a thesaurus and an encyclopaedia – just what you need when you have to be at your most articulate

8 www.freepint.com
Regular newsletters from freepint supply a whole array of business and work-related information. This will help you if you are looking for specialized research sources for particularly difficult fields.

9 Register at www.iviva.com/ where you can access endless resources that will help you build your career, plan your life and tap into new resources.

10 Newspaper websites to make sure you keep up to date with business news and so you can monitor job advertisements.
www.guardian.co.uk/
www.independent.co.uk/
www.telegraph.co.uk/
www.ft.com/
www.executive-grapevine.co.uk

11 The comprehensive directory of head-hunters and recruiters. Have a look at their website and get yourself up to date with who's who in the world of recruitment. These are the people you need to get to know.

12 www.wikipedia.org
Use Wikipedia to become an instant expert on a topic you have never heard of. Broaden your knowledge and be a fast learner. Use this site to set you off.

13 www.touchlocal.com
This is the website that will give you local knowledge, invaluable if you are job hunting in a particular area or if you are going for an interview in a place you don't know.

14 www.viamichelin.com or www.multimap.com
    Make sure you get to the place on time! Check the route to the all-important job interview!

15 www.springwise.com
    Apparently you can get your daily fix of entrepreneurial ideas on this site – excellent reading!

16 http://web.researcha.com/iccquery/
    Use this site to buy company reports of privately owned businesses if you are checking out their financial status.

17 www.ftannualreports.com
    Although you can access the trading statements of a public limited company by going on their website, this is a site that allows you to order reports of businesses you may not have heard of so it is a good way to broaden the remit of your job search.

This list is not comprehensive and it isn't even extensive. It is just a few suggestions of how you might start going down different avenues on the Internet. Allow yourself to browse and see what you might turn up.

3. Radio

My final point is that you could use time when you are in the car or working at home to switch on the radio and find different stations with programmes that will bring you information that you might otherwise miss. Radio 4 has a programme called 'In Business' as well as the business reports on the Today programme. Local radio, the world service, even the advertisements on commercial radio stations could spark off a line of thought. Try out as many different options as you can and see what you can learn.

Open up to the world

We are surrounded and bombarded by information. Information is coming at us from thousands of different directions. The challenge is not really to find those resources; it is to open our minds to them. Open your eyes, open your ears, open your mind and prepare to explore the options that are around us and your career options will suddenly seem more exciting.

Also Available

INDEX